THE Nepale Shamanic]

"The collaboration of Rysdyk and Banstola .has created a compelling read—one that my inner anthropologist recognizes as an ethnography. These two visionaries, Western and Traditional, have given us a look into a non-Western cultural tradition that few of us know about. My inner understanding of myself and my world has been enhanced in response."

HANK WESSELMAN PH.D., ANTHROPOLOGIST, AUTHOR OF
THE SPIRITWALKER TRILOGY, AND COAUTHOR OF
AWAKENING TO THE SPIRIT WORLD

"This book is an accessible chronicle of esoteric cosmology and ritual that preserves the wisdom ways of an ancient people. The abundant and detailed practices and ceremonies that are presented in this book, which might otherwise be lost, make the spirits come alive for the modern practitioner. This is a generous and enduring work."

LLYN CEDAR ROBERTS, M.A., COAUTHOR OF *SPEAKING WITH NATURE*

"If you've been intimidated by the intricate and complex cosmology associated with Nepalese shamanism, this is the book that will walk you through it intelligently, gracefully, and comprehensively. This is an important book to add to the growing effort to preserve indigenous shamanism."

TOM COWAN, AUTHOR OF *FIRE IN THE HEAD*

"This inspirational book reveals the heart of the Nepalese shamanic tradition, showing the essential art of fastening heaven to Earth and releasing all beings from the bondage of the eight fetters by restoring health and harmony to sick people and disenchanted places with loving grace."

CAITLÍN MATTHEWS, AUTHOR OF *SINGING THE SOUL BACK HOME*

"Brilliant shamanic healer and teacher Evelyn Rysdyk has joined forces with Nepalese wisdomkeeper Bhola Banstola to bring us this amazing offering of the ancient practices of Himalayan shamanism. These ancient practices offer a transformation for you, your community, and the world."

MICHAEL STONE, RADIO HOST OF
CONVERSATIONS AND SHAMANIC PRACTITIONER

"Rysdyk and Banstola offer us a profound merging of ancient Nepalese wisdom and modern understanding, through which we may learn to ride the razor's edge between chaos and order that is the dhami/jhankri's path to shamanic empowerment."

HILLARY S. WEBB, PH.D., AUTHOR OF
YANANTIN AND MASINTIN IN THE ANDEAN WORLD

"An astoundingly practical workbook and doorway into the ancient Nepalese shamanic tradition. A book we have waited for for a long time. Rysdyk and Banstola have given us a great gift!"

NICHOLAS BREEZE WOOD, EDITOR OF *SACRED HOOP* MAGAZINE

"A big bow of gratitude for this important and captivating book that combines fascinating stories of transcendent initiations into the author's twenty-seventh-generation Nepalese lineage *and* step-by-step instructions of ceremonies applicable to all shamanic lineages. This book touched my heart!"

ALIDA BIRCH, SHAMAN AND AUTHOR OF *THE CO-CREATION HANDBOOK*

"How lucky to have such knowledgeable and generous guides as Evelyn Rysdyk and Bhola Nath Banstola to lead us on this fascinating journey to explore the ancient spiritual wisdom and ritual practices of Nepalese shamanism."

MAMA DONNA HENES, URBAN SHAMAN AND
AUTHOR OF *BLESS THIS HOUSE*

"This is an inspiring and vital gathering of unique wisdom nuggets and useful practices derived from a mysterious ancient society. A must-read."

ITZHAK BEERY, AUTHOR OF *THE GIFT OF SHAMANISM* AND
PUBLISHER OF SHAMANPORTAL.ORG

"Like discovering an ancient manual and toolbox for reconnecting with your primordial spiritual source, Banstola's childhood encounters with Himalayan spirits of creation, destruction, and death read like a thriller. These authors have made a significant contribution to the literature on shamanism."

ROBINETTE KENNEDY, PH.D., CLINICAL ANTHROPOLOGIST
AND SHAMANISTIC PRACTITIONER

"This book is an outstanding contribution in the field of psychological anthropology"

PREM K. KHATRY, PH.D., RETIRED PROFESSOR OF CULTURE
AT TRIBHUVAN UNIVERSITY, KATHMANDU

THE Nepalese Shamanic Path

Practices for Negotiating the Spirit World

EVELYN C. RYSDYK

with

BHOLA NATH BANSTOLA

Destiny Books
Rochester, Vermont

Destiny Books
One Park Street
Rochester, Vermont 05767
www.DestinyBooks.com

Destiny Books is a division of Inner Traditions International

Library of Congress Cataloging-in-Publication Data

Names: Rysdyk, Evelyn C., author. | Banstola, Bhola Nath, author.
Title: The Nepalese shamanic path : practices for negotiating the spirit world /
    Evelyn C. Rysdyk with Bhola Nath Banstola.
Description: Rochester, Vermont : Destiny Books, [2019] | Includes index.
Identifiers: LCCN 2018020103 (print) | LCCN 2018036293 (ebook) |
    ISBN 9781620557945 (pbk.) | ISBN 9781620557952 (ebook)
Subjects: LCSH: Shamanism—Nepal.
Classification: LCC BF1622.N35 R97 2018 (print) | LCC BF1622.N35 (ebook) |
    DDC 133.4/3095496—dc23
LC record available at https://lccn.loc.gov/2018020103

Printed and bound in the United States by Thomson-Shore, Inc.

10 9 8 7 6 5 4 3 2 1

Text design and layout by Priscilla Baker
This book was typeset in Garamond Premier Pro with Gill Sans, Hypatia Sans,
and Belda used as display typefaces
Cover: "Bhola Dancing with the Mountains" digital painting © Evelyn C. Rysdyk
(special thanks to Sven Geier for his "Vanishing Point" fractal)

To send correspondence to the author of this book, mail a first-class letter to the
author c/o Inner Traditions • Bear & Company, One Park Street, Rochester, VT
05767, and we will forward the communication, or contact the author directly at
www.evelynrysdyk.com.

This book is dedicated to all of our ancestors from around the world who preserved vital bits of wisdom in their stories, myths, and traditions. It is also dedicated to those who are willing to find the truths preserved in that incredible jigsaw puzzle of wisdom—with the purpose of crafting them into a new, sustainable future for all beings.

ॐ

To the elders of our villages, the ascetics and shamans,
To the wisdom-keepers and shamans of the plains,
To the shamans of the high mountains,
To the learned ones of the foothills,
To all who have walked this path before us,
We fold our hands like lotus buds and honor you!

Disclaimer

This book does not replace formal instruction in shamanic spirituality! If this path truly draws you, seek a skilled teacher with whom you can train.

It is necessary that you know how to journey and have a strong connection to a power animal or teacher before you work with this book. If you haven't yet learned this process, I have provided an introduction to shamanic journeying in the introduction to this book (see page 8). I also recommend that you read my book *Spirit Walking: A Course in Shamanic Power* to learn more about shamanic journeying and developing relationships with the helpful, healing spirits. Before you attempt any of the exercises in this book, read the instructions thoroughly, be sure that you understand them well, and be sure to gather all that you will require.

ॐ

The suggestions, processes, and shamanic techniques described in this book are in no way meant to replace professional medical or mental health assistance. This book is intended to be an informational guide and not to treat, diagnose, or prescribe. Always consult with a qualified health care professional regarding any medical or mental health condition or symptoms. Neither the authors nor the publisher accepts any responsibility for your health or how you choose to use the information contained in this book.

Contents

Foreword by Sandra Ingerman   xi

Our Prefaces   xv

INTRODUCTION
The Shamanic State of Consciousness   1
Journeying Basics for Beginners:
The Shamanic Bridge between Worlds   8

PART 1
Awakening

1 Everything Has a Beginning   16
Journey to Meet Banjhankri and Banjhankrini   25

2 Shamanic Awakening Is a Continual Process   28
Journey to Meet a Shamanic Ancestor to Ask
for Empowerment   34

3 Dedicating Yourself to the Spirits   37
Journey to Experience a Personal Dedication Ceremony   42

4 The Four Aspects of the Human Soul   46
Journey to Have a Nepalese Shamanic Experience
of Your Soul   47

PART 2

Flowering

5   Shamanic Sacred Tools and Ritual Objects   52

6   The Khurpa/Phurba   70
Journey to Clear and Empower Your Khurpa   78

7   Using Your Khurpa   81
Khurpa Mudras   82

8   The Dhyangro   88
Journey to Clear and Empower Your Dhyangro and Gajo   90

9   Aina: The Shaman's Mirror   93
Journey to Clear and Empower Your Aina   94

10   The Mala   97
Journey to Clear and Empower Your Mala   101

11   The Trishula or Trident   103
Journey to Clear and Empower Your Trishula   104

12   Consecrating Shamanic Tools and Creating
the Dhami/Jhankri Altar   107
Awakening and Consecrating Your Shamanic Altar   116

13   The Dhami/Jhankri's Costume   119
Journey to Receive a Vision of Ceremonial Attire   123

14   Working within the Nepalese Cosmology   124
Honoring the Elementals with Drumming and Dance   135

15   Ritual of Spring and Renewal   140
Creating a Renewal Ceremony   142

16 Using Your Voice as a Shamanic Tool   **145**

Giving Voice to Your Shamanic Practice   147

PART 3

Bountiful Harvest

17 The Cosmic Plan   **150**

The Mansaune Ceremony   158

18 Primary Feminine Deities   **166**

Journey to Meet Aspects of the Divine Mother Durga   181

Journey to Meet Kali   183

Journey to Meet the Divine Mother as Our Earth   187

19 Primary Masculine Deities   **192**

Journey to Meet Gannyap   199

Journey to Meet Shiva   202

Journey to Meet Vajrakilaya   211

20 Hanuman the Monkey God   **214**

Journey to Meet Hanuman   216

21 The Nagas   **219**

Journey to Meet the Nagas   223

Journey to Meet Nagakanya   229

22 Garuda   **232**

Journey to Meet Garuda   236

23 Local Deities, Protectors, Ancestral Guardians   **239**

*Journey to Meet the Spirit of a Local
    Landscape Feature*   240

Journey to Meet Your Protective Spirits   244

PART 4

Healing through Our Connections to All That Is

24   The Eight Fetters   250

25   Healing and Empowerment through Ceremony   254
     The Khardga Puja Ceremony   258

26   Other Purifying Rituals   264

27   The Shamanic Ransom Ritual   266
     The Kalchakra Katne Ceremony   269

28   Honoring Our Relationship with the Cosmos   277
     The Graha Sarne Ceremony   289

CONCLUSION
Spiritual and Emotional Unification   295

ॐ

Acknowledgments   299

APPENDIX
Celebrating Durga and the Customs of Dashain   301

Glossary   306

Index   319

About the Authors   329

Foreword

By Sandra Ingerman

In 2003 I was leading an event in Brazil, and I knew that a shaman from Nepal would be attending. The shaman turned out to be Bhola Nath Banstola. I was curious and excited to meet him, but what I conjured up in my imagination was not even close to what a remarkable shaman and man Bhola Nath Banstola is.

Bhola Nath Banstola is a twenty-seventh generation indigenous shaman. This young man stepped off the plane, and all I can say is that I was so amazed by his presence. I knew he was truly a shaman and holy man, for the joy and light that shined through his eyes and entire presence I have rarely experienced. He carries an inner light, joy, and a passion to help others heal, reconnect to our Mother Earth, and to bring forth the power of his ancient living tradition.

Over the years, I have watched how Bhola Nath Banstola has touched the hearts of Westerners looking to learn ancient ways of healing and living a balanced and healthy life. Bhola is a perfect bridge for bringing Nepalese shamanism into the West. His deep compassion and understanding of what we are experiencing in the West has shaped his teachings; he brilliantly shares such a wealth of knowledge and practices to take us into the ancient ways that hold so many keys to healing the emotional and physical illnesses plagued by our collective.

Mariarosa Genitrini (Mimi), Bhola's wife, has been a true partner in Bhola's work. Her deep love of nature and her own wisdom in sharing spiritual practices helped Bhola to keep his lineage alive. They started teaching together in 1997 and their work grew widely, touching the hearts and souls of students all over the world.

Evelyn Rysdyk has been a long-term practitioner of shamanism and has a passion for researching how core practices from different lineages around the world can be bridged into the teaching of shamanism in the West. Her gift at research combined with her shamanic journey practice inspired her to help Bhola write and design practices and ceremonies to integrate into their ongoing shamanic work. Evelyn is a remarkable shamanic teacher.

Nepal suffered a devastating earthquake, and the destruction of so many sacred sites and the loss of elders threatened to bring an end to the rich teachings and practices that have been passed down for so long. Bhola, Mimi, and Evelyn received spiritual messages that it was important to keep this rich tradition alive and followed their guidance to write *The Nepalese Shamanic Path*.

The partnership of Bhola, Mimi, and Evelyn—forged years ago—has now created a beautiful way to share stories, rituals, and experiential exercises that will introduce you to the power of Bhola's Nepalese Himalayan shamanic traditions. The shamans of Nepal are not only healers but also receive guidance for others, work with plants as medicine, are storytellers, and carry the richness of all the arts of song and dance.

Together, using a very organic process, Bhola and Evelyn adapted ceremonies, rituals, healing processes, and practices to bridge into the Western world while maintaining the authenticity of the tradition. Bhola's practice was born through direct lineage transmissions from his grandfather and father, from other spiritual teachers, from his dreams, from transformative life experiences, and through his incredible connection with nature. Evelyn added to Bhola's work by sharing her own wealth of shamanic experience, her journeywork and dreams, and her original photographs and artwork. Mimi's photographs, too, capture the essence of the practices. They created a guidebook and road map for self-empowerment, which is truly what the practice of shamanism is about.

As you will learn in *The Nepalese Shamanic Path*, there is a large pantheon of gods, goddesses, and spirits in the Himalayan tradition. Contacting the deities of the East brings us into greater awareness of our true nature, and this connection transcends the limitations of shifts in consciousness that come from our limited perception about ourselves, all of life, and the Earth. The deities of the East function as guides who help to lead us to a path of realization. The practices in the East honor the divine in every human. This understanding extends to all beings in nature as all of life is seen as sentient and must be honored and respected, and we must understand our interdependence and our interconnectedness as well. By working with the material presented in this book, you will learn how as shamanic practitioners we can negotiate harmony by contacting spirits, performing rituals, and making offerings of gratitude to bring balance back into our personal lives and the planet.

The Nepalese Shamanic Path gives step-by-step, illustrated instructions for authentic Himalayan shamanic practices, including physical and spiritual healing, shamanic journeys, and ceremonies. You will learn practices such as the Kalchakra Katne, a shamanic ritual for removing toxic energies from an individual. You will learn exercises to help you meet the ancestors in your shamanic lineage, techniques to use your voice as a shamanic tool, and practices for negotiating the spirit world safely. Evelyn and Bhola also examine the importance of Nepalese cosmology in shamanic ritual and spiritual deities such as Hanuman, Garuda, and the Nagas. They also teach how to work with the sacred objects of the Nepalese shaman.

Bhola and Evelyn recognize that the tradition they are sharing is one not familiar to most of us in the Western world. Their passion, vision, and hope is that you will be inspired to make this work your own and weave it into the shamanic practices you are already doing. You will understand how the universal teachings of shamanism are also embedded in the teachings of Nepalese Himalayan tradition and how they are still relevant in the modern world.

This beautiful collaboration will certainly enrich your life and shamanic work!

SANDRA INGERMAN, M.A., is a renowned shamanic teacher who gives workshops internationally on shamanic journeying, healing, and soul retrieval. An award-winning author of twelve books, including *Shamanic Journeying: A Beginner's Guide*, *Walking in Light*, *The Book of Ceremony: Shamanic Wisdom for Invoking the Sacred in Everyday Life*, *Awakening to the Spirit World*, and *Soul Retrieval*, she lives in Santa Fe, New Mexico.

Our Prefaces

As a girl growing up on Long Island in an urbanized suburb of New York City, my only knowledge of Nepal came from the pages of books and *National Geographic*. For me, the images of its unusual architecture and strange customs epitomized the very concept of foreignness. Like the Himalayas themselves, Nepal seemed an incredibly mysterious place that was distant in both space and time.

By the late 1960s and 1970s, the Himalayan region and its traditions drew closer to home with more Westerners visiting Nepal, the flowering of Tibetan Buddhism in the States, and pop singers "going to Kathmandu." Still, I never would have imagined myself going there, counting a Nepalese shaman among my close friends, or, for that matter, practicing shamanic spirituality for thirty years.

Bhola and I first met well over a decade ago at a gathering hosted by the Society for Shamanic Practitioners. We made an immediate connection. Over the years, I have enjoyed exploring his marvelous culture and shamanic traditions as they relate to my personal practice. Bhola is an extraordinary teacher whose work needs to be more widely experienced.

I am indebted to him for agreeing to collaborate in bringing the teachings preserved by his ancestors into a written form. With this agreement, he chose to contribute to not only our understanding of shamanism but also to our awareness of our collective human history and wisdom.

Before I began writing this book, I thought a long while on what would be the best way to approach the material. The shamanism practiced in the Himalayas is an outgrowth of both the culture and the

Figure P.1. Evelyn and Bhola in Maine, 2009.

region. As such, it becomes a challenge to find an effective bridge that would allow Western shamanic practitioners a viable doorway to the richness the Nepalese traditions can provide. It was important to both of us to present his traditional practices while also preparing a meaningful resource for a contemporary practitioner.

Given I was polishing another manuscript and focused on that during the day, I decided to use my dreamtime to ponder this project. Along with journeying, my dreams are an effective resource for my creativity. I give myself permission to dream about a topic and allow whatever arises to bubble up into my conscious mind for harvesting in the morning. What arose when I asked for a dream about this book was a temporal panorama of ceremonies, songs, and rituals of my time spent with Bhola and in his homeland of Nepal. In seeing this patchwork of the spirits from the region and my own teachers working together over different times, places, and seasons, I immediately realized the perspective being offered by the spirits. I was being asked to view the Nepalese shaman's world through the lens of their methods used to promote healing, balance, and harmony. The spirits of the region, with whom the *dhami/jhankris* or shamans collaborate, also revealed their underlying nature to me in the dream so that I could assist those, like myself, who were not born into the Nepalese culture to understand their powers.

In an effort to better clarify the way Western inculturation might hinder a reader in being able to more fully embrace and understand the material, I turned to the work of the American mythologist Joseph Campbell. During his time teaching at Sarah Lawrence College, he compared the religio-myth structures of Western cultures with the very different perceptions found in those of the East.

Drawing a line at Persia (modern-day Iran), he suggested that the basis for the religious myths of Europe and the Levant (modern-day Cyprus, Egypt, Iraq, Israel, Jordan, Lebanon, Palestine, Syria, and Turkey) lying to the west of that line and those of the Orient (including India and the Far East) lying to the east had foundational differences that influenced not only the religions that arose in there but also the psyches of the regions' inhabitants.

In the East, the ultimate truth, substance, and mystery of being are believed to transcend all description, all naming, and all categories. In that way, the ultimate Divine is beyond any anthropomorphic understanding or behavioral depictions. At the same time, this animating creative energy, which the Upanishads declare is beyond our knowing ("There, words do not reach") is also recognized as the ultimate reality of our being. Therefore, Eastern philosophies, religions, and practices are focused on assisting an individual to realize and experience her- or himself as an aspect of the mystery that transcends any individual perception of self. This awareness suggests that nothing is separate from the ultimate Divine that infuses everything. In other words, each being is a manifestation of "that which is," and the deities of the East are not ends in themselves but rather function as guides and/or metaphors who collaborate with the devoted in that path of realization.

In contrast, the foundations of Levantine and European religio-myths present the ultimate Divine as a separate, anthropomorphic, and sometimes spiteful or cruel being who expects fealty and banishes humans from enjoying the tree or fruit of immortality. At the same time, these forms of the ultimate Divine demand that human beings participate in a quest that is fraught with pitfalls in pursuit of the heavenly prize of being able to sit at the side of the great, sky patriarch in the hereafter. Ultimately, this pits the different descendants of Abraham/Ibrahim against each other in a pitiless and eternal version of *Survivor*. Meanwhile, the European religions of the Greeks, Romans, and, to a lesser extent, the Celts, the Norse, and the Germanic tribes, sought to placate their pantheon of deities so that the gods would allow them to live in peace. In either case, these structures draw a clear line between the ultimate Divine and human beings, divide human beings from one another, and, especially in the Levantine traditions, separate human beings from the rest of the natural world.

In having an awareness of this distinction, we can see that, in many ways, Eastern traditions have more strongly preserved elements of the earlier shamanic perceptions of the Ultimate Reality. For instance, by greeting a stranger with namaste, you consciously acknowledge the divinity that resides in that other being. You are also acknowledging that the person is an aspect of the unknowable Divine that infuses everything. In other words, you are acknowledging him or her as an intangible spirit and tangible human.

This attitude extends to the natural world as the various Oriental deities, particularly those of the Hindu pantheon, work in concert with or are depicted as having animal anatomy. As a result, the devotional structure guides individuals to respect, feed, nurture, and protect all of life, as every aspect is divine and intimately connected to the incarnational cycle of human beings. There is a foundational understanding that everything is profoundly interrelated. As I base my own shamanic practice on the principles of Reverent Participatory Relationship,* I have found that this understanding is helpful in working with the deities and spirits of the dhami/jhankri's world.

Initially, entering into relationships with the huge number of gods, goddesses, and spirits in the Himalayan shamanic pantheon felt somewhat daunting to negotiate successfully. What was useful for me was

---

*More about this concept may be found in my book *Spirit Walking: A Course in Shamanic Power* (San Francisco: Weiser Books, 2013).

to approach these spirits as I had the Norse deities: as accessible representatives of concepts, forces, and ideals that would otherwise be very difficult to enter into relationship with. By having faces, personalities, and ways that they could be honored, these spirits offer new ways to be in relationship with universal energies. In this way, they ceased to feel foreign and became familiar. This was essential as the work of shamans is primarily focused on influencing the spiritual, mental, and physical worlds to negotiate harmony. An awareness of the parties who are participating in the process is therefore vital.

Shamans accomplish this work by contacting the spirits, respectfully negotiating with them, performing rituals, and making offerings of gratitude. Since being alive is a process, not a static state, the shaman always needs to be participating in the balancing act that is life. The harmony being sought in the shaman's work may be within the body of a person for better health, between different people to resolve conflict, between people and aspects of the natural world to create mutually beneficial resolutions, or balancing the elemental forces within the natural world to preserve the life of all creatures.

Bhola and I planted the seeds of this manuscript in 2012, but it took the great Nepalese earthquake in 2015 to provide the urgency to bring it to fruition. With the loss of elders and the disruption of sacred sites in the quake, it became clear that the wisdom of the shamanic traditions practiced in Nepal must be preserved. In these pages, I will share stories, rituals, and experiential exercises that will introduce you to the incredible depth of Bhola's Himalayan shamanic traditions. As you go along, you will meet the deities and archetypes who can become healing teachers and guides for you. In addition, you will have opportunities to integrate his people's powerful rituals and ceremonies into your own shamanic practice.

Although Bhola and I recognize that this volume can only be an entrance into the richly diverse word of Nepalese shamanism, it is our hope that our efforts will not only broaden the scope of your spiritual life but introduce you to practices that you can weave into your personal shamanic practice. We also pray that by exploring Nepalese shamanism, you will learn that even with our myriad different languages and traditions we human beings have so very much in common.

EVELYN

I was even more inspired to write this book with my friend Evelyn and with photographic contributions by my wife, Mimi, after the great earthquake of April 25, 2015, in Nepal. This earthquake not only destroyed properties and killed humans and animals but it also fragmented and shifted the power places. Some wisdom-holding men and women were also lost in the rubble. After having seen this disaster, the idea that "we are guided by impermanence and everything changes" resonated deeply through me. This awakened fear and insecurity in me for many months after the great disaster. Most of my dreams were of disaster and war and of the earth submerging under the ocean. I understood all these dreams were a warning that the shamanic tradition was dwindling, with the loss of wisdom holders and the death of ancient wisdom along with the keepers. This gave birth to my desire to put the oral tradition into a written form for our own brothers and sisters and for the lovers of Mother Earth and all her creations.

Shamanism in Nepal, as in other places, is based on an animistic belief that honors Mother Earth and respects the spirit that resides in all living beings. This universal worldview is key in preserving the ecology of the land and in bringing harmony and universal brotherhood to all things tangible and intangible.

Shamanic sources of power come from honoring Mother Earth and the spirits of the place where the shaman performs his or her ceremonies. The shamans must call on the guardian spirits of Earth and deities who are all partners in the work. The sacred hidden language of the land is felt in the form of rhythms, vibrations, and warm and cool sensations in the physical body. Understanding this language, the shaman has to honor the spirits of the place and ask their permission. If the place is spiritually dead or some malignant spirits have taken over, the shaman must first revive the balance or fill in the gap of what is missing by calling on the spirits of the place.

Dhami/jhankris are the ones people turn to to reestablish this harmony. These shamans are the central figures in their communities for they are not only the healers but also the advisers, plant mendicants, soul conductors, storytellers, dancers, singers, artists, and musicians. They acquire these talents and their spiritual power and wisdom through their personal helping spirits, ancestral deities, elemental spirits, and guides. They can voluntary modify their state of consciousness in order to heal individuals and bring harmony into the community.

Although Nepal is a small country, it is home to many ethnic groups with different traditions and cultures and is one of the richest in the world from a shamanic point of view. All groups practice the oral tradition, with knowledge transmitted through their ancestors, human teachers, and the spirits. The majority of the people still today visit shamans and other traditional spiritual healers before approaching conventional medical centers and hospitals as the greatest cause of disease and disharmony is considered to be spiritual disconnection or distraction. Once the spiritual aspect of the person is taken care of, then, if required, they proceed for further conventional treatments.

As we are part and parcel of all our ancestors, the ancestral deities are a strong source of power and protection for the Nepalese shaman. Bloodline ancestors from the father's lineage and milk-line ancestors from the mother's side are equally important. Without the ancestors' blessings and help, not only would shamanic healing be difficult to accomplish, but loss of equilibrium and imbalances would more likely arise in everyday lives. Our ancestors have left behind very rich, deep-grounded, and authentic practices in the forms of lore, stories, sacred chants, songs, mantras, rhythms, dances, rituals, ceremonies, plant medicines, mineral medicines, sacred geometries, and geomancy that honor nature and her rhythms and changes.

However, ever since the medieval period, with the advent of new civilizations, the propagation of religions, and regional and ethnic wars, the oldest spiritual practice of humankind, shamanism, has been losing ground. From time immemorial, people have sought to nurture good relationships with nature and all that is created through offerings, annual rituals, and seasonal propitiations and through revering the ancesters and honoring Mother Earth. All members of the plant and animal kingdoms were considered part of living a harmonious life. But with the passage of time, greed, envy, and anxiety started taking root in human lives. The harmony started to rupture, thus creating a fragmentation of self. Different diseases emerged, as well as wars, and slowly humans began deviating away from the Source.

To keep the shamanic tradition alive in Nepal and to share this tradition with the wider community, Evelyn and I have written this book.

My wife, Mariarosa Genitrini (Mimi), has been the greatest source of encouragement from the day we met. We started sharing and teaching Nepalese Himalayan shamanic traditions in Italy in 1997. Soon afterward, we broadened our teaching into the European continent and North America. We did this to create a bridge connecting the ancient healing tradition with the modern world. We not only shared the wisdom to a wider audience through weekend classes, conferences, and retreats, but we also escorted hundreds of groups to Asia and especially to the Nepal Himalayas so that participants could have direct experiential learning from different sources and teachers. My heart has been refined and my soul enlightened through my travels to different corners of the globe and meetings with different wisdom holders and transmitters.

My thoughts about this book have evolved much like my own shamanic practice. My practice was born through direct lineage transmissions from my grandfather and father, from both human and spirit teachers, from dream instructions, from my own transformative experiences, and directly from nature's wisdom and omens. In this book, we have adapted ceremonies, rituals, and materials to what is available in the various places where people practice, while maintaining the authenticity of our traditions. As shamanism is a process of empowerment rather than teaching, this book is a practical guide for self-empowerment through journeys, ceremonies, rituals, and healing processes.

Shamanism like myths can be understood and perceived in different ways and forms. When specific supplies become unavailable, ceremonies and rituals can change, songs and chants can change, and the dances and rhythms can also change. The formation of sacred geometrical diagrams, items of offering, appeasement chants, and ways of conducting rituals can change. So performing a healing ceremony can be done in many different ways and forms. In shamanism there is flexibility on the part of the spirits and ceremonies, and chants keep on evolving and changing based on the intimate relationship between the spirits and the shaman.

It is our desire that you become empowered to find your own path to using the traditions of my people in your own practice.

BHOLA

*Namaste! Our Divine Nature recognizes the
Divine Nature in you.*

INTRODUCTION

The Shamanic State of Consciousness

S hamanism is a spiritual tradition that has been practiced across the globe and has endured for tens of thousands of years. It has its roots in animism: the idea that there are spirits in all things. These spirits, which are in animals, birds, plants, and everything else in creation, are available to us for relationship. The shaman knows that we are surrounded by sentient beings who can offer their wisdom, guidance, perspectives, and healing power in support of human life. In return for these gifts, the people offer their respect and nurturance to the spirits. This mutually respectful and honorific interaction is the basis for shamanic culture.

The shamanic state of consciousness is an expanded state of awareness or perception that produces an altered experience of reality. During the shamanic state of consciousness, the brain produces high alpha and theta waves, while the majority of the brain's functions shift into the right hemisphere. Though best known for its spiritual benefits, this state of consciousness literally changes our mind. It enhances creative thinking and imagination, which are critical skills for tackling new or challenging situations and for being able to innovate unique solutions in daily life.

Altering consciousness the way that shamans do is an inherent human capability. Shamans are those who have learned to use these states of awareness to solve the urgent problems of survival. In so doing, they are able to benefit the members of their community.

Since shamans have been intentionally expanding their perceptions of reality for millennia, they have tapped into a transcendent field of knowledge and wisdom. It is for this reason that I believe that ancient shamanic cultures around the world have each preserved pieces of this collective treasure. As we examine the perceptions held by each shamanic culture, we have opportunities to incorporate the wisdom preserved for us by our distant forbearers. This book will explore the shamanic traditions that have been preserved in Nepal.

Lying between the countries of India in the south and the Tibetan Autonomous Region of China in the north, Nepal has been a cultural crossroads for thousands of years. It spans a wide range of geographic zones, from southern steamy jungles to the towering Himalayas in the north. Since Nepal was not opened to the West until the 1950s, it retains much of its original culture. When people from Europe and the United States first traveled there, they came upon a tiny country rich in cultural and spiritual diversity.

The population of Nepal includes over sixty different ethnic groups who practice a wide variety of spiritual traditions. Hinduism, animism, and Buddhism are the major religions practiced in the country; however, followers of Islam, Bön, Christianity, Jainism, and Bahá'í also add their richness to Nepal's diverse spiritual fabric. As true today as it was

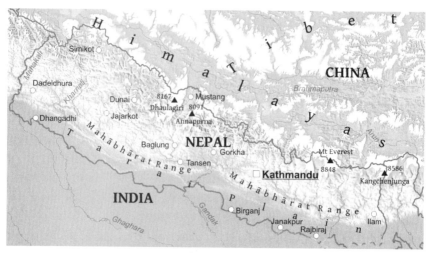

Figure I.1. The country of Nepal.

when the first king of Nepal, Prithivinarayan Shah, said it in the mid-eighteenth century, the country is a "garden for all types of people" (*sabai jaat ko phulbari*).

Although the terms *dhami* and *jhankri* are used all over the region to designate a shaman, some ethnic groups have unique terms for the role. Among the Tamang people, the shaman is a *bonpo*. The Gurung refer to the *khyapri*. The Kham Magar people consult the *ramba* or *rama,* while *bijuwa* is the name for a shaman among the Rai or Khambu people. The Limbu people call a shaman a *phedangba,* and the Tharu people's shaman is an *ojha*.

Regardless of their religion or ethnicity, the majority of Nepali people still turn to a shaman or dhami/jhankri for help. Individuals seek a shaman's help for physical and emotional healings as well as relying on him or her to protect their animals and crops from natural calamities. The shaman's role is important since the Nepalese concept of health does not simply see a person's wellness as something that is isolated to the experience of an individual. Instead, there is an understanding that harmony within a person, family, and local community and with the larger environment is critical to regaining and maintaining health.

Shamans remain central figures in their communities for they are not only healers but also the storytellers, dancers, singers, artists, and musicians. They acquire these talents, their spiritual power and wisdom, through their personal helping spirits, ancestral deities, elemental spirits, and guides. Dhami/jhankris accomplish their work by voluntarily modifying their state of consciousness in order to perceive what aspects of the person, family, or community require rebalancing. The shaman expands consciousness by disciplined methods of drumming, dancing, chanting, and singing. While in the shamanic trance state, the dhami/jhankri functions as an intermediary between the visible and invisible worlds to negotiate harmony and balance.

Within this framework, a shaman's role in a traditional society is multifaceted.

The shaman is a *mediator:*

- Mediating among individuals
- Mediating between an individual and the family or community
- Mediating between the community and another community

Figure I.2. The Nepali dhami/jhankri's dhyangro (drum) and gajo (drumstick or beater) resting on a chammar or white yak tail (photo: Mariarosa Genitrini).

- Mediating between the worlds of the living and the dead
- Mediating between the community and the spirits of plants, animals, and birds.
- Mediating between the community and elemental forces

Mediation may take the form of meeting with and listening to concerns, being an intermediary in conflicts, providing a spiritual perspective on actions or perceptions that are producing conflict, offering healing to one of more parties, and prescribing ceremonial actions.

The shaman is a *healer:*

- Healing imbalances or diseases of the body, mind, or spirit within an individual
- Healing imbalances or diseases of the body, mind, or spirit within a community
- Healing imbalances or diseases of the body, mind, or spirit with the environment
- Healing imbalances or diseases of the body, mind, or spirit with planetary or cosmic forces

The shaman performs these duties using many different methods. A shaman may use herbal medicine or other remedies, or they may use physical manipulations, such as massage or bone setting. They also provide counseling, offer guidance or instruction, and perform ritual actions.

The shaman is a *storyteller* and *preserver of cultural wisdom:*

- Holding the mythic, teaching stories of the ancestors
- Holding the mythic, teaching stories of historical importance
- Holding the teaching stories of human exploits
- Holding the mythic, teaching stories of the deities and personified elemental forces
- Holding the mythic stories of the world's creation

This kind of storytelling offers especially vital links for a society that does not have literate individuals. By preserving and retelling stories, the society's cultural and historical information is preserved for subsequent generations.

The shaman is a *facilitator* and *priest:*

- Facilitating ceremonies for life stages (birth, marriage, death, etc.)
- Facilitating ceremonies for strengthening bonds and upholding cultural traditions within a community
- Facilitating ceremonies to care for spiritual beings and deities
- Facilitating ceremonies to honor and feed elemental forces of nature

Ceremonial actions are performed to resolve conflicts, negotiate with spiritual realms on behalf of the human world, maintain cultural continuity, and produce unity and harmony within a person, family, or community.

Yet with all these duties, the dhami/jhankri is not the source of the power. The shaman is the channel or oracle who brings forth the greater wisdom of the spirits. Bhola's grandfather passed to him this way of explaining it:

I am neither an enlightened yogi, nor realized tantric master.

I have no capacity to offer seasonal fruits and flowers.
I do not know the language of signs, nor do I read minds.
I know nothing.
I am only a carrier of the spirit when it touches me.

The shamanism practiced in the Himalayan region shares attributes with other shamanic cultures from around the world. As an animist tradition, there is a fundamental belief that spirit exists in all things. Shamans in this region also understand that the forces of nature, landscape features, animals and other creatures, the stars and planets, and the spirits of the dead all have integral parts to play in human health and well-being. Along with these aspects, Himalayan shamans also work with deities that have some parallels with Vedic-Hindu religious traditions.

The understanding among the dhami/jhankri is that the deities that they honor actually predate the arrival of Hinduism and have their origins in far older shamanic archetypes. This makes a good deal of sense. Though Hinduism is quite ancient, originating as early as ten thousand years ago, shamanism is estimated to be six to ten times older. Indeed, modern scholars suggest that Hinduism is actually a fusion of earlier spiritual practices and the pantheistic Proto-Indo-European religion.* That being said a great deal of blurring of the edges has occurred over the millennia so that a Hindu, Buddhist, Jain, or Bön practitioner would recognize some aspects of Nepalese shamanism as well as some of the implements used in ceremonies but would have his or her own very different theological perspectives on them.

As with other shamanic cultures, the dhami/jhankris of Nepal devote a great deal of energy to balancing all the spiritual aspects that influence life so that harmony can be regained and maintained. To do this, the shaman needs to stay in contact with all the influences that impact the visible world. This is done for the purpose of assuring continuance—not solely for the human family but for all life-forms and for the survival of nature as a whole. Honoring the sanctity of Mother Earth and maintaining respectful interactions with all beings in the

---

*Craig A. Lockard, *Societies, Networks, and Transitions. Volume I: to 1500* (Boston: Cengage Learning, 2008), 52.

environment, seen and unseen, is crucial to preserving the ecology of the land and the health of the people.

In 1962 Professor A. W. Macdonald wrote that the dhami/jhankris are able "to diagnose illnesses and sometimes to cure them, to give advice concerning the future and to clarify present facts in the light of the evidence which took place in the past. [The shaman] is therefore . . . a privileged intermediary between spirits (which give and cure sicknesses) and men; between the past, present and the future; between life and death and, in another perspective, between the individual and . . . social mythology."*

The land is of primary importance as it is a source of power for the Nepalese shaman. Their ability to do their work depends upon honoring Mother Earth and the spirits of the place where the dhami/jhankri performs her or his ceremonies. The shaman calls on the guardian spirits and deities who inspire her or him: the keepers of the earth, snow-clad mountains, trees, rivers, lakes, and medicinal plants. The sacred hidden language of the land is felt in the form of rhythms and vibrations or as warm and cool sensations in the physical body. Understanding this language is critical for making sure that a place offers a strong physical foundation for performing shamanic duties. Once connected to the spirit of the land, the shaman has to honor the spirits of the place and ask their permission to function in it. If the place is spiritually dead or some malignant spirits have taken over, the shaman must first revive the balance or fill in the gap of what is missing by working on the area's behalf.

This attention to place reflects the shamanic understanding that all beings are part of an intricately interwoven web of interactions. Imbalance in any aspect can cause a weakening of the whole and so impact all the beings in the web. This understanding has many parallels to the Gaia principle of James Lovelock, which purports that living matter on Earth collectively defines and regulates the material conditions necessary for the continuance of life. In this theory, the entire biosphere is considered to be a vast self-regulating organism, and therefore destruction or illness in one aspect can jeopardize the entirety.

It is perhaps for this reason that shamanic practices are experiencing

---

*A. W. Macdonald, *Essays on the Ethnology of Nepal and South Asia* (Kathmandu, Nepal: Ratna Pustak Bhandar, 1983).

a global resurgence. In large part, human beings are no longer attending to being in harmony. For most of our collective human past, people nurtured very good relationships with nature and all that is created. Our ancestors made offerings, revered their ancestors, honored Mother Earth, and understood that caring for the plants and animals was a part of living a harmonious life. The result is that many human beings feel fractured, fragmented, and disconnected from the Source, and the environment has become sick.

Shamanism can provide a platform through which human beings can be restored to harmony. By becoming intrepid explorers of the numinous, we will once again experience the profound sacredness of nature. In doing so we will be drawn to participate in healing the complex interrelationships that sustain all life. It is clear that shamans' drumbeats are calling us to remember our own preciousness and the precious nature of this extraordinary planet. The unique practices of Nepal are one pathway to a renewal of the covenant we once had as stewards of Earth.

JOURNEYING BASICS FOR BEGINNERS: THE SHAMANIC BRIDGE BETWEEN WORLDS

The shamanic journey is a method for exploring hidden realms beyond the limits of our senses and our ordinary perceptions of time and space. The journey functions as a bridge between our everyday state of awareness and an expanded state that provides access to deeper worlds of consciousness, which hold the wisdom of nature, of the ancestors, and of transcendent spirit beings. Practiced by people for tens of thousands of years, it is based in the understanding that everything has a spirit or consciousness that can be available for communication and relationship.

In the journey state, our brain emits waves in the high alpha and theta range and activity shifts more into the right hemisphere. During this process our imagination is heightened as is our intuition, creativity, and ability to problem solve and synthesize information. With continued practice, these beneficial effects also become more sustained even while in ordinary awareness.

The journey through a spiritual landscape provides a kind of interface for the mind to assimilate information, guidance, and insight from the numinous world. The familiar reference of place supports that which lies beyond our senses—the nonlocal world—to be more easily grasped. These hidden realms are typically perceived as having three levels.

The Lower World is a realm beneath the earth that is characterized by a lush and vibrant landscape. It is filled with the spirits of animals, rocks, birds, plants, and those creatures that are extinct or that we think of as mythological. The Lower World feels very primordial in nature. For instance, an animal in the Lower World feels more like an ancestor or spiritual template for the physical animals that live on Earth.

Passing through the sky accesses the Upper World. Many kinds of spirits are found in this level. The spiritual teachers found in the Upper World make themselves available to answer our questions, guide our steps, and encourage our own inherent inner wisdom. Like Lower World spirits, these teachers are safe sources of knowledge. These spirits, who have no need for a form, take a shape that is most useful for our interactions, which is most often humanlike in appearance.

The hidden reality of the world in which we live is called the Middle World. This realm is the place of physical manifestation. It is inhabited by all the spirits of the natural world, the elements, and the guardian spirits of nature we call "the Hidden Folk." The elves, nisse, aspara, dwarves, briksha, faeries, greenmen and greenwomen, gandarva, and other similar beings are those who were honored by our ancestors as protectors and enliveners of the natural world.

Middle World is also the place of physical manifestation. It is the place where the word is made flesh, where quantum vibration becomes physical matter. This refers not only to living beings but also to the energies of feelings, thoughts, and desires. For this reason, we need to be able to work both safely and with humility in this realm. The Middle World is where human beings have, in their unconsciousness, manifested the unbeneficial energies that need to be rebalanced. It is also where the disembodied spirits of the dead, negative emotional energy, and other spiritual and physical hazards reside.

Although the Middle World is rich with spiritual wisdom, journeyers need to learn to travel there safely and with discernment. For these reasons, it is necessary to make strong connections with protective, helpful, and healing spirits in the Lower and Upper Worlds before doing more work in the Middle World.

Journeys are accomplished by using repetitive rhythms that assist us to more easily enter a visionary state. These may include stimuli such as repetitive drumming, rattling, chanting, or dancing. It is also useful to close off or diminish our ordinary sight with a blindfold or other screen so that our inner vision or "strong eye" can become more prominent.

On their visionary excursions, a guardian spirit in the form of an animal or bird typically accompanies a journeyer. These guardians are called power animals. A power animal is different from the animal spirits of the Middle World, being a transcendent spirit that is a teacher, guide, protector, and companion for the shaman. These spirits remind us of a primordial time when people and animals were more closely connected. In her essay "Rock Art and the Material Culture of Siberian and Central Asian Shamanism," Ekaterina Devlet explained that many Siberian tribes believe that in the mythical, timeless period before the remembered time of human beings (a concept somewhat akin to the so-called dreamtime of Australian Aborigines), there were no distinctions in form or essence among people, animals, and birds. Furthermore, there is also a common belief throughout Siberia that when shamans step outside ordinary time and space to enter into the timeless world of the spirits, it gives them access to this deep, ancient kinship bond.

During the journey, a shaman receives information and guidance and then retraces his or her steps to return fully to ordinary consciousness. This moving in and out of this visionary state is what defines the shaman. Here are the directions for journeying to meet a power animal. Your journey will begin in a favorite place in nature and go into the Lower World.

🖂 *Journey to Meet a Power Animal*

This ceremony is best done when you are rested and alert. Please read through the directions carefully several times and gather all that you'll need before you begin. For this exercise, you will need:

- A comfortable place to sit or lie down
- A way to listen to the shamanic journey rhythm (A free download of a fifteen-minute journey drumming audio track

with callback signal is available at www.evelynrysdyk.com
/myspiritwalk.html.)

- A blindfold or bandanna for covering your eyes
- Your journal or a notebook and a pen

↘ Making the Journey

1. First, situate yourself in your comfortable place and in a comfortable position with your blindfold over your eyes.

2. Put on the headphones and have the recording ready to play but do not start it yet. This recording will help you to expand your awareness into the journey state more easily.

3. Take a few minutes to breathe deeply and remember something that fills you with gratitude.

4. Once you have gotten yourself fully into gratitude, allow your memory to take you back to the most magical of your place memories. Choose a place in which you have felt safe. These are often places in nature we have felt to be sacred. Once in that place in your memory, allow yourself to experience it again with all of your senses.

5. Filled with the strong feelings of that place, begin the shamanic journey drumming audio file. While listening to the drumming, engage all of your senses in being in your special place.

    Notice as much as you can. What time of day is it? Where is the sun or moon? Is there a breeze or is it still? Are the scents of flowers, the ocean, or pine trees present? What is the ground around you like? Be as fully present in this place as you are able. Continue to explore. Get to know the trees, stones, and plants of your power-filled place.

6. Look for a place where you can go down to the Lower World. This can be an animal burrow, a hollow tree, or some other opening in the earth.

7. Enter the opening with the intention to travel downward into the Lower World to meet your power animal.

8. Keep going down through the passageway until you come out in a landscape.

9. Continue to repeat your heart's intention about meeting the spirit of your power animal. Feel it already accomplished, and while doing so,

use all of your senses to look for an animal or bird that is revealing itself to you.

10. You will know when you meet a power animal by noticing an animal or bird that stays close. The animal may greet you, speak to you, or make some other strong form of connection. Be persistent until you meet.

11. Continue getting to know your power animal until the drumming changes to the callback signal.

12. Once you hear the change in the drumming, thank the power animal for being with you and retrace your steps back to your starting place. As you retrace your steps, you will return your awareness to ordinary reality.

13. When the callback is finished, take a deep breath, gently remove your headphones and blindfold, and open your eyes.

Take some time to savor the experience and to understand all that you were given. Allow your heart to receive the gifts and write in your journal all that you have experienced.

⌂ Journey Explorations

Journey to your power animal to ask: How do I honor you?

Journey to your power animal to ask: How can you help me in my life?

Journey to your power animal to ask: How may we work together in harmony?

Each time you journey, record the content of your journey and your perceptions about what you received.

If you didn't meet a power animal initially, don't worry. This kind of work can take some time. Be persistent and keep journeying to the Lower World until you do. Indeed, once you meet this being, you'll want to make numerous journeys to it. You are in the process of getting to know your power animal and developing a power-filled relationship. Let your power animal show you around the Lower World. Get to know how it communicates with you and how you are able to understand each other. Be compassionate and gentle with yourself as you learn and practice journeying to your power animal until you feel truly connected with this wonderful being.

Once you have developed a good, working relationship with your power animal, ask the animal in a journey to take you to meet a teacher in the Upper World. Have a simple how, what, where, or why question prepared before the journey to ask the teacher once you meet. (Don't use a when question as spirits do not recognize time in the same way humans do.) When you meet a being in human form, ask her or him: Are you my teacher? If you receive an affirmative answer, then ask the question you have prepared. Remember that anything that happens after you ask the question may be part of the answer.

There are many methods available to you to learn more about the shamanic journey process. These include wonderful books, audios, and even teleconferences. However, if it is possible, the best way to learn is to seek out a skilled teacher who is able to guide you.

PART 1

Awakening

Everything Has a Beginning

In mythic stories, the hero or heroine starts in one place—emotionally, mentally, and physically—but through his or her experiences and challenges grows and changes as the story proceeds. The same pattern holds true in our ordinary life. We begin our lives in innocent awareness as children. As time and experience progress, we develop our thoughts, our perceptions, and our ways of understanding.

If in this process the experiences we have are disturbing and our reaction to them stops us from having new experiences to help to contextualize and alter them, the ideas we have about ourselves, and the world around us, can become fixed or rigid. In this way, through inaction, one actually participates in the loss of our most extraordinary human power—the one that allows us to continue to evolve and flourish. Oftentimes this loss of power is quite subtle. It can manifest as a walking daze of emptiness. Even when people appear to be outwardly going through the motions of living, they are actually unconscious sleepwalkers who are not fully engaged in the vital and precious nature of their life. Once one enters the shamanic path, one's life becomes a process of awakening from the collective unconscious experience of life.

For the Nepalese shamanic initiate, the calling to the path (*deuta-aunu*) can happen in one of four ways. The first method is the calling of blood; that is, the ancestral call that comes from one's place in a shamanic family. In this case, an initiate may be taught from childhood by another family dhami/jhankri or develop shamanic gifts later in life by becoming possessed by a shamanic ancestor or an ancestral shaman's helping spirits.

The second calling is through a sudden and unexplained spiritual illness that overcomes the person receiving the call. This can occur anytime from childhood forward. The strange illness doesn't respond to treatment, and sometimes the initiates enter a kind of spiritual battleground in which they must choose to follow the path or succumb to their malady.

A third path of becoming a shaman, and often the most common way for Westerners, is by following dreams or visions that lead a prospective candidate to seek a human teacher.

The fourth way of receiving the call is to be kidnapped by the primordial shaman, Banjhankri.* The term *jhankri*—one of the most common designations for a shaman—is derived from the name of this male being. He dwells in a wilderness cave with his fierce spouse, Banjhankrini.† These characters are spiritual beings who also have human and animal physical aspects. The power of having a tripartite aspect of the spiritual or divine, animal, and human is known as *trikhandi* in Nepali, which means that which lives in and beyond the three realms of existence.

Banjhankri is typically described as a dwarf three to nearly five feet tall. His size is not his most unusual aspect, however. Except for his face and palms, he is completely covered with golden or reddish hair that grows upward rather than downward over his body. In the fashion of Shiva and some Hindu sadhus, Banjhankri's hair is coiled on top of his head so that it rises into a topknot. His feet are oriented backward on his legs so that his footprints appear to be headed in the

---

*The Nepali shamanic worldview is so complex that there are a myriad of terms in Nepalese to designate the person Westerners simply refer to as a shaman. These include *dhami, jhankri, janne manchhe, guruji, guruba, guruju, heme, dekhne, jhawara, baidhangi, phedengba, khyapri, dhamantari, jyotoshi, jaishi, dangre, dhyangre, japana, khelwa, chalwa, bonpo, lhapa, lhamo, pau, khephry, bijuwa, baidhya, ojha, kulko dhami, phukwa, phukphake,* and many more.

†In the mountain regions of Nepal, Banjhankri is also known as Banaskhandi, "he who dwells in the plant kingdom."

Figure 1.1. Image of the primordial forest shaman Banjhankri on the surface of a dhyangro drum (painting by the author).

Figure 1.2. Banjhankrini, the consort of Banjhankri (painting by the author).

(See color plates 1 and 2)

opposite direction from his progress through the forest. He is some-times depicted with a pail of fresh milk, which indicates his clarity and purity as a sacred teacher or guru for the shaman.

In counterpoint to Banjhankri's light aspect, his wife/consort is an expression of wildness and ferocity. An encounter with the formidable Banjhankrini is fraught with danger. Unlike her diminutive husband, she is over twelve feet tall. She appears to be part bear, part giant ape, and part human. She is covered in a pelt of long, thick, black hair and has long teeth and sharp claws. Banjhankrini also brandishes knives for her work. One is the Nepalese *khukuri,* a kind of short machete with an inward-curving blade made famous by the fierce Gurkha warriors of Nepal. She also carries two *khurungi,* which are small, sharp hand sickles typically wielded by female deities.* She also carries blacksmith's

---

*These are spiritual versions of the *hasiya,* which are small, sharp hand sickles typically used by women for cutting grass.

tongs for handling hot cooking vessels or coals from the hearth and wears a bamboo gathering basket on her back. As with other spirits, each person perceives and experiences Banjhankrini differently.

By representing the two faces of power found in the natural and spiritual realms, this fantastic couple operates in unison to teach the initiate. They represent the cosmic dualities of order and chaos, creation and destruction, lawful and taboo, and domestic and wild. Without Banjhankrini's dark aspect, Banjhankri's light could not be revealed. And without his patient and structured teaching, the forces of dismemberment or dissolution would prevail.

The shaman must learn how to tread the line that holds these opposing energies in harmony. When contained and balanced by a skillful and virtuous practitioner, spiritual energies may be used to heal and create harmony. On the other hand, if a shaman is not balanced within her- or himself and power is mishandled, the shaman may inadvertently stir up forces that sow discord, create strife or illness, and consume the shaman's mind and/or body. Indeed, any kind of power can be harmful when it is wielded without clarity and integrity.

Typically, Banjhankri kidnaps a shaman-to-be sometime between the ages of five and twenty years. The shamanic candidate is taken into the forest cave in which Banjhankri and Banjhankrini live to receive their teachings and to be initiated. Upon arrival in the cave, the abducted male or female child is stripped of his or her clothing. The child is examined for any flaw that may exempt him or her from being taught. Only those abductees who are pure in body, heart, and mind are accepted as students. Once chosen, the period of time that the neophyte spends in the cave may be as little as a few hours to as long as several months, after which the initiate is returned to the ordinary human world.

Since Nepal is a very diverse land, each candidate may have a different ancestry, tribal associations, and traditions. In addition, each candidate will grow to have different gifts as a shaman. For these reasons, the teacher couple will manifest in ways that are specific and unique for each abductee.

For instance, Banjhankri may appear in a golden-haired aspect called Suna Jhankri for those students with a jolly personality and a contented spirit or who can move in and out of the spiritual realms easily and rapidly.

If the candidate is to work with a spirit who doesn't speak but instead uses gestures and signals to communicate, then it will be Lato Jhankri who does the teaching. This might be the case for a candidate who is deaf or who perceives the world more strongly through their kinesthetic senses.

Dude Jhankri is the one-handed manifestation of Banjhankri who teaches the initiate how to drum or beat a brass plate with one hand and how to use medicinal plants and boughs in calling the spirits and for healing.

Langade Jhankri is fast, powerful, and also lame. The shaman-to-be in this case would walk like a crippled person when possessed by his or her healing spirits.

Unlike his golden or reddish brothers, Ritthe Jhankri is dark like the *rittha* (soap nut) beads of the shaman's cleansing mala. He whistles, flutters his eyelids, and twitches with the electric effects of spiritual power. The shaman initiated by this aspect of Banjhankri would behave in a similar manner when possessed by her or his healing spirits.

These are just a few of the possible forms of Banjhankri. The primordial shaman appears differently to each candidate, as each person called to the shaman's path will have unique gifts.

TAKEN BY BANJHANKRI

Although Bhola is an ancestral-lineage jhankri who experienced an illness of spiritual awakening and was subsequently trained by his grandfather, Banjhankri also captured him. What follows is his personal story:

I was a nine-year-old sleeping under a tree when it happened to me. In those days, it took several days to walk to the road that would lead to a town. There we could buy basic necessities that we couldn't grow and occasionally go to the cinema. That day, we were so burdened down with salt, spices, and other goods on our return trip that we were traveling quite slowly. As a result, we were unable to make it to the cave that we usually used to spend the night. You see, there were no houses along the way, and most villagers would either sleep in a cave or take shelter under a tree.

Being the youngest of the twelve or so other travelers, I was positioned in the center of the group under a saal *tree by the river. We boiled some rice to eat with our fermented vegetables (gundruk) and ate and then spread the sheep-wool carpets (radi) we had carried with us and lay down. We covered ourselves with blankets and went to sleep. Like ascetics, we used Mother Earth as our mattress and the sky as our roof.*

At about eleven at night, I experienced a kind of hypnotic trance and a feeling of being taken away. It felt like the period of time in between sleep and being awake. I felt someone coming and calling me. It was an enticing and radiant figure who was dwarfish in size. He held a container over one of his arms and held a shaman's drum (dhyangro) and beater in his hands. His feet didn't touch the earth, and he flew from tree to tree and walked across the surface of the river. He whistled but didn't look back. I was so entranced by the appearance of this radiant being, that I began to follow him. It was like the feeling of falling in love!

After some time, we came to the headwaters of the river and a huge waterfall. There, the being had me dive into the water and go behind the waterfall, where he began beating his drum. His appearance was remarkable! He looked golden all over but with a red face. His feet were turned backward, his head and hair were conical, and his eyes emitted a beautiful light.

The being then began climbing a seven-rung golden ladder up the rock's face that led into a cave. At the cave entrance stood a huge and formidable female creature covered in dark hair. She held a curved knife with three pointed symbols hanging on the tip. Although she was wrathful and ferocious in appearance, she barely noticed me as I entered the cave behind the golden being.

The cave had many chambers and was all glowing and golden like the dwarf. There was a spiral stairway there that took me down to a lower level where a huge flame burned in the middle of a small lake. This surreal vision surprised me! I sensed many other beings around the lake and in the cave beyond it. I was suddenly pushed into the water, and when I came to the surface, I saw a retinue of children playing around the cave. I understood somehow that these were the children of the golden dwarf and the giant female I had encountered at the entrance.

At this point, I was cleansed with a fragrant smoke and dusted all over my body with the branches of a medicinal plant. I was then given some sweet, milky-colored nectar, which I drank from my hand.

Again, I followed the radiant being to an upper chamber that had water streaming from the walls. There was also a beautiful altar with a trident, rudraksha seed malas, quartz stones of different colors, and medicinal plants. A white serpent surrounded the entire altar space. There was no need for a lamp on the altar as every sacred object radiated with its own light.

I was asked to sit in front of the altar with the radiant being facing me. His glowing eyes were fixed on mine. A shivering and thrilling spirit moved through my body. I felt the dance of Mother Earth through the soles of my feet and a flame erupted from the top of my head! My heart was pounding, and the umbilical region of my belly was boiling.

At this moment, I felt connected to the call of my ancestors that had occurred a few years earlier when I was just five years old. I saw an old man to my right and a woman on my left. It was clear to me that they were my ancestors who had come to help me now. The power that filled within me was so strong it roiled my insides. I felt my body disintegrate and appear again, which I witnessed from a vantage point on the ceiling of the cave. All around me the cave was shaking, the altar was shaking, the two ancestral figures began dancing, and I became one with the radiant being.

As his spirit body and mine fused together, we became a single radiant point. The experience was utterly beyond time and space, with time passing in a few seconds while feeling like eternity. The cave began creating its own music, and as it rang out, we danced as one down the waterfall, ran on the water, and flew around the forest.

On reentering into the cave, the radiant being left my body like a setting sun, shifting my sensation and vibration. The radiant being blew some unknowable syllables into my ears and gave a single rudraksha bead, a small meteoric stone, and a splinter of quartz stone. The being blew on my forehead, on my chest, on my umbilical region, under my feet, and on the palms of my hands. By this time, there was no one else present except the being and me, surrounded by the strange rhythm emanating from the cave.

He blessed me with his drum, a bundle of herbs, and animal remains. While beating the drum, the radiant being started walking in the air outside the cave and I followed. I walked on the earth but could not feel it beneath me while the radiant being flew ten feet above me. We both arrived at a huge rock where he left me. As I slowly returned to my ordinary senses, I felt frightened and lonely and was consumed again by the distractions of the physical world. I walked down the rock face into some brush and was stung by nettle plants. This discomfort brought me completely back into my body, and I started crying.

I frantically began calling out to my brother. I heard a response from very far off. It was completely dark. I started stumbling though the shrubs and plants toward the voices I heard. Aroused by my cries, the people had set off to find me, and we met halfway. When they found me, I was shivering, crying, feverish, and nearly inconsolable.

They found me during that in-between time, about three-thirty in the morning. My fellow travelers made a fire, prepared some tea, and began interrogating me. With a whimpering and excited voice, I told them what had happened to me. After listening to my story, they told me that I had experienced abduction by Banjhankri. Into the glowing embers of the fire, they offered butter and incense to Banjhankri, the keeper of the plant spirits and animals, and thanked him for teaching me and for bringing me safely back.

On reaching home the evening of the next day, everybody gathered together in our house and called Banjhankri. The spirit spoke through my mouth and gave the details of the karmic debts that needed to be settled from my past lives and what I had to do in this life.

Later on, my grandfather, who had previously initiated me, helped to weave the teachings of my ancestors and this new experience of being called by Banjhankri into a cohesive whole with a special opening ceremony.

As with many shamanic experiences, Bhola's time with Banjhankri and Banjhankrini may be interpreted on several levels. This meeting with the spirits may first be appreciated at face value. A young boy has his first encounter with tutelary spirits who initiate him on the shamanic path. However, to leave the encounter at that point would miss important layers of meaning.

The cave may be seen as both the multileveled shamanic cosmos and also the ordinary sphere in which the shaman will do her or his work. It is a container for all that is possible; a place where marvelous things occur and challenges are met. The shamanic candidate experiences entering a fantastic realm for the purpose of meeting and interacting with nonordinary beings. These beings can impart wisdom, offer teachings, and reveal hidden information. In this nonordinary world, the elemental forces reveal themselves in fantastic ways so that the candidate understands that they, too, are living beings.

While in the cave, the candidate experiences two energies that seem to be in diametric opposition. One of the energies is light, ordered, and disciplined while the other is dark, wild, and fierce. On the one hand, this binary expression of power is cautionary. Through meeting Banjhankrini, the shaman learns that a misstep could cause destructive energy to consume her or him. This is the dance to keep ego and the need to wield power for one's own aggrandizement in check. Banjhankrini may also be called upon to cut away from the candidate anything that would interfere with him becoming a shaman.

At the same time, the candidate also learns that these powers of creation and destruction are in a perpetual dance that somehow produces fertility. It becomes clear that there is a need for both energies to exist.

Harmonizing these powerful aspects produces myriad manifestations. The children of the divine shamanic couple represent the different fulcra or balance points that may be required in the shaman's work to produce a desired outcome. There is no fixed formula but rather a need to focus on the present circumstance to create a harmonious balance. These divine children also suggest that this work of creating balance and harmony can take many different forms.

VISITING THE DIVINE SHAMANIC COUPLE

As a shamanic practitioner, you already have a teacher and power animal that you can depend upon.* As your practice expands, you will encounter

---

*In Nepal the animal spirits are also referred to as *deo* (deity or demi-god). *Bandar deo* is the name of the monkey spirit; other spirits are *baag deo* (tiger spirit), *singha deo* (lion spirit), *naag deo* (serpent spirit), and *chil deo* (eagle spirit). You may choose to use these designations for your animal helpers.

spirits that you haven't met before, and they will provide their own teaching and guidance. The spirits Banjhankri and his partner, Banjhankrini, have been honored by Himalayan shamans for many millennia. However, these archetypal primordial beings also carry profound wisdom that can be beneficial for anyone who chooses to practice shamanism.

Along with receiving teachings in this meeting, you may also experience a shamanic dismemberment. These experiences usually involve a stripping away of the ordinary way of perceiving reality and a partial loss or detachment from the personality or ego self. While in the shamanic state of consciousness, the journeyer might be partially or completely eaten by animals or demons, burned up in a fire, torn asunder by the forces of wind and ice, or ground to dust. This spiritual annihilation of the old self becomes a ritual doorway for the journeyer to be reborn into a deeper experience of her or his power.*

🪶 *Journey to Meet Banjhankri and Banjhankrini*

This is an opportunity to journey with your power animal or teacher to meet the primordial shaman and his powerful partner.

Please read through the directions carefully and gather all that you'll need before you begin. For this exercise, you will need:

- A way to produce the shamanic journey rhythm†
- A blindfold or bandanna for covering your eyes
- Your journal or a notebook and a pen
- A quiet time and space

🪶 Making the Journey

1. Choose a time when you will be able to work with the spirits.
2. Prepare yourself and all the materials you require. (Once preparations are complete, I prefer to honor the spirits of all the directions and ask them to bless the area where I will be working.)

---

*More about dismemberment as healing may be found in chapter 26 of my book *Spirit Walking: A Course in Shamanic Power.*
†This can be done through live drumming or rattling or by using a recording. A free, fifteen-minute recording of journey drumming using multiple drums with callback signal may be found at www.evelynrysdyk.com/myspiritwalk.html.

3. Begin playing the journey rhythm.
4. Begin in your usual starting place for journeys and call your power animal to you. This spirit will protect you as a guardian and also accompany you on your journey.
5. Ask your power animal to take you to meet with Banjhankri. (This being may be found in any of the realms. Let your power animal guide you.)
6. Once you have met Banjhankri, introduce yourself and ask if he would help you to better understand how he and Banjhankrini work together.
7. Allow Banjhankri and his partner to teach you. If something they say or do doesn't make sense, ask them to clarify until you understand. As a part of this meeting, you may experience a dismemberment. This is an opportunity for a deep and profound healing. Remember your power animal will not allow anything that is unbeneficial to occur.
8. When you hear the drumming change to the callback signal, thank the spirits, retrace your steps, and return to your starting place.
9. Once the callback is completed, take a deep breath.
10. Gently remove your headphones and blindfold. Open your eyes.
11. Record your experiences in your notebook.

You may have a very clear idea of what you learned, or you may have to sit with the experience for a while to understand what you were given. Allow your heart to receive the gifts.

↳ Journey Explorations

Journey with a teacher or power animal to Banjhankri and ask him: How is my shamanic gift meant to manifest in this lifetime?

Journey with a teacher or power animal to Banjhankrini to ask her to dismember you of anything unbeneficial that interferes with your spiritual progress. Record the content of your journey and your perceptions about what you experience.

After your journey, follow up with a journey to your own primary spirit teacher to ask how the dismemberment by Banjhankrini has changed you.

Journey with a teacher or power animal to Banjhankri to ask: What is the best way to keep my perceptions in harmony with my purpose? Record the content of your journey and your perceptions about what you received.

After each journey, thank your power animal, your teacher, and the divine shamanic couple. Then make an offering to the spirits. This can be an offering of incense, food, or something else. Instructions about making offerings and the importance of doing so may be found in my book *Spirit Walking: A Course in Shamanic Power.*

⮑ Process Questions

What was it like to be with Banjhankri and Banjhankrini? Write down your experiences in your journal.

What did you learn about the nature of power? Write down all that you felt.

How does it feel to have begun a relationship with the primordial shamanic couple? Record your impressions.

It is important to nurture an ongoing relationship with these teachers. They are vital links to our global shamanic past. Continue making journeys to them to ask how you can learn more about their understanding of the world, how they understand their relationships with the elemental forces, and most importantly how you may continue to honor them for their teachings.

2

Shamanic Awakening Is a Continual Process

Meeting Banjhankri and Banjhankrini was only one step on the path for Bhola. In my own evolution as a shamanic practitioner, I have found that initiation and growth are ongoing processes. Each new experience I have with the spirits provides another level of opening. It allows me to be able to receive more from the spirits and also deepens my commitment to be in sacred reciprocity with All That Is.

As a nine-year-old child, Bhola's next step was to be tested by his shaman elders about his experience. He was ritually questioned to make sure that his experience was authentic. This ceremony is deemed necessary because Himalayan people believe that malignant spirits can masquerade as Banjhankri (which is why it is important in the previous exercise to journey in the company of your power animal). These false beings also kidnap children who then suffer similar fevers and spiritual illnesses as a real shamanic candidate. To be certain that Bhola was actually captured and initiated by an authentic Banjhankri, a special ceremony of testing and recognition needed to be performed by another shaman. This was to reassure the people of the village that Bhola would be a real healer and not a shamanic poseur who could cause the people harm.

The Diyo-Batti Dinne ceremony was performed at night and required intense preparation. The name of the ceremony means to "grant the oil lamp" and is much like a final examination for gradua-tion. What follows is Bhola's remembrance of that night. (He mentions a number of ritual objects that will be described in the next chapter.)

Bhola's Diyo-Batti Dinne Ceremony
after his Banjhankri Call

It was night. My head felt foggy and my body felt like it was vibrating. My heartbeat was irregular. I felt completely untethered and as though I was caught between the worlds—like the state between sleep and wakefulness. The familiar faces of my family appeared to me as strangers, and I was gripped with a desire to run away. Everything around me felt strange and unwelcoming.

The whole day my family and relatives had been busy collecting the materials necessary for this critical ceremony. They had gathered water from seven different sources (rivers and springs) and boughs from nine different sacred and medicinal plants. A black cow had been milked for the ceremony, and fresh banana leaves had been stitched into shallow bowls. Seven different types of sacred grains were collected, as were multicolored strips of cloths, fresh bamboo branches, red mud from the hill, pure cow butter for incense, totola ko phul *(soul flower seedpods), different types of local blossoms,* ghunring *plants to make altar sticks, and many other things.*

By five in the evening, everyone had eaten except for my grandpa and me. The entire house both inside and out had been smeared with red mud mixed with water and cow dung. All the pitchers and containers inside the house were filled so that no vessel stood empty.

Grandfather's assistants started preparing a special altar under the central pillar of the house near the hearth. Above the hearth a small bamboo shelter (bhaar) was made to protect the seeds, grains, and sacred objects. This shelter also functioned as a canopy to represent the upper realms of the spirits. Fresh banana leafs were arranged on the floor to create the base of the altar and on them were placed three mounds of husked rice kernels.

Several sticks or pukis *had been made from the stems of the* ghunring *plant. Each stick was shaved with a sharp knife at different points along the stem to create fluffy protrusions. Pukis with two fluffs were arranged in front of the two side mounds of rice, and one with three*

Figure 2.1. A construction of ghunring puki staffs.

*fluffs was placed in the center of the middle mound of rice. Another taller puki with seven fluffs was also erected in the center to represent the axis mundi and the seven upper realms of the spirits. In between all the upright pukis, unshaved stems of ghunring were interlaced in a crisscross pattern to represent the earthly realm (*manushya lok). *Then all the ghunring pukis were tied to one another with white cotton thread to indicate that everything, all beings and realms, is connected.*

On the base of banana leaves, all the sacred objects were kept with a butter-burning lamp at the center, and the entire altar was encircled by a long mala of snake vertebrae.

*As the arrangements were made in the house, I was taken to the river for cleansing and was given clean clothes to wear. Besides relatives and family, many other local people had gathered. On a hay or straw mat (*gundri *or* sukul) *a homemade sheep-wool blanket (*radi) *was spread facing the altar in the northeast.*

The entire house was lit with the flickering light of a dazzlingly bright fire in the hearth, and the aroma of the butter incense was intense. The buzzing sound of voices filled my ears as all the people gathered there chatted in excitement. A huge cauldron of water for tea was boiling at the fire to provide tea for all of those who had assembled. The chaos of all the sights and sounds made me want to flee! Just when I thought I couldn't take any more, my grandfather appeared in his jhankri costume of a white shirt and flowing skirt bound at the waist with a wide red sash. He sat at my side and began awakening his malas, rosaries, and bandoliers, after which he crossed them over his shoulders. With his drum on his right side, he took some uncooked rice kernels in his hand and fed the spirits with offerings and prayers.

In separate rounds of tossed rice and prayer chants, he first invoked the ancestors and asked their permission to proceed. Second, he honored the spirits who guarded the house and land. Next, he enlivened all the sacred objects on his altar by sprinkling water and rice. He then brought rice to each corner, window, and door of the house and made his offering to bless and sanctify the space for ritual. Lastly, he placed an oil lamp outside the south side of the house to ward off any malignant spirits or wandering souls who might want to interfere.

My grandfather then faced his altar and bowed down low on the bosom of Mother Earth and began to chant deeply. He held his hands in a lotus blossom mudra as he did this. Before long, he began to look different. He lifted up his dhyangro *drum, blessed its surface with milk and rice, and began playing. The air became electric, and all eyes fell on me.*

The rhythm of my grandfather's drumming pierced my heart, and I began feeling a sense of coldness in my core. A shivering sensation ran through my entire body. The base of my spine felt as though it was trying to break through my body to bury its roots in the earth. The soles of my feet were vibrating, and my torso burned intensely at my belly button. My body was completely overtaken with overwhelming sensations. My loins burned. I felt like I had two eyes on my back and that my third eye (centered on my brow) was trying to painfully extrude some substance. My ordinary eyes were aflame as I filled with power. I was no longer afraid! The people around suddenly looked tiny, and even though the ground seemed to heave beneath me, I was strong.

At this point, a voice began to ask me questions. The voice was coming from my grandfather sitting next to me, but the tone was unearthly. My ancestors began questioning me through him:

Who are you?
Where do you come from?
Where is your place of origin?
Who is your spiritual father and mother?
Who took you to the cave?
What were you given to eat and drink?
What teaching did you receive?
How did you escape the clutch of Banjhankrini?
What power were you given?
If you were given healing wisdom, what is your specialty?
You have already been chosen by your ancestor to carry the jhankri lineage, and then Banjhankri abducted you: Can you hold both powers?
If you were given the seed of wisdom and power, show us only one thing!

Even though I had answered all the questions, the community wanted my new teacher Banjhankri to show them a feat of power. At this time the Banjhankri power completely overtook me, and I danced into the hearth and even ate a burning ember! "Now do you believe?" the spirit in me asked with anger. Banjhankri was furious at having to prove himself. At that moment, a mountain pine and other medicinal plants were thrown into the room with a huge thud! Everyone became terrified!

My grandfather along with others asked to be pardoned for not believing in the power that had taken over me. The power within me was fierce and strong.

More butter incense and the incense from the newly arrived pine needles were offered to the spirits to appease Banjhankri. Little by little, the power was released from me. As it drained away, I felt somewhat hollow and empty, but I felt my own spirit strengthen. Even though moments ago I had been possessed, I was not tired. At the end of the séance, I felt clearheaded and calm and had a full heart.

Before the closing session, the locals asked for divination, healing, and blessing from my grandfather. As the session came to an end, my grandfather gave me protection and blessings, performed a ritual to enhance my life, and gave me a sacred song.

The relationship between my ancestral lineage and Banjhankri's power had been established. Both of these doors of power were now open.

Bhola's opening ceremony is a good way to see the balance between inspiration from the spirits and the concrete guidance that an experienced shaman—in this case, Bhola's grandfather—can provide. No matter how the Nepalese shamanic candidate is called to the path, it is always necessary to have a human teacher in the physical world. The human teacher assists the shamanic candidate in learning how to harness and balance the power from the spirits, without losing a connection to the self. Shamans need to be adept at riding the razor's edge between chaos and order while remaining mentally, physically, and spiritually balanced. One has to work with the numinous and wild spiritual energies within a safe and organized container. A shamanic candidate's human teacher or mentor can support and teach the neophyte how to navigate the potential pitfalls that may occur on this journey.

It is the human teacher who questions shamanic candidates about who they are and what they are doing and teaches them them how to maintain balance, how to appease the wild spirits, and how to perform the rituals and ceremonies that affect the fabric of reality. If shamanic candidates do not learn how to create an internal and ritual structure to harness power, they will likely be consumed by it.

If you are serious about following the path of the shaman, then it is vital to find a teacher you can trust and with whom you can train.

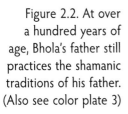

Figure 2.2. At over a hundred years of age, Bhola's father still practices the shamanic traditions of his father. (Also see color plate 3)

This book is no substitute for the step-by-step guidance that a skilled teacher can provide in helping you work with the threads of reality in a safe, sane, and disciplined way.

That being said, for the time being, this next exercise will introduce you to a shamanic ancestor who can begin to support your explorations.

🐚 Journey to Meet a Shamanic Ancestor to Ask for Empowerment

This is an opportunity to journey with your drum or rattle to connect with your shamanic ancestors. Read the instructions all the way through to the end before beginning the exercise.

You will start by creating an energetic space for your shamanic work. Clear away clutter, and light a candle or burn a bit of incense to bless the area. Also remember to silence all of your electronics.

For the next step, you will go outdoors to make an offering. While you offer a bit of uncooked rice or other grain to the natural world, you will fill your heart with thanks. This is best accomplished by remembering those things in your life and in the natural world that fill you with thankfulness. Your feelings are your prayer. It is important to keep at it until you can really feel the emotions of gratitude. Once you have experienced gratitude, you will settle in where you will be doing your journey.

The journey begins by asking your power animal or teacher to take you to meet one of your shamanic ancestors. Once you meet the ancestor, ask his or her name and share yours. After you have been properly introduced, it is important to share from your heart your desire to participate in creating harmony in the world. After sharing you may ask your ancestor to bless your path. Listen closely to any wisdom your ancestor offers.

Once you return you will be making another small gratitude offering in thanks to your power animal and for the opportunity to meet and be blessed by your ancestor. For this exercise, you will need:

- Your preferred method for creating the shamanic journey rhythm. This may be a recording or by performing your own drumming or rattling.
- A blindfold or bandanna for covering your eyes

- Offering materials (This can be some uncooked rice kernels, flowers, birdseed, or other nature-safe food offerings.)
- Your journal or a notebook and a pen

⟐ Making the Journey

1. Choose a time when you will be able to work with the spirits.
2. Prepare the space so that it feels clear of distracting energies. This includes making sure all your electronic equipment is silenced.
3. Make a gratitude offering outdoors.
4. When you experience feelings of gratitude, settle into your place to journey.
5. Begin playing the shamanic journey rhythm.
6. Now call your power animal to you. This spirit will protect your body and also accompany you on your journey.
7. Ask your power animal to take you to one of your shamanic ancestors to receive a blessing.
8. Once you meet your ancestor, introduce yourself.
9. Once you have properly met, begin sharing your desire to participate in creating harmony in the world.
10. Ask the ancestor to empower you on your path.
11. Listen closely to wisdom they may share.
12. When you feel complete, thank the spirits with whom you have spent time.
13. Return to ordinary consciousness.
14. Once you are back from your journey, make another offering to give thanks for your power animal, for meeting your ancestor, and for receiving a blessing.
15. Take time to record your experiences.

⟐ Journey Explorations

Journey with your teacher or power animal to your shamanic ancestor to ask: What is the best way for me to cultivate internal balance for all aspects of my spirit, mind, and body?

Journey with your teacher or power animal to your shamanic ancestor to ask: How do I recognize when I am out of balance?

Journey with your teacher or power animal to your shamanic ancestor to ask: How did your shamanic practice serve your people?

Record the content of your journeys and your perceptions about what you received.

After each journey, thank your power animal, your teachers, and any other spirits who have revealed themselves to you. Then make an offering to the spirits. This can be an offering of incense smoke, bits of food outdoors, or flower petals.

▷ Process Question

What were your feelings and bodily sensations? Write down in your journal what you experienced upon receiving a blessing from your shamanic ancestor.

3

Dedicating Yourself to the Spirits

Now that you have met your shamanic ancestor and received a blessing, it is time to dedicate yourself to the spirits. For a Nepali dhami/jhankri, this involves creating a kind of energetic, spiritual container that protects and enhances all of the shaman's interactions. In this way, the dhami/jhankri recognizes that her or his body is held within the cosmos and that the cosmos also exists inside the body.

The dhami/jhankri reinforces this deep and profound connection through a ritual that rededicates the mortal self to the elements of the cosmos and the shaman's spirit to the spirits of All That Is. Indeed, the shaman's body, the shaman's altar, sacred ritual diagrams, and healing ceremonies are all re-creations of the larger sphere of reality and, as such, allow the shaman to commune and converse with all of creation. When a dhami/jhankri begins working, the preparation is actually a rededication ceremony. This ceremony reinforces the shaman's sense of profound connectedness to the cosmos, to the deities and healing spirits, and to the elemental forces.

LAYERS OF PROTECTION

The first thing the dhami/jhankri does to prepare for work is to set up her or his altar, light the oil lamp, and change into shamanic garb.

Figure 3.1. Functioning as the center of the cosmos with representations of the elemental forces, animals, birds, and deities, the dhami/jhankri altar (thaan) is a sacred space that houses the shaman's implements (photo: Mariarosa Genitrini). (See also color plate 4)

Before the shaman takes a physical seat (*asan*) on a cushion in front of the altar, permission is asked from Mother Earth, the spirits of the directions, and from the local land spirits and local deities. The dhami/jhankri then creates a spiritual seat by way of a vivid visualization and through his or her personal power songs. This visualization invokes three levels of light around, above, and below the body. This also affords levels of protection and enlarges the shaman's spiritual body, giving the shaman a more substantial presence in the spiritual realms.

The first level of light that is closest to the body is brilliantly golden. This is the light of the sun, of the deity Shiva, of all the stars in the heavens, and all the radiance from the divine. It is the light that created and constantly re-creates all matter. This level of protection energizes and renews the shaman's spiritual body.

The second level beyond the body is a sparkling silver-colored light.

This level recalls the light that twinkles across the surface of the waters or the light that is reflected to us by the moon, It is the light of the air and of Parvati, the aspect of the Great Goddess who is the mother of Gannyap (Ganesha) and the partner of Shiva. This level assists in harmonizing the shaman's power.

The final, outer layer is gray iron or rust-colored light. Iron is revered as a superb apotropaic—that which can repel evil and negative influences. This layer offers the protection of the impenetrable qualities of stone and of the great mountains, the powerful properties of meteoric iron revered by the shamans of the Himalayas and of the grounding qualities of the physical body of Mother Earth.

After this ritual of overlapping energies to surround the shaman, the next phase is to observe and bless the body's connection to the aspects of creation. To accomplish this, the dhami/jhankri observes his or her body from head to toe three times. This is done to assess the spiritual power housed within the physical body.

Next, the dhami/jhankri performs a blessing ritual. To do this, the shaman takes rice kernels (*akshyaata*) in the left hand. Then the right hand is placed over the left. While holding the rice in this way, the dhami/jhankri begins to chant the power songs and mantras of protection. While chanting, the shaman touches his or her body from head to toe with the left hand.

The spontaneous songs and chants are for protecting the shaman's physical body and binding or connecting his or her helping spirits to the dhami/jhankri. They are chanted seven to twenty-one times. This is Bhola's own version:

> *Om Ghara Ke Gharai Baadhu*
> Om, support me to bind the house and the
>   housekeeper*
>
> *Bana Ke Banail Baadhu*
> Bind the forest dwellers
>
> *Mana Ke Manai Baadhu*
> Bind the mind inside the mind

---

*The physical body is the spirit's house.

Kali Baadhu
Bind Kali on my favor

Kalyana Baadhu
Keep supporters in my favor

Bana Ke Mahapate Baadhu
Bind the lord of animals in the forest

Ishwar Mahadeo Gaura Parvataki Bacha
I take (renew) my oath in the name of Lord
Mahadeo and Gaura-Parvati.*

The empowered rice kernels are then offered as a blessing by sprinkling a few kernels onto what is to be blessed and protected. First, a few of the rice kernels are offered on top of the dhami/jhankri's head, then on both shoulders and knees, and finally under the cushion on which the shaman is seated. This process of offering to the self strengthens the mind, the voice, and the body so that the shaman can work with vigor. In addition, by invoking these guardian deities and spirits with songs and mantras, the dhami/jhankri strengthens his or her connection with them, which further empowers the shaman's ability to battle with any malignant or evil spirits.

Next, a few rice kernels are offered to the altar as the center or axis mundi of all the realms and to all the cardinal directions. A few kernels are tossed high over the altar for the heavenly spiritual beings, and then a few kernels are placed into the shaman's cloth shoulder bag (*jhola*).

AS WITHOUT, SO WITHIN

In Nepalese shamanism it is believed that the inner and outer worlds are mirrors for each other. The natural world with all its rivers, mountains, forests, and elemental forces is within the shaman's body. The same is true for the deities and for heavenly bodies such as the sun and the planets. All of these energies are held within the body in specific

---

*"Lord Mahadeo and Gaura-Parvati" refer to the divine couple: Shiva, the primary male deitiy for the dhami/jhankri, and Parvati, one of the forms of the primordial Great Goddess Shakti-Durga.

places. This ritual activates their participation and fortifies the body prior to the dhami/jhankri's invocation of his or her tutelary deity, which invariably leads to a trance state.

In the following, Bhola describes the various energies that Nepali shamans invoke or activate for their work and where they are housed in the body.

The Shaman's Body as Sacred Container

In the heart region (mutu-chati), *the presence of ancestral deities* (kul deuta/devata) *may be housed and honored.*

In the umbilical region (agni deo) *are housed the spiritual energies of fire arrows, lightning, and volcanoes. [The phrase* agni deo *literally means "fire spirit." This refers to both the external fire spirits of nature and to the umbilicus area where the "fire in our belly" is housed. This is the fire of creativity, passion, courage, rebirth, and renewal.]*

On the underside of the feet is our connection to Dharti Mata, the physical aspect of Mother Earth, which is the soil and stones on which we walk, raise our food, and build our homes.

On the right shoulder (daya kuma) *sits the White Bhairung (also known as Seta Bhairung), a wrathful aspect of Lord Shiva who uses his fierce energy to defend the weak, to defeat disease entities, or to protect.*

*On the left shoulder (*baya kuma*) sits Black Bhairung (also known as Kala Bhairung). This aspect of Shiva is called upon to defeat witchcraft and sorcery or to turn negative energies back to the one who sent them.*

*The sun as Shiva the great teacher (Mahadeo Guru) is housed on the head (*sira*)*

*In the mouth (*mukh*) is the home for the goddess of wisdom, learning, and communication (Saraswati Mata).*

*Bhimsen Deo, deity of rainfall and of the energy that can move through impediments, like a river cutting through a the mountain or a plow creating furrows in Mother Earth's body, is housed in the knees (*ghuda*). This energy is also connected to Mother Earth's material richness, to wealth, and to bestowing abundance.*

*In the hands and arms (*hata-pakhura*) is housed Hasta Deo, the power of the hands in action.*

*In the eyes (*jyoti netra*), the powers of ordinary and shamanic sight as well as the ability to penetrate the darkness are honored.*

*The seat of mind-soul (*trikaldarshi shivaji*) resides in the center of the brow at the third eye region (*teshro netra*).*

*The spine or vertebral column (*meru danda*) represents and is a reflection of Kalpa Vriksha or the world tree or tree of immortality whose roots are up and trunk is down.*

Besides illuminating and empowering the retinue of spirits and deities that are also part of the shaman's spirit body, the dhami/jhankri sings the songs of all the bodily organs so that all aspects of physical nature are fully present and focused on the duties to be performed.

Finally, the shaman's helping animal power spirits are invited to stay and support from the left-hand side of the shamans. The spiritual guide or teacher stands to the right and the dhami/jhankri's ancestors protect from behind.

With all of this in place, the path that lies ahead is made luminous and open. Here the dhami/jhankri dances with the dhyangro drum. Whirling round and round in an ecstatic dance, the shaman becomes empowered by all of her or his helping spirits. The dance is also an offering to them for their willingness to partner with us here in the physical world.

A MORE ACCESSIBLE DEDICATION CEREMONY

We Western practitioners of shamanism may feel daunted by such an elaborate dedication ceremony; however, it is possible to break down this ceremony into a simpler and yet still effective version that is more in tune with our understanding of the spiritual realms. This ceremony also doesn't require an altar or shamanic tools.

❦ *Journey to Experience a Personal Dedication Ceremony*

This is an opportunity to experience a dedication ceremony that you can do each time you "power up." Since you will be tossing a few rice kernels around, you may want to do this exercise in a place that is easy to tidy after your work. This ceremony will also include honoring the spirits in the directions.

Please read through the directions carefully and gather all that you'll need before you begin. For this exercise, you will need:

- A way to produce the shamanic journey rhythm in the background
- A comfortable place to be seated
- A candle or oil lamp
- Matches
- A handful of uncooked rice kernels
- Your journal or a notebook and a pen
- A quiet time and space

⌑ Performing the Ceremony

1. Choose a time when you will be able to work with the spirits.
2. Prepare yourself and all the materials you require.
3. Begin playing the journey rhythm softly.
4. Call your power animal to you to support you during this ritual.
5. Now imagine that a brilliant sun blazes above your head. Feel that it is illuminating, opening, and clarifying your mind.
6. Next, invite the wisdom of your primary teacher to sit in your third eye region. Try to feel your teacher's presence in that place.
7. Visualize that your throat and neck are bathed in a blue-colored light.
8. Next, imagine that the full moon is sitting in your chest. It fills the area from the base of the throat down to your solar plexus and encompasses your heart and lungs.
9. In the region of your belly button, imagine a blazing fire whose flames flicker in rhythm with your pulse.
10. Invite the power of a righteous hero or heroine warrior to reside in your knees. This can also be a cultural hero or role model you admire.
11. On and under the soles of your feet, imagine that you are connected to Mother Earth. It is as if your feet and her body are made of the same energy. Feel that connection.
12. Now imagine that just beyond your skin is a radiant, golden light. It is the gold of the most beautiful sun of summer. Enfold your entire body—above, below, and all around—with this light. It even encompasses the chair in which you are seated.

13. Feel the radiance of this light energizing and renewing your body. It is the energy of creation, re-creating you in this moment. Breathe in that nourishment.

14. Once you have experienced this golden layer, imagine a new layer forming all around it that is silvery in color. This layer is calming and harmonizes the energy that you are receiving from the golden light so it is perfectly attuned for your body. As you are imagining this light, also recall the feelings of seeing a beautiful full moon, of filling your lungs with crisp, clean air, and of observing the glassy reflective nature of ice.

15. Allow this calming energy to enfold your golden envelope.

16. Now visualize that the golden and silver envelopes around you are encompassed by a third gray or rusty iron layer. This layer is like a warrior's shield. It holds the protective energy of Mother Earth's bones, her rocks and mountains, as well as the inherent ability of iron to repel negative influences. (As your practice grows, this protective layer will assist in keeping you from being attacked by unbeneficial spirits who may be drawn to your growing light, as well as from the spirits of the wandering dead.)

17. Allow yourself to experience this grounding and protective energy embracing your radiant and peaceful body.

18. When you are ready, begin playing the callback signal. Thank the spirits, and bring yourself back to your ordinary reality.

19. Once the callback is completed, take a deep breath.

20. Take a few moments to notice your own energy. How has it changed?

21. Gently remove your blindfold and open your eyes.

22. Record your experiences in your notebook.

You may have a very clear idea of what you learned, or you may need to sit with the experience for a while to understand what you were given. Allow your heart to receive the gifts.

☙ Journey Explorations

Journey to your teacher or power animal to ask: How does this preparation affect my physical body?

Journey to your teacher or power animal to ask: In what circumstances do I use the spirit dedication/protection ceremony?

Journey to your teacher or power animal to ask: How do iron objects
affect unbeneficial spirits?

Record the content of your journeys and your perceptions about
what you received.

After each journey, thank your power animal, your teacher, and any other
spirits who have revealed themselves to you. Then make an offering to
the spirits. This can be an offering of incense smoke, bits of food outdoors, or flower petals.

⊾ Process Question

What were your feelings and bodily sensations? Write down in your
journal what you experienced while performing this ceremony.

The Four Aspects of the Human Soul

Dhami/jhankris understand the concept of soul somewhat differently than most Westerners. They think of the soul as having four aspects. The idea of a multipart soul is quite widespread outside the confines of Levantine religious beliefs.

For instance, soul plurality is a common belief across Northern Europe. The ancient Norse believed that people had tripartite souls. The *animating principle* was the aspect of the person that left with the final breath and was part of the fabric of the cosmos and so also a part of the gods and nature. The *free soul* or *dream soul* would be freed from the body during sleep or trance. The *conscious soul,* which held the emotions and the will, was located in the physical body. That part was only released when the body or *haugbui* was fully destroyed through immolation or complete decay. At that point the conscious soul was free to journey to the realm of the dead.

Similar ideas about the human soul having three aspects are observed across Siberia and central Asia. The Evenks, Nenets, Enets, Nganasans, Selkups, Mongolians, Buryats, Khakas, and Finnic cultures all share the belief of a tripartite soul. The Manchu also believe that we have three soul aspects, while some neighboring Siberian tribes believe that four or five soul aspects exist.

According to the Inupiaq, Yup'ik, and Aleut of North America, we all have two souls with a third soul that manifests once a person is named. In Africa the Yoruba people's tradition honors five soul aspects as do the Illa people of Zambia.

In Nepal the four aspects are:

Atma: This is the Nepalese term for the immortal soul that contains the thoughts, hopes, wishes, and dreams that blossom inside of us.

Saato: This is the Nepalese term for the mind-soul. It is the part of us that is connected to the Upper World. This soul aspect is the one that can be lost or taken away by other entities. In Nepali language soul loss is called *saato jannu* and a soul retrieval ritual is called Saato Bolaunu.

Mutu, mukhya, or mul: This is the Nepalese term for the heart-centered soul, which is connected to the Middle World and to present time. This soul is connected with the primary spirit teacher.

Hangsa: This is the Nepalese term for the aspect of the soul that is centered in the umbilical region. It is connected to the Lower World and holds our emotional way of being. It can also be the seat of emotional poisons such as anger, envy, and hatred.

To further complicate matters, dhami/jhankris believe that the soul transitions from one body to another through cycles of death and rebirth. They believe that our physical characteristics are a gift from our parents while we inherit our soul body from our past life experiences. Therefore, we can carry information, characteristics, behaviors, prejudices, and attractions from our soul's journey through its own evolution.

To have a better understanding of what may initially feel like an alien concept, it is always best to have a first-person experience from your own spirit teachers.

❦ *Journey to Have a Nepalese Shamanic Experience of Your Soul*

In this exercise you will work directly with your spirit teachers who will help you, through a personal experience, to better understand the dhamai/jhankri viewpoint of soul. Before you begin, surround yourself with your golden, silver, and iron spheres. Sing your sacred songs, make an offering of uncooked rice to the spirits, and honor all of the helping spirits in the directions.

Please read through the directions carefully and gather all that you'll need before you begin. For this exercise, you will need:

- A way to produce the shamanic journey rhythm in the background
- A comfortable place to be seated
- A handful of uncooked rice kernels
- Your journal or a notebook and a pen
- A quiet time and space

⮕ Performing the Ceremony

1. Choose a time when you will be able to work with the spirits.
2. Prepare yourself and all the materials you require.
3. Begin playing the journey rhythm softly.
4. Call your power animal to you to support you during this ritual.
5. Do a journey to your primary teacher to ask for an experience of your soul as it is understood by dhami/jhankris.
6. Once you feel complete in your understanding, thank the spirits with whom you worked and return to ordinary reality with the callback signal.

Once your journey is complete, remember to make an offering to the spirits for their help and support.

⮕ Journey Explorations

Journey to your teacher or power animal to ask: What is the best way to keep my soul strong?

Journey to your teacher or power animal to ask: How can this new understanding enrich my experience of life?

Record the content of your journeys and your perceptions about what you received.

After each journey, thank your power animal, your teacher, and any other spirits who have revealed themselves to you. Then make an offering to the spirits. This can be an offering of incense smoke, bits of food out-doors, or flower petals.

⊾ Process Questions

What thoughts or feelings were stimulated by this new understanding of your soul?

How does this experience shift your ideas about your life?

PART 2

Flowering

5

Shamanic Sacred Tools and Ritual Objects

Every shaman works in two realities. They maintain strong relationships with beings in the spiritual world and also maintain a grounded connection to the physical world of nature, plants, animals, birds, and human beings. Both aspects are required, and the balance must always be attended to.

When performing their shamanic work, shamans often use objects that enhance and channel the spiritual or cosmic energies. In essence, these objects support a "translation" of the nonphysical forces into the physical plane. When empowered by the shaman in ceremony, these objects don't just represent the spirits but embody them, giving the spirits a place to reside in the physical world. In essence, they function as an interface or doorway between spirit and matter.

Sacred implements also can support a shaman to go deeper into the intangible worlds through journeys to the numinous realms of spirit where the dhami/jhankri navigates the complex interrelationships that are continually creating our physical existence. Sacred objects also assist in expressing complex ideas and intangible feelings. For instance, when we light an oil lamp or a candle as a part of a ceremony, we are literally invoking the light, emotionally and transcendentally.

Tools also help to provide a tangible bridge for the nonshaman participants in a ritual or healing. Through witnessing the manipulations

Figure 5.1. A simplified dhami/jhankri altar with nearly all the objects contained within a hand-beaten copper plate (thaal) that has been lined with rice kernels (photo: Mariarosa Genitrini). (See also color plate 5)

of objects and the atmosphere created by these objects, those who may not perceive the spiritual energies are still able to have an understanding of the proceedings.

A shaman may have many different kinds of sacred implements, such as sacred plants, special stones, animal parts, drums, musical instruments, masks, and costumes. It is important to remember that these implements alone do not enable a shaman to heal or otherwise wield spiritual powers. Tools do not make the shaman! Shamanic implements are extensions of the shaman's body and of his or her spirit helpers. They are used to enhance and deepen the relationships that the dhami/jhankri has already nurtured with his or her healing spirits. It is through those relationships that spiritual power is able to flow through the shaman during his or her work.

That being said, what follows below is a brief list of some of the many ritual objects and unique terms used in Nepalese shamanism.

Thaan: The dhami/jhankri's altar. The *thaan* is the sacred ground, map, and axis that unites all realms, all time, and all directions. It typically contains the shaman's healing implements, representations of the five elemental forces (air, fire, water, earth, ether), and symbols of the dhami/jhankri's helping spirits and invoked deities. (The next chapter goes into greater depth about the altar.)

Aina or melong: A bronze mirror. An *aina* or *melong* is used to reflect away negative forces, to provide a great hall for the deities when they enter sacred space, to be a safe haven for a shaman's soul while he or she journeys, and as a surface on which a shaman can see information during a divination or disease-causing spirits during a healing. Smaller versions may be worn for protection and may have either auspicious symbols or animals on their reverse side.

Akshyaata: Uncooked rice kernels. In Nepali *akshyaata* means "carriers of truth." A dhami/jhankri uses the rice to receive a clear divinatory diagnosis (*jokhanna*) by touching a patient's head with some kernels. Akshyaata are also used in healing, divination, and the transference of spiritual energies. When the rice kernels are used as offerings on altars, they represent Mother Earth.

Amliso: The shaman's broom. The flowers of the *Thysanalaena agrestis* plant, a perennial grass, are not only used in cleaning houses but are also used to cleanse the spiritual body of an ailing person. This grass is also called the witch plant because it is thought to be effective against sorcery or negative witchcraft. Shamans use it to transform the dark energies into light, using the leaves to transform regular water into healing water or *amrita*.

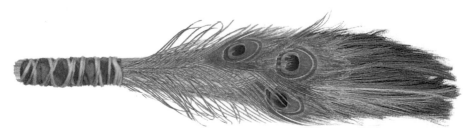

Figure 5.2. A dhami/jhankri broom made from the soft, flowering grass of the *Thysanalaena agrestis* plant.

Figure 5.3. The chammar is a shaman broom that may be made from either a black or white yak tail.

Figure 5.4. A chatri yarn cross that has been wound with five-color rainbow threads (pancha rangi). (See also color plate 6)

Chammar: A yak tail. It is used to cleanse the spiritual body of the person and to foster clarity of mind. During the medieval period, members of the royal class used the *chammar* as a fan and fly whisk. In some temples and households, the yak tail is used to cleanse and fan statues of deities. In West Nepal yak tails form the crown of spirit pillars known as *gaanj*.

Chatri or chata: A yarn cross. Also known as a spiritual umbrella (*chatri* means "canopy" or "umbrella"), it may be used as a spirit catcher to trap malignant spirits or as an instrument for holding healing energy and protection. It can have various shapes and be made up of different colored yarn depending upon its purpose.

Damaru: A small, two-sided hand drum used by lamas and some shamans in the Himalayas. These may be made of wood with goatskin drumheads or of two human craniums with human skin. Tibetan *chod* practitioners typically use the latter form. To play the *damaru,* the drum is held upright in one hand while rapidly rotating the wrist, which causes the two ball-shaped beaters, suspended from cords, to strike the drumheads.

Dhanus and kand: A bow and arrow. The *dhanus* and *kand* are both the weapon and symbol of the forest-dwelling deity Sikari, as well as some other wrathful deities and spirits. They are used as a spiritual antidote for the effects of food poisoning, for repelling spiritual attacks, and for supporting extreme, focused concentration.

Dhupauro: An incense burner made of clay or any metal. Sacred plants or incense are transformed into divine purifying smoke.

Dhyangro: A shamanic drum. The *dhyangro* is unique to Nepal. This two-sided drum has a handle (*murro*) that resembles and may be used as a ritual dagger (*khurpa*). The two sides represent the male and female aspects of creation. Usually, the drum surface is made from the skin of a deer or wild or domesticated goat, with the handle having different iconographic representations. The drum is often played in front of the shaman's torso. One drumhead faces the body while the drumstick (*gajo*) is used to beat the forward-facing head.

Diyo, palla, panas batti, or sukunda: Oil lamps. An oil lamp is another essential element in a dhami/jhankri's altar. The flame is called *dirpa* or *jwala,* and the lamps that hold the flame can have different forms. A *diyo* is a bowl-shaped oil lamp made from earthenware pottery or copper with a simple spout that holds the wick. A *palla* is a smaller, simple earthenware bowl lamp that is used as an offering; a number of pallas are lit for outdoor ceremonies. *Panas batti* are pillar-like oil lamps that may be either simple or decorated with deities, and a *sukunda* is an elaborate oil lamp with a well for storing extra oil. These sukundas may

Figure 5.5. Holding a dhyangro drum and drumstick (gajo) to receive the spiritual energy of a sacred waterfall (photo: Bhola Banstola). (See also color plate 7)

Figure 5.6. The earthenware oil lamps (diyo) hold the central flame for the altar.

be simple or decorated with a deity or peacock. Small bronze or copper spoons known as *sumicha* are used to refill the area that holds the wick. The handles of these spoons may also be decorated with a deity or auspicious symbols.

Dumsiko kanda: A Himalayan porcupine quill. Used for protection of the self and the house, for better concentration and focus, and as a link between the birds and mammals. It is one way for the shaman to keep connected to the middle-world spirits.

Gajo: Drumstick. This curved S-shaped drumstick is made from the bent and dried stem of a cane plant. A gajo is often wrapped at either end with red and white cloth strips. Some dhami/jhankris employ two gajos at the same time.

Janawar ko singh and dara: Animal horns and teeth. The horns and teeth of some animals have great healing effects and are also included in preparation of protective amulets and talismans. Many times they are represented on the shamanic altar.

Jhola: A cloth shoulder bag worn across the chest containing blessed rice kernels (akshyaata) and other small sacred talismans. It may also be decorated with small seashells.

Jhyamta: A set of cymbals that may be used to accompany the drum.

Kalasa: A water pitcher. This sacred water pitcher is believed to hold the elixir of immortality (amrita). The shamans divert one of their souls into the *kalasa* before embarking on a journey of healing. Two kalasas with flowers and sacred leaves are kept near a hand-beaten copper plate (*thaal*) on the altar or at the front of

Figure 5.7. Jhyamta cymbals.

the altar. The kalasa on the left side of the altar represents the female; the one on the right represents the male.

Khadga: A sharp ritual knife. The word *khadga* also refers to an obstacle on one's life path.

Khurpa, phurba, kila, or kilaya: Ritual daggers. A more detailed explanation is provided in the following chapter.

Khurungi: A curved sickle. The khurungi is wielded by female deities and is used for clearing spiritual entanglements and for extraction processes.

Mala: A strand of prayer beads, similar to a rosary. These prayer beads are for protection, for honoring the deities, and for harmonizing the body. Most malas have 108 beads, but a mala can also have 78 or 54. Shamans in the Himalayas use malas made from the seeds of a sacred plant called rudraksha (*Elaeocarpus sphaericus*), the black seeds of the rittha or soap nut tree (*Sapindus mukorossi*), and even lotus seeds. *Kamalgatta* or lotus (*Nelumbo nucifera*) seed malas are thought to spiritually purify the soul and also to invite abundance and prosperity. Shamans are generally the only ones who wear rittha or soap nut malas. These soap nut malas cleanse the aura and protect the wearer from spiritual pollution. The *sarpa mala* or *naga mala* is a prayer rosary made from snake vertebrae that have been strung like beads. It represents the naga or snake deity, the keeper of the Lower World and earth realm. It also reminds the shaman that everything is influenced by constant transformation and change. Clear quartz crystal (*shila dhunga*) malas can also be used to demonstrate clarity and purity of purpose during a ritual.

Mayur ko pankha or mayur: Tail feathers of the peacock. These feathers are symbolic of shamanic power, shamanic sight, soul flight, journeying, healing and dispelling ignorance, anger, fear, and darkness. They also represent spiritual and physical purity, graciousness, clarity, wisdom, and light.

Nali haard: A femur bone from the left leg of a human being or an animal used to gather and subdue the disease-causing, wandering spirits of humans and animals. In some rituals it is also used as a trumpet to call healing spirits.

Pancha rangi: Five-colored rainbow thread used in ceremonies.

Each thread or strand is composed of five individual threads (yellow, blue, red, green, and white), each representing one of the elements. The addition of a black thread (the void or origin of all colors) creates a *chha rangi* or six-colored strand. If violet is added as well, then it becomes *sapta rangi,* the seven-thread strand. Bhola says about the pancha rangi:

> *In shamanic practices of transference* (mansaun) *or extraction* (bhed jhiknu) *or during depossession processes, we use five colors. Using these threads, we make a spirit bridge between the patient and the object where the spirits are transferred or released to. Even during empowerment, protection, and honoring ceremonies we use these rainbow colors. In Nepalese shamanic tradition, we have a deep understanding that our outer spiritual body is palpable and made of rainbow colors that reflect our inner spiritual being. In the same way the universe is made up of these same colors, so using a rainbow strand helps to create a bridge between these worlds.*

Sankha: Conch shell trumpet. The sound of the conch trumpet supports the recall of primordial memories and awakens dormant emotions deeply embedded in the unconscious. It is also the symbol of authority, and when it is blown by the dhami/jhankri, it clears the presence of any dark forces in the house or property during healing rituals. During the death procession to accompany the dead to the cremation ground, the same conch shell is blown to collect soul essences and to open the path of the soul for a safe journey to the other realms.

Shaligram or shila: This black stone fossil ammonite is found in the Kali Gandaki or Narayani River of Nepal. The spiral shape of these fossils represents the cycles of birth and annihilation. These stones support the shaman's descent to the Lower World and ascent to the Upper World. Having a coiled or spiral shape, these fossils also represent the naga deity unfolding creation and holding Earth. In some folk traditions, they are considered to be the "ladders to the heaven." The stones are also used as symbolic representations for the god Vishnu in his twenty-four aspects.

Shila dhunga: A clear quartz crystal that represents a celes-

Figure 5.8. A conch shell trumpet (sankha) with carved Gannyap figures decorating its surface.

tial mountain that connects the Lower, Middle, and Upper Worlds. Another representation of the axis mundi, this crystal can become a home for the shaman's healing deity or a way to "see" the spirits that cause shamanic illness. These stones are also called *dhami dhunga* or *jhankri dhunga,* meaning "shaman's stone," and can also be white crystals.

Thaal and nanglo: A thaal is a hand-beaten copper plate, often with raised, auspicious decorations. The *nanglo* is a large, round, shallow winnowing basket made from bamboo. Both the plate

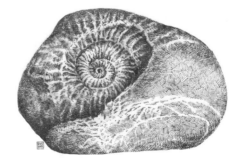

Figure 5.9. Fossil ammonite known as a shaligram (pen-and-ink drawing by the author).

Figure 5.10. An abundance-increasing offering arranged on a winnowing basket (nanglo) (photo: Mariarosa Genitrini). (See also color plate 8)

and the basket can function as shamanic altars, containing the uncooked rice and all the sacred objects. Nanglo are also used to make certain offerings. On larger altars, a thaal or nanglo is the central feature of the altar.

Trishula or trident: A divine symbol that encompasses the three worlds (Upper, Middle and Lower); the three moments of birth, death, and rebirth; the three aspects of Lord Shiva (Brahma, Vishnu, and Mahadev); and the three states of creation, preservation, and destruction for reconstruction again. The trident also represents the fire element and the state of illumination.

Vajra or dorje: *Vajra* is a Sanskrit word meaning both "thunderbolt" and "diamond." It is a ritual weapon that symbolizes both the properties of a diamond (indestructibility) and a thunderbolt (irresistible force). In this way, the vajra (*dorje* in Tibetan) represents the undeniable and eternal spiritual power that is available for the shaman. Shaped in a vaguely dumbbell form, vajras feature prongs that emanate from a lotus- or water-monster called Makara and then loop back to a central shaft prong at either end. They come in several variations having from three to nine prongs at each terminus. There is also a variation where the prongs are not looped back onto the central prong. These open-prong vajras are referred to as "wrathful" as they more closely resemble the original indestructible thunderbolt that blazed like a meteoric fireball across the heavens in a maelstrom of thunder, fire, and lightning.

A creation story with a vajra is told by Bhola:

> *Before Time, when the whole Universe was covered in*
> *   darkness,*
> *The swirling wind brought forth the vajra-thunderbolt.*
> *It was so big that it covered the entire Universe.*
> *From nowhere and nothing, fire came to live in this*
> *   vajra.*
> *Above the fire, a watery lake was born,*
> *And in the lake, foam frothed and solidified.*
> *And from this solid froth the soil was born.*
> *From the soil, the mountain, Sumeru Parvat was*
> *   created.*
> *On this mountain, the directions emerged,*
> *North, West, South, and East—the four directions.*
> *In each of these directions, humans came forth.*
> *The world above was inhabited by the Gods and*
> *   Goddesses.*
> *The world below was occupied by the Naga King, the*
> *   Naga Queen, and their court.*
> *The worlds that were born in between were inhabited*
> *   by the Shikari [hunting] spirits.*

Vajra dhunga: An iron meteorite. These meteorites are called thunder stones or lightning stones and are closely associated with the symbolism represented by the vajra or dorje. Representing the fire element and light or illumination, they protect from any alien attacks and illusions and support balance and harmony. Sometimes the iron meteorite is fashioned into an ax head. The *vajra dhunga* can also be used in place of a khurpa in many of the shamanic rituals as it also represents the instrument of both Indra, the deity of sky and rain, and Marut, the god of clouds and weather.

Vishva-vajra: An object that is formed from two vajra crossed at right angles to each other. It represents the stable foundation of Mother Earth and is a protective symbol that cannot be destroyed but itself can destroy all evil.

PLANTS AND SEEDS USED ON SHAMAN ALTARS FOR CEREMONIES

Baar: Banyan tree (*Ficus benghalensis*). This tree is considered to be male, and its leaves are often combined with *pipal* (bodhi) tree leaves and mango leaves to make ceremonial water offerings.

Bans: Bamboo varieties native to Nepal (plants in the subfamily Bambusoideae). Bamboo is known as the "herb of all worlds with multipurpose." Various parts of the bamboo are used in healing rituals, birth rites, and death rites and as food for humans and animals. It is widely used in house construction and in making fences, boats, bridges, and so on.

Ghunring: A stiff grass similar to thin bamboo (*Neyrandia madagascariensis*). Its stems are used to make pukis, sticks that are used on a shaman's altar to represent aspects of the cosmos and their interconnections. The pukis are made by shaving each stem with a sharp knife held perpendicular to the stem. Shaving in this manner produces fuzzy fluffs along the stem. The number of fluffs may indicate past, present, and future, a connection to the ancestors, the multiple realms of existence, or other things as designated by the individual shaman. These pukis are placed upright in piles of rice and interconnected to one another with unshaven stems of ghunring and cotton thread.

Katus: A nut-bearing plant (*Castanopsis hystrix*) that grows in tropical regions of Nepal. The leaves are used as an offering and to clear away heavy or negative spirits.

Kaula: A decoction of the leaves and bark of this plant (*Machilus odoratissima*) is used to sever the connections a patient has to ghosts or ghouls. The liquid is sprinkled over the patient's body.

Kera: Either the banana (*Musa acuminata* hybrids) or plantain (*Musa balbisiana* hybrids) tree. In shamanic healing rites, the kera represents the world tree that connects all the realities. It may also be used as an agent of sacrifice in rites and healing rituals when a container for an unbeneficial spirit in needed. Banana leaves may also be placed on the ground as a clean covering onto which a dhami/jhankri's altar is then constructed.

Pala-byu: Any unspecified flower, leaf, or vegetal offerings. These may be whatever flowers happen to be in bloom or thriving in the local area.

Pipal: Bodhi tree (*Ficus religiosa*), which is considered to be feminine in nature. Ceremonial plates are made by combining pipal leaves with those of the baar or banyan tree (the male aspect) and with leaves from other plants like mango. The leaves of the bodhi may also be used alone for offerings in the sacred water vase (kalasa) or in the creation of house- and land-protection ropes. These ropes are woven from the fibers that are created by beating sheets of the bark with sticks. They are used as barriers to keep away harmful spirits from fields.

Saal: A tree (*Shorea robusta*) that is both evergreen or deciduous depending upon the moisture conditions in which its grown. The very sturdy leaves of this tree have been traditionally used in Nepal to make plates and vessels to serve rice or curry. These leaves are woven together and pinned with bamboo slivers to make sacred offering baskets, bowls, and even covered boxes. These vessels are referred to as *tapari*. The plant also exhudes a resin called *saal dhup,* which is used for incense.

Sata byu: Seven types of sacred grains. They may be used as an offering, as a substance that accepts illness in a ceremony of transference, or depossession in the sacred mandalas. By offering the grains, you are transferring your illness or possessing spirits into the rice and then into the mandala. As it is rice, it also feeds the spirits that carry away the harmful energy. They may also be offered directly to Mother Earth.

Supari: Betel nut, which is the seed of the areca palm (*Areca catechu*). Traditionally chewed by agrarian people in Asia as a mild narcotic that stains the mouth a dark red, these seeds may be used as an offering and as an invitation for the deities to take their place in the sacred altar space. Along with offering the deities the seed equivalent of a mildly alcoholic drink, placing the betel nut on the altar represents the hardness of the individual ego that must be surrendered to our divine nature as represented by the deities.

Tapari: Plates or bowls that have been woven from the leaves of sacred plants. These leaf plates are used to hold offerings for sacred places or on altars, or the containers themselves can be given away as part of an offering to the spirits. The sturdy leaves of the saal tree are most often used to make *tapari*.

Titepati: Mugwort (*Artemisia vulgaris*). It is used as an offering, for cleansing the environment, as incense, and as a medicinal plant.

Totola ko phul: The flower of this plant (*Oroxylum indicum*) is considered to be the most sacred and purest. Both the flowers and seeds are used. The seeds have a white fibrous covering and are found hidden inside the long spadelike fruit of the plant. Shamans call this seed and its diaphanous covering a soul flower. The flower can assist in calling a person's soul aspects back to the body. Dhami/jhankris may give this to a patient after performing a soul retrieval or power retrieval.

Tulsi: Holy basil plant (*Ocimum sanctum*). It is used for cleansing and healing and as a medicinal plant because of the great amount of oxygen it produces.

As you can see, there are quite a lot of implements that a dhami/jhankri may use in her or his work. The ritual tools, sound-making instruments, and herbs vary depending upon which tribal group the shaman belongs to. Instead of a dhyangro, the Kham Magar and Chepang shamans use a frame drum that is more similar to a Siberian or Mongolian drum, while Tibetan lhapa use the smaller damaru drum and shang bell simultaneously. Variations among other implements and their uses are also seen across Nepal's ethnic groups and even among individual shamans within those groups.

The shaman's ritual objects may be bestowed by the shaman's ancestral teacher or elder, chosen through the relationship the dhami/

jhankri has with his or her helper spirits, or they may be selected simply on the basis of availability and practicality. For instance, a shaman working in the rural mountains is much more likely to use a natural antelope horn or carved wooden khurpa than one made of metal, and his or her plant helpers would be quite different from the ones used by a dhami/jhankri from the lowland areas.

When a shaman has been chosen through spiritual transmissions from his or her own lineage, the initiate can use all tools used by his or her forefathers because the same ancestral deity has bestowed empowerment. If the shaman is too young or physically challenged, then a human mentor or teacher working along with the selected members of the community or family members can collect sacred tools and objects on the initiate's behalf. Bhola, having been raised by his shaman grandfather, began receiving his tools at an early age.

> *I used my grandfather's drum and his sacred objects until the age of twelve. When I reached my thirteenth birthday, I started receiving instructions in my dreams that I must have my own drum. Messages and visions about this drum were also made clear during séances performed by my grandfather.*
>
> *I was shown the proper way I would make my dhyangro. In our house, we had deer hide,* given to us by a hunter, that became the drum's two heads. I received guidance to use wood from the koirala tree† to make the rim, jhankri kaath‡ for the drum handle (murro), and cane sticks to attach the hide to the rim. I was shown how to*

---

*Drumheads are made from wild animals and are often either mountain goat (*ghoral*) or deer hide. Animals that have not been domesticated are considered to be purer and therefore more able to sustain the possession by a dhami/jhankri's healing spirits.

†The koirala tree (*Bauhinia variegata*) has medicinal bark. It is alterative, anthelmintic, astringent, and tonic and used to treat amoebic dysentery, diarrhea, and other stomach disorders. A paste of the bark can be used for cuts and skin diseases. The wood from this tree is also used to make household implements and charcoal and for firewood. The bark may be used for tanning and dyeing.

‡*Actinodaphne angustifolia*. The wood of the *bhalayo* or marking-nut tree (*Semecarpus anacardium*) may also be used to make the khurpa or murro (drum handle). The bhalayo can cause strong allergic reactions in people, and it is said to cause negative spirits to flee. There are two types, the *kaag bhalayo* (raven/crow), which is associated with death and dissociation, and the *rani bhalayo* (queen), which is more compassionate in nature.

prepare the six colors of fabric strips to hang on the drum handle. I was also shown how to place a rudraksha seed, silver coin, and rice kernel inside the drum to enliven it. Once the drum was completed, my grandfather showed me how I could "dress" the drum by weaving peacock feathers and porcupine quills through the cane lashing around the outer rim.

Once I had my drum-making instructions, I had to be prepared, too. On the day after the new moon of Chaitra, the twelfth month of the Nepali calendar, my people's main ancestral deity Masto instructed me to eat only one vegetarian meal a day for fifteen days, till the full moon of the first month Vaishake Purnima. The night before that full moon, a very clear vision came to me. It showed me where to go and how to obtain the wood for the rim and handle for the new drum. After bathing on the next morning, we started our sacred journey.

On the journey to the forest, we carried all necessary items, including rice kernels, milk, water from seven different sources, flowers, a porcupine quill, spear, a temporarily made bow and arrow, incense, and yellow and red strips of cloth. On reaching the demarcation line separating the realm of forest spirits and the human habitations, we found plenty of trees that were the correct species. Now the question was to identify which among them was the right tree.

We made a fire, offered incense, and started the invocation. As the drum was meant for me, I made a special invocation to the spirit. I called to the ancestors, to the naga realms, to the hunting spirits of the forest (sikhari), to the mistress of the universe (Sansari Mai), to the forest-dwelling primordial shamans (Banjhankri), to the forest goddess (Bandevi), to the mistress keeper of the green (Hariyali Ki Dhani), to all land-dwelling beings, to the water beings and sky-flying beings (thala basne, jala basne, nava/aakash udne), and finally to the keepers of the mountains and rivers (danda ra khola ko rakhwa).

After this intense invocation, the long porcupine quill was thrown like a javelin into a stand of koirala trees. The quill struck one of the trees and remained attached there, quivering like an arrow that had found its target. We made offerings and asked the tree's permission to cut its flesh. We then cut down the tree and made the rim of the drum. Following the same steps, we also secured the wood for the drum's handle.

My khurpa (shaman's healing dagger) was made for me from kaulo *wood.* A coppersmith made my copper trident, while a snake vertebrae mala* (sarpa mala) *and all necessary sacred objects were gathered together along with plant boughs that my father taught me were sacred.*

My first ceremony with my new drum, new shamanic costume, and new sacred altar space (thaan) *was intense. The consecration, empowerment, awaking, and inserting the spirits into the drum and other sacred objects was one of the most powerful experiences I have ever experienced.*

In integrating Nepalese traditions into my own shamanic practice, I journeyed to find out what objects would be useful to me and what spirits would participate in their collection and empowerment. The spirits with whom I worked were happy to help me choose those objects that enhanced our work together. The spirits that I trusted helped me to integrate the ones that were a good fit and cautioned me against those that were not. In all cases, these objects were cleared, cleansed, and empowered by my helping spirits before I began working with them. There was a period of time with each object during which I got to understand how the implement and I would work together. Some ritual objects I connected with right away. These were very useful and made my work easier. Others required a period of time to establish a working relationship.

Guidance about how to build your tool kit of shamanic ritual implements is something between you and your spirit helpers. For this reason, it is important to do journeys about what they would like you to learn to use. Having stated that, the next chapters will provide guidelines on the process of procuring, clearing, and consecrating objects. Specifically, this book will also provide insights about working with a khurpa dagger and a few of the other key ritual objects.

---

*The tree of paradise (*Machilus odoratissima*).

6

The Khurpa/Phurba

The khurpa, also called a *phurba, kila,* or *kilaya,* is a kind of ritual dagger. It may be seen as a representation of the axis mundi or world tree. This central column of the cosmos unites the realms of the Upper, Middle, and Lower Worlds. In addition, it functions as the hub for the cardinal directions, the wheel of existence, and the still point around which the stars move. In essence, it represents that which unites and holds the cosmos together. It provides a counterbalance to the forces of chaos that are simultaneously pulling the cosmos apart into its constituent components.

While attending to the balance between these primal forces in the human world, dhami/jhankris use the khurpa as a stake to anchor themselves to the center of all worlds as they engage with the forces of chaos and disease. Among Nepal's many different tribal shamans, it is common practice to position the khurpa vertically, point down, into a basket or bowl of rice or other soft grain if the khurpa is wooden. If it is a metal khurpa, it is placed upright in a triangular stand or pushed point downward into the ground. In this position, the khurpa provides stability on the altar or ceremonial space. In the Himalayan traditions, only those initiated in its use, or otherwise empowered, may wield it. The khurpa affixes the energies of the heavens to Earth, thereby establishing energetic continuity and balanced flow. Working in this way, the khurpa unites energies that have been torn apart, dislocated, or dissociated.

Wooden khurpas are made from either jhankri kaath or bhalayo

Figure 6.1. A carved wooden khurpa (pen-and-ink drawing by the author).

tree wood. Bhola has said that because shamans do not carry their healing tools all the time, they use what is available by invoking a khurpa mantra or the spirit teacher's (*guru-gyan*) healing wisdom. In this way, a sickle, a khukuri (Nepali knife), a khurungi (curved sickle), an iron meteorite (vajra dhunga), an antelope horn, and even a peg that would be used to fasten a rope restraining an animal may be used for subduing, clearing, and extracting unhealthy spirits. Indeed, even the handle of the dhyangro drum is a khurpa that helps the shaman ground and protect during the shamanic sessions.

In a healing, the khurpa can be used to gather negative spiritual energy as one might gather wool on a spindle. This gathered energy is then staked into the ground so that the negative influences are

Figure 6.2. Metal khurpa with the three faces of Vajrakilaya/Dorje Phurba. This deity, who represents the action of the khurpa, is also seen as a manifestation of Kaal Bhairung, the wrathful aspect of Shiva.

themselves anchored to Earth where they can be transmuted. The khurpa thus functions like the sacred mountains of the Himalayas, which folk tradition likens to great pegs that hold Earth itself together. The khurpa can also bring the force of healing energies directly into a patient as well.

Indeed, these instruments are very powerful shamanic implements when they have been inspirited. Bhola had a particularly powerful experience when he first learned how to use the khurpa in healing and initially found performing healings on other people very challenging.

When I learned one of the many khurpa mantras, I felt the sound of thunder and lightning flash in front of me! My body shivered, and through khurpa the lightning spirit was transmitted to the patient to dispel unhealthy and negative spirit presences.

When I started healing on others I felt very shy. Having my body shaken by spirits from the beginning of the healing ritual to the end used to be very difficult. My mind had doubts about whether healing actually occurred or not; however, the spirits would instruct me to do this and that and reassured me that all would be fine. Although the results of the healings were instant, generating trust in myself took many years.

VAJRAKILAYA/DORJE PHURBA

The khurpa may be seen as a representation of the Buddhist deity Dorje Phurba, also known as Vajrakilaya, who embodies the enlightened activity of all the Buddhas. This wrathful deity is able to remove obstacles, destroy the forces hostile to compassion, and purify spiritual pollution. In essence, he is the living presence of the khurpa's action while in the hands of the shaman. In Nepal this deity would be also seen as a version of Kaal Bhairung, the wrathful, moving-energy aspect of Shiva. The working shaman becomes a manifestation of Dorje Phurba—moving through the realms to defeat chaos and disease while bringing harmony. In essence, the khurpa and shaman become one entity.

Made of iron, copper, clay, bone, horn, quartz crystal, wood (usually wild juniper, which is purported to have holy properties), or other materials, the khurpa is a unique dagger having three distinct sections: a pommel, a handle, and a triune blade. This is of special importance as the number three is also sacred to Shiva, the primary god of the Hindu religion, who is also honored as a powerful tutelary spirit by Himalayan shamans.*

The three sections of the khurpa may be seen to represent specific elements or features:

TABLE 6.I. THE THREE SECTIONS OF THE KHURPA

	Pommel	Handle	Blade
Human Body	Head	Torso	Legs
Shamanic Universe	Upper World	Middle World	Lower World
Physical Direction	West	Center	East
Temporal Direction	Past	Present	Future
Gender Energies	Male	Neutral	Female
Planetary Aspects	Sky	Earth	Waters

To represent all of the above energies, the khurpa has different thematic representations in each of its three segments. Every individual khurpa is unique and so has its own combination of images. What follows is an explanation of imagery that may be present on the different khurpas you may discover in your search for the "right one."

Pommel: Head of the Khurpa

A Nepalese shamanic khurpa has various protective, healing, or harmony-producing representations on its pommel. As such, the top end of the khurpa may be used to impart a blessing on a person, place, or object.

Vajrakilaya or Dorje Phurba is the Himalayan deity of purification. This entity is usually shown in three forms or with three faces: one joyful, one peaceful, and one wrathful. In Buddhism these three faces represent the many aspects of compassion.

The umbrella is one of the eight auspicious symbols of Tibetan Buddhism. This image represents protection from harmful forces and

---

*More details about phurba/khurpa may be found in chapter 14 of my book *A Spirit Walker's Guide to Shamanic Tools* (San Francisco: Weiser Books, 2014).

illness as well as the expansiveness and unfolding of space or heaven. It is an image of protection.

The sacred mushroom cap represents the sacred medicinal mushrooms used by Himalayan shamans. In this way, the mushroom stands as an allegory for both vision and healing.

The horse's head is a representation of the wind horse, which has its origins in the shamanic traditions of central Asia. It is an allegory for the human soul—the part of the shaman that can travel through the realms—and also a force that assists in creating order and harmony. Mongolian legends report a magical horse, which was born as a foal with eight legs and the ability to fly—an interesting parallel to Odin's eight-legged flying steed Sleipnir. This wind horse was the spiritual child of a shaman woman, and it helped her to escape the clutches of an evil ruler. In Tibetan Buddhist traditions, the wind horse's appearance is supposed to bring peace, wealth, and harmony.

A horse's head may also refer to Hayagriva, a Buddhist bodhisattva or fully enlightened being. He is depicted with a human body and a horse's head or as a wrathful face with a horse's head above. He represents the triumph of pure divine wisdom. His blessings are sought by students or devotees when they are beginning the study of both sacred and secular subjects.

The monkey image is an early image representing Buddha as well as Hanuman, the Hindu god who lifted mountains and whose energy is said to remove the fear of demons.

The snow lion represents unconditional cheerfulness, fearlessness, and a mind that is clear and precise. Its holds the energies of the sacred mountain elevations.

The *chorten* or *stupa* is a reliquary for a saint's bones or relics or a Buddhist shrine. In Nepali shamanic traditions, this image correlates with the symbolism of the *kalachakra* symbol, which protects the bearer against negative influences.

The guardian or ancestor is similar to the wooden guardian cult figures found on houses in Nepal. Holding the namaste gesture of prayer, this figure reminds us of the divinity that we all carry as well as the oneness to which all life belongs.

Gannyap or Ganesha is a Hindu deity with an elephant's head who is also honored by Buddhists as Ganapati, a powerful worldly protector, as well as by shamans. In the Nepalese shamanic tradition, it is Gannyap who is honored first among the deities. Gannyap is the remover of obstacles, ensurer of success, and lord of beginnings. He also puts up beneficial obstacles to impede negative forces. It is said that Gannyap holds the cosmic eggs of past, present, and future inside his belly and that he is a representation of om, the seed syllable of creation. He is sometimes portrayed beside the Mahakala or wrathful form of Buddha.

Bird forms are especially seen on khurpas belonging to the shamans of the midwest hill tribes in Nepal. They represent the energies of air and the above or Upper World direction.

Handle: Middle of the Khurpa

The vajra symbol is often at the core of the khurpa's handle, representing the incorruptible, diamond lightning bolt. It can cut any substance but not itself be cut and is therefore an irresistible force. It represents the flash of insight, the firmness of spirit, and spiritual power.

This vajra or dorje also has three parts, echoing the triune nature of the khurpa. The vajra or dorje is also implied through the representations of either knot work or two lotus blossoms on either side of a sphere. This image invests the energy of the khurpa with the symbolic nature of a diamond's indestructibility and that of the irresistible force of the thunderbolt. This image is believed to represent firmness of spirit and spiritual power.

The trident or *trishula* represents the powers of Shiva, who is often the protector of Himalayan shamans. The sacred number three is represented again here, as well.

Blade: Bottom of the Khurpa

Repeating the triune theme, the blade of a khurpa has a triangular, three-sided point. As it is the end of the implement that emanates power, the middle of the khurpa often ends with the face of a fierce being from whose mouth the blade originates. This ferocious being may be a wrathful aspect of Gannyap/Ganesha/Ganapati, ensuring the success of the healer; the sea monster Makara, who is associated with the Lower World; or Garuda, a being that defeats the disease-causing serpent spirits. In addition, since the blade is preceded by the vajra, it emanates protective and harmonious energy as well.

Makara is a hybrid sea creature generally depicted as a terrestrial animal in the front (stag, deer, crocodile, or, most often, elephant) and an aquatic animal in the back, usually having a fish or seal tail—though sometimes a peacock or even a floral tail is depicted. Tradition identifies Makara with water, the source of all existence and fertility.

Nagas are snake nature spirits and the protectors of springs, wells, and rivers and as such are guardians of treasure. They bring rain, and thus fertility, but they are also thought to bring disasters such as floods, sickness, and drought. The nagas on a khurpa are under the influence of the being just above them and are therefore benevolent in nature. Shown entwined, they are working on behalf of harmony, fertility, and creation and in this form are reminiscent of the Rod of Asclepius and the Caduceus of Hermes.

Garuda is a protective entity represented in shamanic, Hindu, Buddhist, and Bön traditions. It is a mythical, semidivine birdlike creature that is the enemy of the serpent spirits or nagas. Garuda is typically invoked to counter illnesses provoked by negative naga spirits.

Whichever being is represented, the blade's position in the mouth of the being implies that the khurpa is the "voice" or power of the deity manifesting in the world—in other words, the deity's protective energy in action.

CHOOSING A KHURPA

Finding khurpas was once the exclusive privilege of those who traveled abroad. Thanks to our ever-shrinking world, they are now available through shops that provide dharma supplies to Buddhists, Himalayan craft stores, meditation suppliers, and various online vendors. You will want to choose this tool carefully. It is useful to look at a few before buying one, so it is best to shop around. You will want to decide on size, material (metal, wood, bone, crystal, etc.), and the imagery represented on the khurpa. It is also useful if the khurpa is about 7 to 12 inches long (17–30 cm) and has a slim handle so that you can easily curl your fingers around it. This will become important as you learn khurpa gestures.

Once you have secured your khurpa, do the following journey to your teacher to get instructions for clearing and then empowering this spiritual implement. It is imperative to check what the spirits who will be supporting you in your use of the khurpa want and to follow their directions carefully. When the ritual is done, tie cloth to the handle (usually red and white) to secure it for sacred purposes.

When putting your sacred ritual tools away after use, you may want to wrap them in red cotton cloth. This color represents purity and is very auspicious. Red is the color of action in the world and also represents Shakti or power. In Hindu traditions, deities that are protective, brave, charitable, and adept at destroying evil are dressed in red.

🌺 *Journey to Clear and Empower Your Khurpa*

This is an opportunity to work directly with your helping spirits to clear and dedicate your khurpa. Before you begin, surround yourself with your golden, silver, and iron spheres. Make an offering to the spirits, sing your sacred songs, make an offering of uncooked rice, and honor all of the helping spirits in the directions.

Please read through the directions carefully and gather all that you'll need before you begin. For this exercise, you will need:

- A way to produce the shamanic journey rhythm in the background
- A comfortable place to be seated
- A small handful of uncooked rice kernels
- Your journal or a notebook and a pen
- A quiet time and space
- Your new khurpa
- A strip of red cotton cloth and a strip of white cotton cloth, both about ½ inch (1.3 cm) wide by 6 inches (15 cm) long

🍃 Performing the Ceremony
1. Choose a time when you will be able to work with the spirits.
2. Prepare yourself and all the materials you require.
3. Begin playing the journey rhythm softly.

4. Call your power animal to you to support you during this ritual.

5. Do a journey to your primary teacher.

6. Once you are in the teacher's presence, ask him or her to assist you in clearing the khurpa of any unbeneficial energies.

7. Once the object is cleared, ask the teacher to empower the khurpa. The teacher may merge with you to breathe upon the dagger, to offer a song or chant, and to move around with the dagger, or the process may be accomplished energetically. Allow your trusted teacher to guide the process.

8. After the khurpa is empowered, tie the red and white cloth strips around the handle to "tame" the power of the dagger for use. (Think of this like the bridle on a horse, which allows you to direct the animal's direction, bringing the raw power into a useful energy. Representationally, it keeps the khurpa, which is now a living thing, under the dhami/jhankri's control.)

9. Thank the spirits with whom you worked and return to ordinary reality with the callback signal.

Once the journey is complete, remember to make an offering to the spirits for their help and support.

ᴌ Journey Explorations

Journey to your teacher or power animal to ask: What is the best way to care for my khurpa?

Journey to your teacher or power animal to ask: What do the symbols that are represented on my khurpa mean for my own practice? Ask the teacher to introduce you to the spirits that are represented on the khurpa.

Journey to your teacher or power animal to have him or her take you to meet the living spirit of your khurpa.

Journey to your teacher or power animal to ask: How do I care for my khurpa?

Record the content of your journeys and your perceptions about what you received.

After each journey, thank your power animal, your teacher, and any other spirits who have revealed themselves to you. Then make an offering to

the spirits. This can be an offering of incense smoke, bits of food outdoors, or flower petals.

⮞ Process Questions

What drew you to the khurpa you have chosen?

Under what circumstances does your spirit teacher want you to use
the khurpa?

7

Using Your Khurpa

The khurpa may be used in several different ways by the dhami/ jhankri. It is used by the shaman to cure disease, perform extraction, conduct exorcism, defeat negative influences on a person or place, sanctify food or drink, assist in meditation, and tether the shaman so that she or he may safely return to this reality.

In the hands of a shaman, the khurpa augments intent. Along with being used as part of healing an individual, a khurpa can assist the shaman in clearing a space of harmful entities. Following a shaman's intent, a khurpa can also sanctify a drink or healing potion on behalf of a patient when the tip of the blade is placed into the liquid—thereby removing any unbeneficial energy and making it spiritually pure. The pommel of the khurpa can also impart a blessing or calming influence upon an overly excited patient or calm a space's energy. Patients who are dissociated or ungrounded may be told to hold the khurpa, or the shaman may lay the khurpa on the patient's prone body, aligned with his or her midline, to organize and harmonize the patient's energy system. As is the case with every shaman's tool, the khurpa is a living entity whose applications can shift and change based upon immediate circumstances and the needs or intent of the shaman who wields it.

Although learning the full breadth and depth of working with the khurpa can only be accomplished by working with a human shamanic teacher, there are a few ways that any shamanic practitioner may safely use the khurpa with positive results.

🔱 *Khurpa Mudras*

In working with the khurpa, the dhami/jhankri also uses specific hand gestures or mudras. A mudra is a symbolic or ritual gesture that is common to Hinduism, Buddhism, and Himalayan shamanism. The word is derived from Sanskrit and means "seal" or "gesture." In other words, it is a symbolic gesture usually made with the hands and fingers that assists in manifesting and anchoring energy. In some Himalayan traditions, there are as many as 180 different mudras that are used in this way.

Before you begin, roll the khurpa between your hands with the blade pointed away from your body to awaken the dagger and your own energies.

🔱 Khurpa Mudra for Invoking Helping Spirits

For this mudra, the khurpa is held in the right hand. The middle and ring fingers are curled around the handle with the thumb. The index finger and pinkie are pointed straight.

In Himalayan traditions, the right hand holds masculine energy and the handle of the khurpa represents the Middle World and Earth. As a

Figure 7.1. Khurpa mudra for invoking helping spirits.

result, this gesture is strongly directing beneficial energy to manifest in the Middle World and ordinary reality. This khurpa mudra can be used when you are honoring the spirits or preparing to do shamanic work and to awaken the spirit of the khurpa, itself.

☌ Khurpa Mudra for Protection

For this mudra, the khurpa is held in both hands. The right hand is exactly as it was for the previous mudra. The left hand does the same gesture below the right on the blade part of the khurpa. Your index fingers and pinkie are pointed straight but in opposing directions. By adding the left or feminine hand to the blade, which also represents water, the eastern light of dawn, and the Lower World, you are simultaneously invoking illumination, flow, and grounding. (Think of this gesture like Gandalf declaring, "You shall not pass!")

This khurpa mudra can be used to ground you and to offer extra protection before merging with helper spirits and can be used as part of space clearing rituals.

Figure 7.2. Khurpa mudra for protection.

Figure 7.3. Khurpa mudra to invoke union and harmony.

⤷ Khurpa Mudra of Communion or Unity

For this mudra, the khurpa is held in the right hand once again with the middle and ring fingers curled around the handle with the thumb. The index finger and pinkie are pointed straight. The left hand is held so that the tips of the index fingers and pinkies touch.

This mudra is for union and harmony. The touching fingers are creating a perfect circuit of energy. This gesture is the union between male-female, sacred-secular, and formless-corporeal. This mudra dispels all dissonance and discord in and around the dhami/jhankri. It is appropriate for use while merging with your helping spirits.

⤷ Khurpa Mudra to Awaken Positive Earth and Water Energies

For this mudra, the khurpa is held in the right hand as in the first mudra for invoking spirits. The middle and ring fingers are curled into the palm and held down with the thumb while the index and pinkie grasp the khurpa. In this position, the dagger's blade tip is struck on the floor. This awakens the naga spirits who hold sway over the waters and energy currents of Earth's body. This can be used to help awaken a house that has been empty for a while or to positively energize a place after it has been spiritually cleaned.

Figure 7.4. Khurpa mudra for awakening positive energies of earth and water to energize a space.

▷ Khurpa Mudra to Call in Heavenly Energies

In this gesture, the khurpa is held vertically with blade pointing downward between the palms and fingers of upraised hands. The effect is of sandwiching the khurpa in a namaste or prayer gesture.

In this mudra, the khurpa is drawing in light, heavenly energies. This

Figure 7.5. Khurpa mudra to invite in heavenly energies.

mudra can be used to call in healing energies, to carry back a soul essence or power animal during a retrieval healing ceremony, or to bring more light into a space.

◺ Khurpa Mudra to Charge a Glass of Water

This gesture would follow the previous mudra to call in heavenly energies. The khurpa is held with four fingers grasping the upper handle and pommel. The thumb is held on the very top of the pommel as you might when clicking the button on a ballpoint pen.

When transforming a glass of water into a healing elixir, the blade of the khurpa is touched to the surface of the water and the energy that was captured in the khurpa is discharged into the water by releasing the thumb.

Figure 7.6. Khurpa mudra to charge a glass of water.

◺ Khurpa Mudra for Personal Meditation

To complete this gesture requires that you hold a vajra in the left hand while the hands are positioned like the mudra of unity (fig. 7.3, on page 84) but without touching the tips of the left and right index and pinkie fingers.

ᐯ Khurpa Mudra for Creating a Ritual Intention

This same gesture as above but the mudra is done with each hand holding a khurpa in the first mudra position (fig. 7.1, on page 82). This mudra can be done with hands crossed over the chest and the blades pointed outward and down.

This is a peaceful, balanced pose that aligns with the great Mother Goddess's energy. It is used for clarifying or declaring one's intentions for a ritual and then embodying that intention with your whole being.

ᐯ Khurpa Mudra for Creating a Ritual Intention and Dancing with the Spirits

This mudra begins like the previous one but with the arms uncrossed and mobile. In this position, the dhami/jhankri can stand and dance the power of the helping spirits, and the mudra can be very useful for raising power and honoring the helping deities and spirits.

Make notes about how each of the mudras felt as you performed them. It is important to integrate as you go along. As you are building your skill and your use of sacred objects, keep checking in with your spiritual guides to see if they have more information for you about using your khurpa.

In chapter 19 you will have more opportunities to work with the embodiment of the khurpa's action in the form of Vajrakilaya/Dorje Phurba.

ᐯ Process Questions

What mudras felt the most powerful for you?

Under what circumstances does your spirit teacher want you to use each of the khurpa mudras?

8

The Dhyangro

Himalayan shamanic drums known as dhyangro are one of the most unique shamanic instruments. These two-sided drums have deep frames and are held by a handle attached to the rim. The handle or murro is actually a specialized, large, wooden khurpa that is made in the same fashion and from the same variety of woods. In overall form, the dhyangro has some similarities to the Bön *rnga* or the Tibetan Buddhist *lag-na*, in that it has two drumheads and a handle, but differs due to the khurpa-shaped murro.

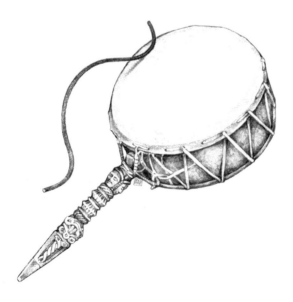

Figure 8.1. Dhyangro drum and gajo beater (pen-and-ink by the author).

This handle has additional length at the top, which fits inside the drum. It is secured in place with rattan and wooden pegs. The part of the murro that is below the head functions as the handle and also allows the dhyangro to be spun back and forth to allow each drumhead to be played in turn. The murro may also be used as a healing

Figure 8.2. Bhola playing his dhyangro (photo: Mariarosa Genitrini).

instrument. It can stand in for the khurpa in ceremony, such as for healing, blessing, or any in any other way that the shaman's dagger might be called into play.

Before the drum is fitted with its playing heads, various charms, sacred beads, or stones are added to enliven the instrument and cause it to rattle as it is spun. These typically include a copper coin, a rudraksha bead, and some rice kernels or mustard seeds. This "feeding" is part of making the drum an empowered, living being and not simply a musical instrument.

Dhyangro drumheads are made from deer or goat rawhide. The dual drumheads represent the male and female aspects of creation. The gender of the skin is not determined by the gender of the animal source of the hide but rather by the relationship to the handle's three-sided blade. The drumhead that is aligned with a flat side of the murro or khurpa blade is female, while the side of the drum aligned with an edge of the blade is male.

A unique feature of the dhyangro is that it is played most often in front of the dhami/jhankri's torso. One drumhead faces the body while the drumstick (*gajo*) is used to beat the forward-facing head. In this way the sound of the drumbeats are directed into the shaman's body.

Although dhyangros are not as common as other shamanic drums, thanks to the Internet's many vendors of imported instruments as well as online auctions such as eBay, it is much more possible for a Westerner to obtain them. If you choose to include a dhyangro with its gajo beater in your shamanic practice, you will want to clear it and dedicate it to your shamanic practice.

Journey to Clear and Empower Your Dhyangro and Gajo

This is an opportunity to work directly with your helping spirits to clear and dedicate your Nepalese shamanic drum. Before you begin, surround yourself with your golden, silver, and iron spheres. Make an offering to the spirits, sing your sacred songs, make an offering of uncooked rice, and honor all of the helping spirits in the directions.

Please read through the directions carefully and gather all that you'll need before you begin. For this exercise, you will need:

- A way to produce the shamanic journey rhythm in the background
- A comfortable place to be seated
- A small handful of uncooked rice kernels
- Your journal or a notebook and a pen
- A quiet time and space
- Your new dhyangro and its gajo beater
- A strip of red cotton cloth and a strip of white cotton cloth, both about 1 inch (3 cm) wide by 12 to 16 inches (30–40 cm) long

⬥ Performing the Ceremony

1. Choose a time when you will be able to work with the spirits.
2. Prepare yourself and all the materials you require.
3. Begin playing the journey rhythm softly.
4. Call your power animal to you to support you during this ritual.
5. Do a journey to your primary teacher.
6. Once you are in the teacher's presence, ask him or her to assist you in clearing the drum of any unbeneficial energies.
7. Once the object is cleared, ask the teacher to empower the dhyangro. The teacher may merge with you to breathe upon the drum, to offer a song or chant, or to move around with the dhyangro, or the process may be accomplished energetically. Allow your trusted teacher to guide the process.
8. After the drum has been empowered, tie the red and white cloth strips around the handle (close to the drumheads) to "tame" the power of the drum for use. (Think of this like the bridle on a horse, which allows you to direct the animal's direction, bringing the raw power into a useful energy. Representationally, it keeps the dhyangro, which is now a living thing, under the dhami/jhankri's control.)
9. Get up and dance with the drum while performing the journey beat. (Remember to beat the side facing away from you while you hold the drum in front of your torso.)
10. When you feel you have finished dancing, thank the spirits with whom you worked and return to ordinary reality by drumming the callback signal.

Once the journey is complete, remember to make an offering to the spirits for their help and support.

⌂ Journey Explorations

Journey to your teacher or power animal to ask: What is the best way to care for my dhyangro?

Journey to your teacher or power animal to ask: What do the symbols that are represented on my dhyangro's handle mean for my own practice? Ask the teacher to introduce you to the spirits that are represented on the murro.

Journey to your teacher or power animal to have him or her take you to meet the living spirit of your dhyangro.

Record the content of your journeys and your perceptions about what you received.

After each journey, thank your power animal, your teacher, and any other spirits who have revealed themselves. Then make an offering to the spirits. This can be an offering of incense smoke, bits of food outdoors, or flower petals.

⌂ Process Questions

What drew you to using a dhyangro in your practice?

Under what circumstances does your spirit teacher want you to use the dhyangro?

9

Aina

The Shaman's Mirror

In several Asian and Siberian cultures, shamans wear polished metal disks on the front and sometimes on the back of their costumes. The mirror reflects negativity and amplifies access to the positive energy the shaman seeks for working. Mirrors have been used in this fashion all across Asia from Siberia to China into the Himalayas and down into the foothills of Nepal and northern India.

In Asia, many shamans still wear at least one mirror, which is sometimes suspended on a cord and worn around the neck. Such is the case

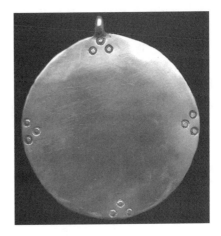

Figure 9.1. Aina shaman mirrors may be small enough to wear as a pendant or as large as a saucer.

with Bhola, who wears a small shaman's mirror or aina (in Tibetan, melong) as part of his ritual dress. Depending upon the region, shamans' mirrors are of different sizes and have different names.

Wherever it is used, an empowered aina can reflect away negative energies or be used to draw positive energies into a space. When a shaman's mirror has been made with a convex and a concave side, the convex side faces outward and the concave faces inward. The concave side focuses positive energy into the wearer's body or the altar, and the convex side repels any negative energy.

Another form of aina used in Nepal is the *lokur chuni,* a cast metal disk of brass, bronze, or silver, which is polished on one side like an aina and has a complex design of protective symbols on the reverse, concave side. This can be worn around the neck, sewn onto a coat, hung in a room, or strung inside of a frame drum. As with all shamanic objects, the use is determined through the relationship the dhami/jhankri has with his or her helping spirits and with the spirit within the object that is being used.

Bhola's altar always has a large aina, which functions as a portal through which beneficial spirits may enter the room for healing as well as for his personal protection. The mirror is either set upright in a bowl of rice or leans upright against the lamp or rim of the copper plate (thaal).

Mirrors can also be tools for divination during a shamanic session. Gazing into a reflective or luminous surface to receive spiritual information is called scrying. An inspirited dhami/jhankri uses her or his inner sight to perceive the illness afflicting a patient or search for lost objects and errant souls. Crystals, pools of water, or ordinary mirrors may all be used for this purpose when cleared and empowered by a shaman. As with all of the shaman's empowered regalia, a mirror may also be used to heal when the energies stored in it are transferred to whatever or whoever requires the dhami/jhankri's help.

❦ Journey to Clear and Empower Your Aina

This is an opportunity to work directly with your helping spirits to clear and dedicate your aina or melong. Before you begin, surround yourself with your golden, silver, and iron spheres. Make an offering to the spirits, sing your sacred songs, make an offering of uncooked rice, and honor all of the helping spirits in the directions.

Please read through the directions carefully and gather all that you'll need before you begin. For this exercise, you will need:

- Your dhyangro and gajo to beat the journey rhythm or another way to produce the rhythm
- A comfortable place to be seated
- A small handful of uncooked rice kernels
- Your journal or a notebook and a pen
- A quiet time and space
- Your new aina
- Heavy-duty red carpet thread or rainbow thread about 30 inches (75 cm) long (Nepalese shamans use balls of very lightweight cotton rainbow threads in their work. The individual threads are extremely thin and rolled on the ball together. A good substitute is Coats & Clark Star Mercerized Cotton Quilting Thread Multicolor Thread 1200 Yd. Over The Rainbow. It is a single thread with multiple colors dyed along its length.)

☙ Performing the Ceremony
1. Choose a time when you will be able to work with the spirits.
2. Prepare yourself and all the materials you require.
3. Begin playing the journey rhythm softly.
4. Call your power animal to you to support you during this ritual.
5. Do a journey to your primary teacher.
6. Once you are in the teacher's presence, ask him or her to assist you in clearing the aina of any unbeneficial energies.
7. Once the object is cleared, ask the teacher to empower the shaman's mirror. He or she may merge with you to breathe upon the mirror, to offer a song or chant, or to move around with the aina, or the process may be accomplished energetically. Allow your trusted teacher to guide the process.
8. After the aina has been empowered, tie the thread through the loop at the top of the aina to "tame" its power for use. (Think of this like the bridle on a horse, which allows you to direct the

animal's direction, bringing the raw power into a useful energy. Representationally, it keeps the mirror, which is now a living thing, under the dhami/jhankri's control.)

9. Place the aina around your neck as you would a necklace. The mirror should lie over your heart.

10. Get up and dance with the drum while performing the journey beat. (Remember to beat the side facing away from you while you hold the drum in front of your torso.)

11. When you feel you have finished dancing, thank the spirits with whom you worked and return to ordinary reality by drumming the callback signal.

Once the journey is complete, make an offering to the spirits for their help and support.

⌂ Journey Explorations

Journey to your teacher or power animal to ask: What is the best way to care for my aina?

Journey to your teacher or power animal to ask him or her to introduce you to the spirit of the aina. Record the content of your journeys and your perceptions about what you received.

After each journey, thank your power animal, your teacher, and any other spirits who have revealed themselves to you. Then make an offering to the spirits. This can be an offering of incense smoke, bits of food outdoors, or flower petals.

⌂ Process Questions

What drew you to using a shaman's mirror in your practice?

Under what circumstances does your spirit teacher want you to use your aina?

10

The Mala

Strings of beads are used by the faithful of many spiritual traditions. These tools are common to Buddhists, Hindus, Sikhs, Muslims, and Catholics, as well as dhami/jhankris. Typically, these rosaries or malas are used to focus intent and to count a prescribed number of prayers, mantras, or meditations. Each time the prayer or mantra is spoken aloud, one bead is run through the fingers. This physical action assists the users in more fully embodying their prayers.

Malas or prayer beads may be made of many materials. Wood, shell, root, crystal, seeds, bone, horn, pottery, precious stones, amber, and metal are all used to make prayer bead strands. For some practitioners, the spiritual purpose of the mala can determine what substance is chosen. For instance, if you are working with peaceful deities, you might choose a mala with white or crystal beads, while if you were chanting mantras to increase life span or deepen wisdom, a gold, copper, silver, or amber mala might be used.

Typically, malas used by Himalayan practitioners have 108 beads. The number 108 is thought to have special numerological significance and considered special and sacred in Hinduism, Buddhism, Taoism, and other religions such as Islam, which refers to God with this number. Since 108 is divisible by three, manifestations such as past-present-future, birth-life-death, and body-mind-spirit and the three shamanic realms of the Upper, Middle, and Lower Worlds are contained within it.

Prayer beads may also have counter beads strung along the length of the strand to keep track of the specific number of circuits made around the mala. Known as *chupshed* in Tibetan or *chopshee* in Nepal, these special counting beads can be assigned the role of tracking hundreds or thousands of prayers.

SHAMANIC USES OF PRAYER BEADS

The art of disciplined alteration of consciousness is essential for any shaman to accomplish her or his work. While you may be most familiar with the use of repetitive drumming or rattling to expand awareness, the repetition of words or chants can have a similar effect in altering consciousness. Indeed, it is common for dhami/jhankris to sing while drumming to enhance the depth of the shamanic trance. However, it is just as possible to enter the shamanic state of consciousness through singing or chanting alone. After chanting for a few minutes, the consciousness of a disciplined shamanic practitioner can easily slip into the realm of the spirits.

This use of chanting to alter states of consciousness is a two-way street: counting on a mala can also have the effect of bringing the bearer into laserlike focus on the present moment. By fingering the beads and counting or chanting, the practitioner slows the breath, and the perceptions of the moment can become expanded and clear. This brings the spirit walker more keenly into ordinary reality.

Malas as Part of Shamanic Garb

Among Himalayan shamans, malas of rudraksha seeds are not only used for meditation and prayer but also as part of a shaman's protective, ceremonial attire. Bhola wears several very large malas crossed over his heart in a bandolier style, along with a strand of large brass bells. The malas are made of a combination of rudraksha seeds and the dried fruits from the soap nut tree indigenous to the Himalayan mountain ranges. Soap nut seeds have been used since time immemorial for washing clothes and as a gentle natural wash for body care. In spiritual terms, a rosary made from these beads helps to cleanse the area around the shaman, keeping it clear of all negative influences.

Rudraksha seeds are considered sacred to the Hindu god Shiva who is the primary male deity honored by dhami/jhankris.* The word *rudraksha* is a combination of the Sanskrit words for Shiva (*rudra*) and eyes (*aksh*) and means the "tears of Shiva," which the deity shed in a moment of bliss.

Rudraksha malas are also traditionally used to subdue or tame harmful energies. Since shamans are responsible for combating chaos, healing illness, and moving the spirits of the dead from our world, they are often thought of as gaining mastery over unbeneficial spirits. This idea is common in many areas of the world. Among central Asian shamans, for example, a ceremonial horse switch is part of their traditional paraphernalia to control harmful energies. As a rider might control a horse, in the same way, rudraksha malas are used by Himalayan dhami/jhankris to subdue disease-causing or disruptive spirits.

By using rudraksha seeds, which are sacred to Shiva, and soap nut seeds together, Bhola ritually enfolds himself in the blessing and protection of the Divine while maintaining a spiritually clean space around himself as he does his shamanic work.

Bhola keeps another strand of prayer beads close at hand when he is teaching workshops. He reaches for them after he has drummed, danced, and sung forth his power. Although his intent is to express his gratitude, he is also settling back into his body and his ordinary reality consciousness through working the beads. Used in this way, his mala helps him to attain a calmer, centered, and more grounded affect, which is more suitable for presenting information.

Some dhami/jhankri also use a mala for divining the source of illness or other information. A simple divination practice using malas, which involves bead counting, may be found in my book *A Spirit Walker's Guide to Shamanic Tools.*

Malas have become very accessible in today's world, and rudraksha malas are available through many sources including merchants of Ayurvedic, meditation, and shamanic supplies. Rittha (soap nut) malas,

---

*The practice of Nepalese shamanism is both animistic and polytheistic. It honors the spirits of nature, the ancestors, and tutelary spirits as well as many gods and goddesses who control the forces of nature and the workings of the cosmos. The god Shiva is one such deity acknowledged by Himalayan shamans as the supreme deity or creator; more will be introduced later in this book.

Figure 10.1. Rudraksha malas for sale in Kathmandu, Nepal (photo: Mariarosa Genitrini).

kamalgatta (lotus seed) malas, and naga or sarpa (snake vertebrae) malas are often more difficult to find.*

Using the Mala to Chant Mantras

Once you have empowered the mala, you will want to chant mantras that can be of use in your shamanic practice. Here is one that you can learn very easily. I have written it as it would sound in English. There are other mantras throughout this book.

There are important guidelines that need to be followed when you chant any mantra. First, make sure you begin with a clear mind and chant with an open heart. Make sure to give the chanting your full attention and concentration. Since chanting the words of a mantra are akin to spell casting, it is important to pronounce every syllable to the best of your ability. It is important as you are weaving magic through these syllables that you do this for the benefit of all living beings. Have a clear intention that your chant is a positive blessing for everyone. Never chant when you are angry, preoccupied, or with a desire to harm.

Om Mah-nee Pad-may Hum

This mantra is perhaps the most well known to Western people. It assists in bringing peace by purifying the one who chants the mantra from the

---

*Some good mala suppliers can be found at www.shamansmarket.com, and www.rudrakshamayurveda.com.

"sins" of pride or ego, jealousy, desire, ignorance, greed, and aggression or hatred. This mantra can bring balance, calm, and harmony.

⚜ *Journey to Clear and Empower Your Mala*

This is an opportunity to work directly with your helping spirits to clear and dedicate your new mala. Before you begin, surround yourself with your golden, silver, and iron spheres. Make an offering to the spirits, sing your sacred songs, make an offering of uncooked rice, and honor all of the helping spirits in the directions.

Please read through the directions carefully and gather all that you'll need before you begin. For this exercise, you will need:

- Your dhyangro and gajo to beat the journey rhythm or another way to produce the rhythm
- A comfortable place to be seated
- A small handful of uncooked rice kernels
- Your journal or a notebook and a pen
- A quiet time and space
- Your new mala
- Rainbow thread about 5 inches (13 cm) long (The chapter 9 exercise offers more information about the thread; see page 95.)

◣ Performing the Ceremony

1. Choose a time when you will be able to work with the spirits.
2. Prepare yourself and all the materials you require.
3. Begin playing the journey rhythm softly.
4. Call your power animal to you to support you during this ritual.
5. Do a journey to your primary teacher.
6. Once you are in the teacher's presence, ask him or her to assist you in clearing the mala of any unbeneficial energies.
7. Once the object is cleared, ask the teacher to empower the mala. They may merge with you to breathe upon the mala, to offer a song or chant, to move around with the mala or the process may be accomplished energetically. Allow your trusted teacher to guide the process.
8. After the mala has been empowered, tie the thread at the junction

where the strand was tied together. There is often a larger bead or tassle in this place. The addition of the rainbow thread tames its power for shamanic use, keeping the living object under the dhami/jhankri's control.

9. Place the mala around your neck as you would a necklace, or wind it around your right wrist.

10. Get up and dance with the drum while performing the journey beat. (Remember to beat the side facing away from you while you hold the drum in front of your torso.)

11. When you feel you have finished dancing, thank the spirits with whom you worked and return to ordinary reality by drumming the callback signal.

Once the journey is complete, make an offering to the spirits for their help and support.

◤ Journey Explorations

Journey to your teacher or power animal to ask him or her to introduce you to the spirit of your mala.

Journey to your teacher or power animal to ask: What mantra would be most useful in my practice?

Journey to your teacher or power animal to ask: How many repetitions of this mantra are best for me to chant? How often should I chant this mantra?

Record the content of your journeys and your perceptions about what you received.

After each journey, thank your power animal, your teacher, and any other spirits who have revealed themselves to you. Then make an offering to the spirits. This can be an offering of incense smoke, bits of food outdoors, or flower petals.

◤ Process Questions

What drew you to using a mala in your practice?

Under what circumstances does your spirit teacher want you to use the mala?

11

The Trishula or Trident

The *trishula* or trident is the three-pronged sacred weapon of the Hindu deity Shiva. In a general sense, the trishula represents the male aspect of the primary deity in his three aspects of creator, preserver, and destroyer (Brahma, Vishnu, and Mahadev).* Its three prongs also represent several other triads, including the three moments of birth, death, and rebirth; the three Shaktis (powers) of will, action, and wisdom; the point where the three main *nadis* or energy channels (*ida, pingala,* and *shushumna*) that channel kundalini energy through the chakras meet at the third eye; and the three shamanic spiritual worlds (Upper, Middle, and Lower). The trident also represents the fire element and the state of illumination.

With the trishula, Shiva is able to defeat negative energies. The trishula in the hands of Shiva can also destroy the three worlds of human existence: the physical world, the world of the past, and the world of the mind. It is said that, when these three planes of existence are destroyed, a single nondual plane of existence emerges that is pure bliss.

OBTAINING YOUR TRISHULA

Although the jhankri's trishula is usually handwrought from copper or iron, purveyors of Hindu *puja* (ritual worship) supplies are excellent

---

*As Shiva is part of the supreme Mother Goddess, she in her form of Durga or Kali is also shown wielding a trishula. Shiva and Pavrati's son Ganesh also wields the weapon.

Figure 11.1. Large trishulas are erected to both honor and represent Shiva's presence (photo: Mariarosa Genitrini).

sources for purchasing a trishula made from brass. If you are fortunate to live near an Indian grocery shop, they may carry puja supplies or be able to order you what you need. Hindu Vedic shops also carry brass trishulas. They sometimes come with a separate base or stand, which allows them to be positioned easily on an altar. eBay and Amazon are other excellent sources.

Journey to Clear and Empower Your Trishula

This is an opportunity to work directly with your helping spirits to clear and dedicate your new trishula. Before you begin, surround yourself with your golden, silver, and iron spheres. Make an offering to the spirits, sing your sacred songs, make an offering of uncooked rice, and honor all of the helping spirits in the directions.

Please read through the directions carefully and gather all that you'll need before you begin. For this exercise, you will need:

- Your dhyangro and gajo to beat the journey rhythm or another way to produce the rhythm
- A comfortable place to be seated

Figure 11.2. A rustic Shiva altar with two trishulas (photo: Mariarosa Genitrini).
(See also color plate 9)

- A small handful of uncooked rice kernels
- Your journal or a notebook and a pen
- A quiet time and space
- Your new trishula
- Rainbow thread about 5 inches (13 cm) long (The chapter 9 exercise offers more information about the thread; see page 95.)

ᙁ Performing the Ceremony
1. Choose a time when you will be able to work with the spirits.
2. Prepare yourself and all the materials you require.
3. Begin playing the journey rhythm softly.
4. Call your power animal to you to support you during this ritual.
5. Do a journey to your primary teacher.
6. Once you are in the teacher's presence, ask him or her to assist you in clearing the trishula of any unbeneficial energies.

7. Once the object is cleared, ask the teacher to empower the trishula. They may merge with you to breathe upon the trishula, to offer a song or chant, to move around with the trishula or the process may be accomplished energetically. Allow your trusted teacher to guide the process.

8. After the trishula has been empowered, tie the thread just below where the prongs come together. The addition of the rainbow thread tames its power for shamanic use, keeping the living object under the dhami/jhankri's control.

9. When you feel you have finished the process, thank the spirits with whom you worked and return to ordinary reality by drumming the callback signal.

Once the journey is complete, make an offering to the spirits for their help and support.

⤴ Journey Explorations

Journey to your teacher or power animal to ask: What is the best way to care for my trishula?

Journey to your teacher or power animal to ask him or her to introduce you to the spirit of your trishula.

Record the content of your journeys and your perceptions about what you received.

After each journey, thank your power animal, your teacher, and any other spirits who have revealed themselves to you. Then make an offering to the spirits. This can be an offering of incense smoke, bits of food outdoors, or flower petals.

Process Questions

What drew you to using a trishula in your practice?

Under what circumstances does your spirit teacher want you to use the trishula?

Plate 1. Image of the primordial forest shaman Banjhankri on the surface of a dhyangro drum (painting by the author).

Plate 2. Banjhankrini, the consort of Banjhankri (painting by the author).

Plate 3. At over a hundred years of age, Bhola's father still practices the shamanic traditions of his father.

Plate 4. Functioning as the center of the cosmos with representations of the elemental forces, animals, birds, and deities, the dhami/jhankri altar (thaan) is a sacred space that houses the shaman's implements (photo: Mariarosa Genitrini).

Plate 5. A simplified dhami/jhankri altar with nearly all the objects contained within a hand-beaten copper plate (thaal) that has been lined with rice kernels (photo: Mariarosa Genitrini).

Plate 6. A chatri yarn cross that has been wound with five-color rainbow threads (pancha rangi).

Plate 7. Holding a dhyangro drum and beater (gajo) to receive the spiritual energy of a sacred waterfall (photo: Bhola Banstola).

Plate 8. An abundance-increasing offering arranged on a winnowing basket (nanglo) (photo: Mariarosa Genitrini).

Plate 9. A rustic Shiva altar with two trishulas (photo: Mariarosa Genitrini).

Plate 10. The portion of the Himalayas containing Mount Everest, known in Nepali as Sagarmāthā, as seen from space (photo credit: NASA).

Plate 11. Bhola drumming to honor the elements and the directions.

Plate 12. Dharti Mata, Mother Earth, giving birth to all life (photo: Mariarosa Genitrini).

Plate 14. A mask-wearing, ascetic devotee of Hanuman dancing at the Pashupatinath temple complex in Kathmandu.

Plate 13. Gannyap statue depicting the deity with ten arms and two heads (a second smaller head can just be seen above his primary head), Kathmandu, Nepal.

Plate 15. On Nag Panchami small posters like this one are hung over doorways and blessed with milk to honor the nagas for their blessings and protection.

Plate 16. The flour dough clay ransom effigy.

Consecrating Shamanic Tools and Creating the Dhami/ Jhankri Altar

The altar or thaan is the central pillar, cosmic map, and spiritual "control panel" for the dhami/jhankri. A shaman may create an altar for a healing, for a ceremony, or as part of a daily ritual. In doing so, the shaman is actually creating a diagram of the cosmos. The objects on a thaan are arranged in a ceremonial manner that becomes the shaman's map of the realms, the ground on which spirit work is performed, and a second home for the spirits. The altar may be a permanent fixture in a room or be put together for a specific purpose. In either case, it is a sacred meeting place between the ordinary and spiritual realms created by the shaman and containing all her or his ritual objects.

The form of a shaman's altar may be a reflection of that person's cultural traditional, may be constructed from the guidance provided by the shaman's tutelary deity, or may be the result of a shamanic journey, vision, or dream. Each altar is unique, and yet there are also some similarities.

Altar spaces usually have a central pivot point or world tree that represents the connection of heaven and Earth. Arranged around it are often objects that represent the elemental forces (earth, water, fire,

Figure 12.1. Bhola preparing his altar for a presentation in Europe
(photo: Mariarosa Genitrini).

air, and ether/spirit), places from which the shaman draws power, and representations of the spirits with whom the shaman works. In addition, different tools may also be placed on the altar, such as drums, malas, bells, mirrors, and other objects that are significant to the dhami/jhankri.

Every object and piece of shamanic paraphernalia is made alive through spiritual empowerment. For the dhami/jhankri, this means singing sacred songs and powerful chants to awaken the spirits.

THE BASIC STRUCTURE OF A NEPALESE DHAMI/JHANKRI ALTAR

Typically, an altar is constructed after personal purification but before any actual shamanic work. The ground or table on which it is built is cleaned thoroughly as is the area around where the altar will be created. The exception to this is in the countryside where, before setting up a shamanic altar, the head of the household would smear the earthen floor with a mixture of cow dung and red mud to sanctify the place. In this case, the idea is to assure a beneficial outcome for the ritual by replicating the actions that are taken to prepare a field to create a fruitful harvest.

The space that will hold the altar is then blessed with sacred water, incense smoke, or special songs and prayers. These prayers honor Mother Earth, the spirits of the house or structure, the land, and the ancestral spirits who take care of and inspirit the space on which the altar will be built.

With the dhami/jhankri sitting in the south, facing the prepared space in the North, the objects of the altar are arranged on a spiritually clean surface. In the countryside of Nepal, such a surface might be created by arranging fresh banana or saal leaves on the ground. A clean cloth, whether a simple fabric or an elaborate textile, could also serve as a foundation for an altar, as could a low table (see fig. 3.1, page 38).

As a fundamental fulcrum for shamanic work, an altar usually has aspects that honor and represent the five elements of creation (earth, water, fire, air, ether), a vertical element that stands in for the world tree, and objects that reflect the connection to the spirit helpers, deities, power animals, and ancestors.

A copper plate (thaal) or large, flat winnowing basket (nanglo) is often the first object to be placed and is usually centered on the altar space. This vessel is filled with uncooked rice kernels (akshyaata) and this becomes an earth-honoring foundation for other objects. Mother Earth (Bhumi Devi) is also honored with crystals and stones.

Next to be placed is the diyo or oil lamp. The lamp is positioned on the south side of the altar, closest to the dhami/jhankri. The flame of the oil lamp represents the element of fire, divine light, spiritual illumination, and purity. The oil lamp can be a very simple affair. A small copper or clay bowl of oil with a cotton wick whose lit end rests on the lip of the bowl is the most common form. Other more elaborate brass oil lamps can also be used, as well as those that feature the elephant-headed god Gannyap. Whatever its form, this object is placed near the dhami/jhankri and another lamp may be placed at the center of the rice-filled plate.

An incense burner (*dhupauro*) is placed nearby. Burning incense blesses the space and also honors air. Feathers and a yak tail brush are also considered air-honoring objects, as they can move the air, creating a wind.

Behind the oil lamp, a copper vase weighted with rice or stones and holding peacock or other feathers is used to prop up the khurpa. A Tibetan-styled triangular phurba stand could also be used to hold the khurpa upright. The khurpa symbolizes the axis mundi, connecting Earth with heaven. Another container weighted with water filled with large leaves becomes a stand for the trident. If the thaal plate is not large enough to hold these objects, they are placed just beyond the plate's rim. In circumstances where extra vessels cannot to be used, the khurpa and trident may be placed so that they rest on the edge of the plate with their points facing toward the oil lamp's flame.

Large porcupine quills may also be placed in an upright fashion to honor the animals and the Middle World spirits.

A brass shaman's mirror or aina/melong is rested against the edge of the plate behind the oil lamp or against one of the vertical vessels. The aina is positioned so that the light of the oil lamp is reflected in its surface. This creates a spiritual portal in which the dhami/jhankri can see a great hall filled with healing spirits and deities. Another aina is placed closest to the shaman. This mirror offers protection by reflecting away negative spirits as well as revealing their location.

Two water pitchers (kalasa) with clean water are placed near the plate. These pitchers honor the water element. The one on the left side of the plate represents the female energies and the one on the right represents the male. This water becomes a blessed elixir (amrita) or water of immortality. A small metal or earthenware water bowl is also typically placed nearby.

Quartz crystals (shila dhunga), ammonite fossils (*shaligram*), animal teeth, claws, or horns, curved knives (khurungi), and other objects that serve the dhami/jhankri may be arranged within the thaal. Beyond the edge of the thaal may be placed a conch shell trumpet (*sankha*), shaman's broom (*amliso*) or yak tail brush, large malas, cymbals, and the dhyangro drum and its gajo beater, as well as other objects meaningful to the individual dhami/jhankri. These implements are arranged in an order that the dhami/jhankri feels is correct based upon his or her personal mythos or the relationships the shaman has forged with spiritual entities.

As the dhami/jhankri sets up the altar, she or he sings songs to honor the deities and to awaken the objects and remind them of their duty to serve.

BHOLA'S METHOD FOR BUILDING AND AWAKENING THE ALTAR

Traditional dhami/jhankris receive their tools in several ways. These objects may be gifts from their teacher or mentor, may have been passed to them by ancestral shamans, may be given to them by their community, or may be shown to them in visions or dreams from the shamanic reality (*nindra*). Until needed, these sacred objects are safely stored in a bamboo chest called a *daelly*.

Before embarking on healing or other ritual duties, the dhami/jhankri recites long mantras and sings sacred songs to bring her or his physical, emotional, and spiritual body more fully into the present moment. This process or ceremony is called Sarir Jagaunu Deuta Chadanu. After the shaman is fully enlivened and empowered, the spirits of the home and property are honored.

The elements of the shaman's paraphernalia are cleansed and

awakened next, followed by a spiritual purifying of the sacred space. This includes honoring the elemental spirits who embrace the shaman as well as the healing objects. At this point, the shaman begins drumming and singing the sacred invocations that bring all the helpful spirits into harmony for the ceremony.

First, an honoring chant to the diyo or oil lamp is offered. The songs honor that the fire is placed in and represents the direction of the south. This is the direction of the ancestors. Fire is honored for illuminating and opening the path of the dead, for illuminating all the levels of tangible and intangible realities, for burning the dark forces hindering the shaman's path, and for killing beings at the right time and deciding their rebirth.

The dhami/jhankri also asks, through song, that he or she be able to hold a fire arrow (*agni baan*) to be released in times of obstacles and sings that she or he will eat the fire whenever attacked by malignant spirits or sorcerers. Eating the fire spirit allows the shaman to become more powerful than these enemies. Other songs thank the fire for illuminating the dhami/jhankri's body and soul, for illuminating the place where the ritual is to be performed, for illuminating the shaman's path, and for being a *sakshi* or witness of the shaman's work.

The trident is honored in a way that celebrates its triune nature. These include creation, preservation, and destruction, as well as the three levels of the shaman's reality and those of our human existence—birth, death, and rebirth. The trident is also honored as an instrument representing the fire element of Shiva and as the standard of the shamanic ascetic.

The white quartz crystal stones represent the uprising power of Mother Earth as well as the attributes of clarity, vision, and transparency. These stones along with other stones on the altar also represent masculine power and stability. Sometimes the shamans look into them for answers as spirits linger around them.

A *nali haard* or femur bone of the left leg of a human being or an animal is also kept on the altar to gather and subdue the disease-causing, wandering spirits of humans and animals. This bone is awakened for the altar by summoning the spirits of the lord and lady of the cremation grounds. (This divine couple is referred to as *citipati* in

Tibetan.) Whenever there is need, the bone is blown like a trumpet to protect the place and also for healing.

Whenever they are available, shaligram or black ammonite fossils are also placed on the altar. Their main purposes are to protect the dhami/jhankri, to clear the place from any harmful spirits, and to support the shaman's focus during journeys through the spirit realms. Sometimes a shaligram is immersed in a bowl of water that is then used for purifying a place or for healing. These stones have great spiritual significance, and it is believed that taking the spirit of a shaligram into your being can produce a rapid spiritual perfection or *siddhi*. For this reason, sadhus (Hindu ascetic yogis) sometimes literally consume the stones.

A serpent vertebrae mala (sarpa mala or naga mala) is used to maintain the boundary between the spiritual and mundane worlds. It also represents the energies of change, offers protection, and represents the transitions of death and rebirth, as well as offering the blessings of abundance and wisdom. Shamans may wear this mala around the neck and also use it for healing diseases caused by disruptive earth and water spirits. Chanting mantras that honor the spirits of the nagas activates this unique rosary.

The two water vases are then placed on either side of the altar. Healing and helping spirits are called into the water to support healing processes, and the water itself is turned into a healing substance. During difficult healing journeys the shaman keeps one of his or her soul parts in one of the water vases in case of encountering dangers during the journey. If the journeying dhami/jhankri is trapped or captured by malignant spirits, the shaman's helper or *sahayogi* has to sprinkle water on the shaman and give him or her a drink to assist the shaman's soul to safely return to the body.

Sacred fire ash that has been collected from healing rituals or by burning sacred medicinal plants is applied on the third eye, below the eyes, and on the throat of the shaman for protection and to dissolve the individual ego into the universal mind. During this action, the shaman sings a song about where the sacred plants grew and also chants protective charms.

The shaman activates the healing and protective powers of feathers from sacred birds such as the peacock or eagle. These represent the in-between worlds of the humans and spirits. The characteristics and powers of the respective birds are invoked in song.

The khurpa (phurba) may also be kept on the altar. If a khurpa is not available then the shaman activates the dhyangro drum's handle, which is also a khurpa. The shaman invokes the powers of the drum handle and the khurpa for grounding purposes and for subduing disturbing spirits. The khurpa is wielded to protect from different directions, to active the spirits of the body, and to protect the altar.

Mirrors or aina are kept right in front of the shaman. If these aren't available, the water bowl plays the function of the mirror. In these reflective surfaces, it is possible for the dhami/jhankri to see the reflections or shadows of disease-causing spirits. The helping spirits of the dhami/jhankri are sung to empower these objects.

Metal coins, betel nuts, and other offerings are also placed on the altar as invitations to the tutelary deities.

BINDING AND PROTECTING THE ALTAR AND SACRED OBJECTS

Once the altar is prepared, a protection mantra is chanted seven to twenty-one times to bind the objects to the shaman and to place protection over them. What follows is Bhola's ancestral version of this chant:

Om! Ashana Baadhu
Om! Bind and protect the sacred cushion

Thana Mandira Baadhu
Protect and bind the sacred altar and shrine

Diyo Kalasa Baadhu
Protect the oil lamp and sacred water vase

Dhyangro Gajo Baadhu
Protect my drum and drum beater

Jhyali-Jhyamata Baadhu
Protect my cymbals and other instruments

Jala Mala, Ghanti Ghamara Baadhu
Protect my mala rosaries, bells, and bandoliers

Sira Ko Mukut Pheta Baadhu
Protect my turban and headdress

Bhoto Jaama Patuka Baadu
Protect my shirt, frock, and waist belt

Bokshi Daini Ka Gyana Baadhu
Bind the unhealthy effects of witches and sorcerers

Preta Pishacha Masana Ko Bato Baadhu
Block the paths of vengeful, malignant, and un-crossed-
    over spirits

Gyana Chale Gyana Baadhu
If hostile forces attack, protect me from them

Baana Chale Baana Pharkau
If attacking darts or arrows come, send them back to
    the sender

Aakasha Baadhu, Patala Baadu
Bind the Upper World realms and subterranean realms
    in their places

Ghara Ka Muul Dwar Baadhu
Put a gate over the main door of the house

Chara Sura Baadhu, Dashai Disha Baadhu
Bind the four corners and ten directions

Bokshi Daini Ko Gyana Baadhu
Bind the ill intention of witches and sorcerers

Phuro Mantra, Ishwar Mahadeo Ki Bacha.
with the power of the mantra and oath of Ishwar
    Mahadeo.

Since this has specific references to Bhola's own area, it is best to
work with your own teachers to craft a protection song or chant that
accomplishes the same purpose. Crafting your own chant is a part of
the following exercise.

CEREMONY FOR AWAKENING AND CONSECRATING YOUR SHAMANIC ALTAR

Including Nepalese objects in your shamanic work is best accomplished through engaging with your familiar spiritual allies and asking what objects would be beneficial in your practice, as well as how they might be used.

Appropriate journey intentions to receive the information you require are shown below. Be sure you have received all of the information from these journeys and have assimilated what you have received before you proceed to the awakening.

◣ Journey Explorations

Journey to your teacher or power animal to ask: What are the best dhami/jhankri tools for my practice? Make a list and gather whatever objects that have been suggested to you. You may receive a combination of Nepalese objects and others that are familiar or especially sacred to you. Follow the suggestions of your spirits and of your own heart.

Journey to your teacher or power animal to ask: What is the best arrangement for my shamanic objects on my dhami/jhankri altar (thaan)? Record what you learn in the form of a simple diagram that can be easily stored with your sacred objects.

Journey to your teacher or power animal to ask: Please give me my own protection chant/song. Practice the song or chant until you have completely internalized it before moving forward to the next exercise.

Once you have finalized the contents and arrangement of your altar and have internalized your protection chant or song, it is time to set it up and perform an awakening ceremony. A version of this ritual will be done each time you set up your altar for work.

🪷 *Awakening and Consecrating Your Shamanic Altar*

As you have done before other sacred actions, surround yourself with your golden, silver, and iron spheres. Make an offering to the spirits, sing your sacred songs, make an offering of uncooked rice, and honor all of the helping spirits in the directions.

Please read through the directions carefully and gather all that you'll need before you begin. For this exercise, you will need:

- Your dhyangro and gajo to beat the journey rhythm or another way to produce the rhythm
- A comfortable place to be seated
- A small handful of uncooked rice kernels
- Your journal or a notebook and a pen
- A quiet time and space
- All of your altar objects and a copper plate (thaal), flat winnowing basket (nanglo), or special cloth on which they are to be arranged
- The diagram of how the altar is to be arranged

⌦ Performing the Ceremony

1. Choose a time when you will be able to work with the spirits.
2. Prepare yourself and all the materials you require.
3. Begin playing the journey rhythm softly.
4. Call your power animal to you to support you during this ritual.
5. Do a journey to your primary teacher.
6. Once you are in the teacher's presence, ask him or her to assist you in setting up your thaan.
7. Take each object in turn and perform a *fu mantra*. This involves holding the object in both hands and then touching the forehead (third eye) and heart. After touching these parts of your body, blow prayers onto the object. These can be as simple as a short prayer of gratitude for their service in your work.
8. Continue this process until your altar is complete.
9. Light the oil lamp or candle.
10. Now, perform the protection song or chant seven to twenty-one times while blessing your body, the altar, and the tools with rice kernels.
11. When you feel you have finished the process, thank the spirits with whom you worked and return to ordinary reality by drumming the callback signal.

You are now ready to use the altar for your shamanic purpose. You may also want to set up a simpler altar whenever you are planning to do journeys.

Whenever your work is complete, make an offering to the spirits for their help and support.

⌂ Journey Explorations

Journey to your teacher or power animal to ask: What is the best use of my thaan? Under what circumstances is it best to set up my thaan before journey work?

Journey to your teacher or power animal to ask him or her to introduce you to the spirit of your thaan.

Journey to ask your teacher: What spirits will work with me through this altar?

Record the content of your journeys and your perceptions about what you received.

After each journey, thank your power animal, your teacher, and any other spirits who have revealed themselves to you. Then make an offering to the spirits. This can be an offering of incense smoke, bits of food outdoors, or flower petals.

⌂ Process Questions

What called you to use a Nepalese dhami/jhankri altar in your practice? How can using an altar deepen your experience of the spirits?

13

The Dhami/Jhankri's Costume

A dhami/jhankri's costume is perhaps the most individually unique element of the shaman's paraphernalia. The act of donning a special article of clothing, or a complete costume, on occasion, alters the shaman's appearance and is a physical reminder or reflection that the shaman has become *another*—that is, the dhami/jhankri has become the embodiment of the healing spirits with which she or he works. This alteration of physical appearance signifies that the dhami/jhankri has become *holy;* the shaman has taken on the mantle of spirit.

Like their brother and sister shamans around the globe, traditional Nepalese dhami/jhankris don a ritual outfit before performing shamanic duties. Although regional and ethnic differences exist, there are some similarities. Bhola's dhamai/jhankri costume is primarily white and red. White is associated with the Divine Feminine, purity, and Mother Earth, but it is also the color of Lord Shiva's skin. Red is associated with both Lord Shiva and his masculine energies and his role of taking action in the world and with the goddess Shakti and the flow of energy and power. Putting these colors together provides a perfect balance to enfold the shaman.

Bhola wears a long-sleeved, collarless, bright white shirt made from a finely woven cotton fabric. It is fastened at the V-shaped neckline and at the waist with ties of the same fabric. This garment is called a *bhoto*.

A collarless, bright white shirt dedicated to your shamanic practice could be substituted for the traditional bhoto.

Beneath the waist, Bhola wears a *jama* or flowing floor-length white skirt. It is also fashioned from a finely woven cotton fabric. The skirt has 108 pleats sewn to a narrow waistband and is worn wrapped in an overlapping fashion around the waist. It is then tied in the same

Figure 13.1. Bhola in his ritual attire blessing a space prior to performing a ritual.

manner as the bhoto shirt. The jama may be worn over white shorts or white tights. A loose pair of white trousers can also be worn in place of the jama.

Where the bhoto and jama meet, Bhola wears a long cummerbund of red cotton fabric called a *patuka* that is wound around his waist. It is six inches wide and several yards long so that it can be wound at least three times around the waist (seven or nine are preferred) and then fastened by tucking the end into the band. This protective belt for the belly is also a wonderful place to rest the handle (murro) of the dhyangro while playing the drum.

Over the bhoto, Bhola wears his rudraska and rittha malas and a bandolier of chain onto which metal bells (*ghanti*) and metal amulets have been secured. This heavy bandolier is worn from the left shoulder to the right side of the body. When the shaman stands, the bandolier and malas fall to about the center of the waistband. A very long rudraksha mala is worn on the same side as the bandolier. On the other side of the torso, several long rittha malas and rudraksha malas are arranged from the right shoulder to the left side of the body so that they cross over the bandolier. They fall to the same length as the bandolier on the other side. A small, sturdy, white fabric shoulder bag is sometimes also worn on the left side to hold rice kernels or other objects. This is usually a bit longer to allow easy access to the contents.

On his head, Bhola wears a *feta*. This is a headband fashioned from two long pieces of cloth, one white and one red. They are approximately four inches wide and double the height of the person wearing it. These are tied, white first and then red, around the forehead, much like one might tie a bandanna. Once tied around the head, they both reach the floor.

Over the top of the feta, Bhola wears a headdress or *pagari*. The pagari holds peacock feathers (*mayur* or *mayur ko pankha*) and porcupine quills (*dumsiko kanda*), which are set upright in a red- or white-colored band of the headdress. The peacock feathers represent spiritual and physical purity. In shamanic terms, they also symbolize shamanic power, soul flight, journeying, healing, and the action of dispelling ignorance or darkness. The long quills of the Himalayan porcupine (*Hystrix brachyuran*) are used to assist in protection, as a link to the animal world and to the dhami/jhankri's Middle World spiritual allies, and as an aid for keeping focused during long sessions of shamanic work.

Each dhami/jhankri has a somewhat different version of ritual attire. The colors and form of the garments may vary; however, the wearing of crossed malas and a bell bandolier, a headdress or turban, and a small shoulder bag are nearly universal. Ritual garments are a direct outgrowth of the dhami/jhankri's relationship with the spirits and their power. Furthermore, a shaman's paraphernalia increases the power available as the clothing, implements, and instruments, such as the drum, have been enlivened. This empowerment invests the objects with the essential energies of the shaman's helping spirits.

Bhola's first experience with his own shamanic attire was a powerful experience:

> Our dresses are mostly white with a little red and sometimes no red. White is a color of wisdom, purity, and auspiciousness. It is also the color of renouncers and ascetics. In my culture, dead bodies are covered with white fabric, and white often symbolizes the spiritual pollution of death. When an immediate family member dies, such as a parent, the children of the parent wear white throughout the year as a sign of mourning. When I begin a ceremony dressed completely in white, I have a sense of my own death. However, I also know that everything I wear during ceremonies and healing sessions has been purified and empowered with its own spirit, and so I feel protected. I feel the presence of my helping spirits in close proximity, right next to my skin. Once I have put on the malas, the turban, the headdress, and the medicine bag and have inserted my khurpa in my waistband, I feel completely transformed into a warrior and traveler. Being fully enrobed in my regalia brings me feelings of profound oneness and openness.

As you grow in your practice, you will eventually require some form of shamanic clothing to augment your connections to power. Your attire can be similar to Bhola's costume, or you can create your own special vest, shirt, overcoat, dress, apron, or some other form of clothing that has been decorated in a sacred way guided by your helping spirits and fully empowered. The best way to find out what will work for you and the spirits with whom you work is to journey to them to ask questions.

If you study with a traditional dhami/jhankri and if you qualify in your practices, then your shaman teacher will grant you permission to put on this traditional attire during a special ceremony along with giving you an oil lamp (diyo batti). However, if your practice is based on different indigenous traditions or core shamanic teachings, your personal tutelary deity or your closest spirit guide may provide you with a clear vision of ceremonial attire. As has been stated earlier, it is always recommended that you have a fully trained human teacher to support your learning along with your personal spiritual guides in nonordinary realities.

Here are some suggested journeys that can assist you in becoming clear:

🪷 *Journey to Receive a Vision of Ceremonial Attire*

ᗩ Journey Explorations

Journey to your teacher or power animal to ask: What shamanic ritual clothing is right for me?

Journey to your teacher or power animal to ask: At what times am I to use my ritual clothing?

Journey to your teacher or power animal to ask: How do I make (or find) my ritual clothing?

Journey to your teacher or power animal to ask: How is this ritual clothing to be decorated?

Journey to your teacher or power animal to ask: How do I care for this ritual clothing?

Record the content of your journeys and your perceptions about what you received.

After each journey, thank your power animal, your teacher, and any other spirits who have revealed themselves to you. Then make an offering to the spirits. This can be an offering of incense smoke, bits of food outdoors, or flower petals.

ᗩ Process Questions

What called you to having shamanic ritual garb?

How will this ritual clothing deepen your experience of the spirits?

14

Working within the Nepalese Cosmology

In Nepalese shamanism, the inner and outer worlds are unified. The dhami/jhankri honors the three worlds of the spirits that lie outside the body as well as the reflections of those realms that live within the body. In this way, the Upper World is the area above the heart, which is connected to the future. The Middle World is the torso from the heart to the umbilicus and represents the present moment. The Lower World is everything from the belly button to the feet and is the realm of the past.

The dhami/jhankri is aware that harmony begins "at home." There needs to be attention on the creation of harmony within the shaman. This means healing emotional burdens of the past, present, and future and attending to mental, emotional, spiritual, and physical health.

From that center, the dhami/jhankri widens the circle of attention to keeping relationships with other beings harmonious. These relationships include family, friends, and community and also relationships with other beings (animals, birds, reptiles, etc.), the ancestral spirits, the local spirits of place, the spirits of natural forces, and deities.

What follows is Bhola's ancestral version of the chant-song that is used to welcome in the participation of the spirits in his work. This is sung as he drums and includes the directions and all the spirits of nature that he honors. You may choose to use the English translation and substitute your local spirits with whom you have relationships:

Jaya Kul Deo, Jaya Guru!
Victory ancestral deity, victory teacher!

Patal Dekhi Daki Bolai Lyau Naga Raja, Naga Rani
Let me invite from the Lower World the serpent king and
   queen

Uttara Disha Dekhi Daki Bolai Lyau Dharti Mata
From the North I invite Mother Earth

Paschima Disha Dekhi Daki Bolai Lyau Jala Devi
From the West I invite the water deity

Dakhina Disha Dekhi Daki Bolai Lyau Agni Deo
From the South I invite the fire deity

Purwa Disha Dekhi Daki Bolai Lyau Vayu Deo
From the East I invite the wind/air deity

Antariksha Ma Udne Harul-Gadul Daki Bolai Lyau
I invite the regal eagle from the spaces in between

Pitri Loka Dekhi Pitri Vayu Daki Bolai Lyau
I invite ancestral spirits from their realm

Surya Chandra Graha Mandal Deo Pukara Gari Jau
I invoke the sun, moon, and celestial beings

Hariyaliki Dhani Bana Devi
the forest goddess, keeper of the greenery

Banai Khene Bana Jhankri, Suna Jhankri, Latte Jhankri
the primordial forest-dwelling forest shaman, gold-colored
   shaman, shaman with matted locks

Sirin Shikari, Simi Bhume
the hunting spirit, those of the swamps and those who
   dwell in the earth

Rukha Pata Khola Naa Kheli Hidne
those spirits that play in the trees, leaves, river, and rivulets

Himala Ko Danda Kanda Kehli Hinde Himali Deo
the spirits of the Himalayas and those spirits that roam
among their peaks

Madhye Pahad Mahabara, Chure, Silwalik Ghumi Hidne
the spirits that roam in the foothills of Mahabara, Chure
and Siwalki ranges

Mala Madhesa Terai Ma Kheli Hidne Deo Dewani
the spirits that roam and play in the plains of Terai.

[Here, Bhola honors the rivers:]

*Purwai Disha Bagi Jane Teesta Nadi, Mechi Nadi, Sapta
Koshi*
I also invoke the rivers of the east flowing down: Teesta,
Mechi, Sapta Koshi

Madhye Bhag Ko Bagmati, Trishuli, Kali Gandaki
the flowing rivers of the middle region: Bagmati, Trishuli,
Kali Gandaki

Paschhim Bhag Ko Karnali, Bheri, Seti, Mahakali
the rivers flowing down from the west: Karnali, Bheri,
Seti, and Mahakali

Tamrai Saran, Tamrai Pau, Tamrai Pichha
I honor you, I bow before you, I follow you!

[Here, Bhola honors the sacred mountains (*parvata*):]

*Kanchan Janga, Sagar Matha, Gauri-Shankar, Ganesh
Himal*
I honor the sacred mountains! The Five Treasures of the
Snow, Head of the Horizon, Parvati-Shiva, Ganesh
Himal

*Annapurna, Machapuchhre, Neelgiri, Gaurishankar,
Dhaulagiri*
Annapurna, Machapuchhre, Neelgiri, Gaurishankar,
White Mountain

Saipal, Api, Gauri-Mandakini, Lailash Parvat, Manaslu
Saipal, Api, Gauri-Mandakini, the Kailash ranges,
    Mountain of the Spirits

[Next, he honors the sacred lakes and ponds (*taal, pokhari,
    or kunda*):]

Manasarovara, Rara Pokhari, Khaptad, Seyphoksundo
I honor the sacred lakes of Manasarovara, Rara Lake,
    Khaptad, and Seyphoksundo

Muktinatha, Jwala, Tilicho Tal, Fewa-Rupa Taal
the flames of Muktinath, Tilicho, Fewa-Rupa Lakes

Gosainkunda, Saraswati Kunda, Tso Rolpa Kunda
Gosainkunda Lake, Saraswati Lake, Rolwaling Lake

Duudh Pokhari, Latta Pokhari, Paanch Pokhara
Milk Lake, Matted-Hair Lake, the Five Lakes

Bhairung Kunda, Surya Kunda, Shiva Kunda
Bhairung Lake, Sun Lake, Shiva Lake

*Panchakanya Pokhari, Nag Pokhari, Trishule Pokhari,
    Siddha Pokhari*
Five Virgin Lake, Serpent Lake, Trident Lake, Lake of the
    Enlightened One

Kamal Pokhara, Satyawati, Ghoda-Ghodi, Raja Rani Pokhari
Lotus Lake, Truthful Lake, Horse Lake, King-Queen Lake

*Indreni Taal, Mahadev Pokhari, Gokyo Taal/Ramsaar,
    Saalpa Pokhari*
Rainbow Lake, Mahadeva Lake, Gokyo Lake, Salpa Lake.

[He honors the sacred waterfalls (*jharna* or *changa*):]

*Devi Jharna, Hyatung Jharna, Namaste Jharna, Rupse
    Changa, Pakali Changa*
I honor Devi's Waterfall, Hyatung Falls, Namaste Falls,
    Rupse Falls, Pakali Falls

[Caves are next on the list. These are called gufa in
   Nepali:]

*Halesi Gufa, Chobar Gufa, Mahendra Gufa, Mustang
   Gufa, Siddha Gufa*
Halesi (Maratika) Cave, Chobar Cave, Mahendra Cave,
   Mustang Cave, Siddha Cave

[He also honors the valleys (*upatyaka*):]

Bajua Ki Badimalika, Makalu Ko Barun
Badimalika in Bajura, Barun at the base of Makalu [great
   dark]

*Sudhur Paschim Ko Khaptad, Solu Ko Khumbu, Langtang
   Upatyaka*
Khaptad in far west, Khumbu Valley in Solu, Langtang
   Valley

Manang Upatyaka, Sindu Palchok Ko Paanch Pokhari
Manang Valley, Paanch Pokhara, Sindupalchok

Rara Nikunja, Rolwaling Upatyaka, Kathmandu Upatyaka
Rara National Park, Rolwaling Valley, Kathmandu Valley

Chitwan Upatyaka, Terai Upatyaka, Anya . . .
Chitwan Valley, Terai Valley, [and so on]

This prayer can go on for quite some time with mountain passes
(*bhanjyang*) connecting and joining other valleys being invoked next,
as these passes are not only crossed by humans and animals but even
the spirits roam through and occupy these areas. Indeed, local spirits
of the village, or small shrines, and other very local features would also
be honored.

Bhola's above example demonstrates the intimate connections that
shamans maintain with the spirits that surround them. Without the
power that is sourced from these spirits with whom the dhami/jhankri
has engaged in reciprocal relationships, none of their work—no healing
or balancing—would be possible.

Figure 14.1. The portion of the Himalayas containing Mount Everest, known in Nepali as Sagarmāthā, as seen from space (photo credit: NASA). (See also color plate 10)

DRUMMING TO HONOR THE ELEMENTS

In the Nepalese cosmology there are five elements: earth, water, fire, air, and ether (spirit). The elements are honored each time the dhami/jhankri works. Each element corresponds to a different direction and is honored with drumming and song.

The element of earth is honored in the North. This element is honored as Mother Earth, Bhumi Devi.* She is represented as a very old grandmother holding a bamboo basket on her back, full of medicinal herbs and grain. She is holding a curved sickle in her right hand

---

*In one of the practices Sansari Mai is invoked, instead of Bhumi Devi. Sansari Mai, the mistress of the universe or the universal goddess, has the same characteristices, and her abode is a tree. She carries on her back a bamboo chest containing medicinal herbs and grains and holds a curved sickle in one hand and tongs in the other. She goes to the North, the direction of the earth element. She takes the form of Bhumi Devi and transfigures into a woman holding a child to her bosom as the nurturing mother. The rest of the directions and elementals and their characteristics are the same.

and tongs in her left hand. She is the white goddess who is dressed in white cloth; however the color usually used to represent the North direction is yellow. She travels all over the world carrying abundance, nurturance, and prosperity to everything that has been created. Her journey is one of transformation and is replicated by a dhami/jhankri each time he or she prepares for doing healing work. The earth elemental of the North is stability, and starting in this direction provides a stable foundation for the power that will fill the shaman's body. It is also the direction in which an extraction of unbeneficial energy from a patient is performed. For this direction, the drum is beaten in a slow, one-one pattern (boom—boom—boom—boom).

The dhami/jhankri moves counterclockwise as this flow is considered to be the path of the spirit and of transformation. Leaving the northern direction, the water elemental is honored in the West. The water element supports us to accept the situation where and how we are now, to be accommodative, to be fluid, and to be able to honor the situation and to let go. The spirits who control the waters are the serpent spirits or nagas. The water spirits are helpful to make concrete relationships and to be able to live a comfortable and happy life by being able to let everyday slights and wounds slide away "like water off a duck's back." The water element is critical in the process of accepting a situation, then releasing and letting go.

The water element is represented by serpents and honored in the West. The Nepalese call them nagas. The nagas are the keepers of the water, and since water is critical to Earth's fertility, they are also the keepers of the land. In her journey, Mother Earth, as the white goddess Bhumi Devi, travels from her home in the North to the water where she encounters a blue-colored naga. The color usually used to represent the West direction is blue. She holds the blue-colored snake in her hand, and the naga becomes her walking stick. In the same way, we confront our issues, recognize them, and then let them go, transforming that which was once harmful into beneficial energy. The drumming rhythm for the water is like the heartbeat or waves of water. It is a pattern of two beats with a pause between (boom, boom—boom, boom—boom, boom).

Moving counterclockwise again, Mother Earth now comes to the South that is the home of the fire elemental. It is represented by the color red. Fire is the spirit, the power of change and transformation, the power of passion, the power of creativity, and the power to make things happen. The South is the direction of our deceased ancestors. The fire elemental has three eyes. One of the eyes illuminates the Lower World, one illuminates the earth realm here in Middle World, and the third one illuminates the Upper World. When Bhumi Devi reaches the South, she is given the capacity to see what the present and

Figure 14.2. Bhola drumming to honor the elements and the directions.
(See also color plate 11)

foresee what lies ahead. The fire element is so powerful in transformative processes that the dhami/jhankri always lights either an oil lamp or candle to honor the spirit, illuminate the path, and reveal possibilities. Here, the shaman begins to move and sway like the flame, filling with more power. The dhami/jhankri changes the drumming to a rhythm of three beats followed by a pause (boom, boom, boom—boom, boom, boom—boom, boom, boom).

Turning again counterclockwise, the dhami/jhankri follows Bhumi Devi to the East. East is the place of the spirit of the wind, the air elemental. The East is represented by the green of spring shoots, and the air element is represented by a white horse. Here Mother Earth, the white goddess, gets on the back of the white horse of the wind.*

When the dhami/jhankri faces the East to honor the air and wind, the rhythm of the drum changes. This is because in closing the circle, the shaman begins incorporating the energies supporting the tutelary deity or the ether element. Here the drumming is a more rapid one-one beat that is like the shamanic journey rhythm (boom, boom, boom, boom).

In the East, heaviness is transformed into positivity, and anger transforms into love. Jealousy dissolves, and the heart becomes fully open and altruistic. The East is the seat of spiritual consciousness, and so the shaman incorporates the power of all of his or her spiritual supports in this direction. As the spirits are incorporated, the breath of the shaman becomes softer and the beating of the heart becomes stronger and stronger. During this time a special kind of spiritual energy moves up and down in the body that reminds the dhami/jhankri to anchor deeply to Mother Earth. With a strong and deep connection, the shaman can rise up even farther and expand widely. When shamans do the healing process invoking this element, they use the spiritual broom, bird feathers, or the tail of a sacred animal like the yak to cleanse the body of the person before healing work is undertaken. Here, there is no exact rhythm because when the dhami/jhankris integrate their helping spirits, the rhythm becomes joyful, enthusiastic, and passionate. A version of the drumming is like the

---

*The monkey deity Hanuman is also invoked in the East, especially when awakening and empowering plant medicine.

rapid drumming for a shamanic journey (boom, boom, boom, boom).

At this point, Bhumi Devi riding on the back of the white horse goes to the Lower World domain of the Naga Raja and Naga Rani (serpent king and queen). The serpent king holds a luminous jewel (naag maani) in his mouth, which illuminates the realm. The light-emitting jewel creates a very powerful and clear rainbow. After offering her honor to the king of the serpents, Bhumi Devi gets onto the rainbow bridge and comes back on the surface of Earth under a huge tree. She climbs the tree and continues her journey to the Upper World where she encounters a circular-shaped crystal palace with four doors. The four doors are located in the four cardinal directions and have the same directional colors as in the earthly realm. She spontaneously chooses a door and enters into another realm within the Upper World where a great palace stands. At the center of the palace is a golden-colored throne where Shiva-Mahadeva is sitting. Here the union of Bhumi Devi and Shiva-Mahadeva occurs. The shamans call this the union of the male (purusha) and the female (prakriti) principles or the union of opposites. In Sanatana-Dharma, Hinduism, and Tantric practices, this moment is represented by a half-man and half-woman form called Ardhanarishwara. After this union, Bhumi Devi separates herself and descends down to the earthly realm under a huge tree.

Dhami/jhankris follow this path of the Bhumi Devi to incorporate and honor the elemental spirits. Sometimes the shamans immediately journey to the Upper World realm to get information after a short preparation. But following the path of Bhumi Devi in which she transfigures into elemental beings and unites with the male principle is a longer and deeper way.

Incorporating all of the elements and the spiritual support of the tutelary spirits makes the shaman very strong and powerful. It is at this time that the shaman goes into a shamanic state of trance during which answers and visions are bestowed.

Finally, the fifth element of ether, the spirit that is in all things, is honored by facing upward. This honors the sky and cosmos that embrace Bhumi Devi and all of her many children. She is held by the cosmos and is constantly creating with the spiritual energies of the ether, and all of her many children are blanketed by the wide sky. Ether is pure and is represented by white.

Ether is both the action and purview of the dhami/jhankri. It involves attending to the invisible forces that shape and reshape our reality that may either bring health or cause disease. The shaman's work is about keeping harmony among all the spirits so that healing, well-being, nurturance, fertility, and peace continue to flow in the world. This is done because even a healing spirit can be destructive when it is out of balance—just as either too much or too little rain can be devastating to a community. If healing is being done, this is the time when a soul retrieval would be performed to bring the patient into wholeness. Here the shaman's drumming becomes more syncopated (BOOM, BOOM—boom, boom—BOOM, BOOM—boom, boom).

Following this path, when Bhumi Devi returns to the base of the tree, she sends back different elemental spirits that she had incorporated to their respective directions: the earth spirits go back to the earth; the water spirits go back to the water realm; the fire spirits go back to the fire realm; the air spirits go back to the air realm. The Lower World realm spirits go back to that realm, and the Upper World male principle goes back too. This is the time that shamans release the helping and elemental spirits and other spirits of the sacred objects and ceremonial clothing.

During this period in the ceremony, the drumming rhythms undergo a winding down. The shaman drums from a four-beat rhythm sequence (boom, boom, boom, boom—boom, boom, boom, boom), then to a three-beat rhythm (boom, boom, boom—boom, boom, boom), then a two-beat sequence (boom, boom—boom, boom), and finally a slowing one-beat sequence. (boom—boom—boom—boom). During this winding down, the shaman is gradually brought back to ordinary reality. When the drumming is done, the shaman is able to check in with the patient, offer healing water (amrita), and provide a talisman or special mantra to close the ceremony.

HONORING THE FIVE ELEMENTS

The following exercise is a ceremony of honoring the five elements with the intent of creating a luminous space. When the dhami/jhankri offers this ceremony for a group, everyone sings the songs that enliven their healing objects. Next, everyone bows down to honor our ancestors, ancestral deities, spiritual guides, animal protectors, Mother Earth, and the other protectors or helpful spirits in all the realms. The whole ceremony is accompanied by singing, dancing, drumming, and rattling.

⚜ *Honoring the Elementals with Drumming and Dance*

As you have done before performing other sacred actions, surround yourself with your golden, silver, and iron spheres. Make an offering to the spirits, sing your sacred songs, make an offering of uncooked rice, and honor all of the helping spirits in the directions.

Please read through the directions carefully and gather all that you'll need before you begin. For this exercise, you will need:

- Your dhyangro and gajo to beat the journey rhythm
- A small handful of uncooked rice kernels
- Your journal or a notebook and a pen
- A quiet time and space
- All of your altar objects and a copper plate (thaal), flat winnowing basket (nanglo), or special cloth on which they are to be arranged (or at the very least a lit candle or oil lamp, a bowl of water, a feather, and a stone) placed in the center of your space

⛰ Performing the Ceremony

1. Choose a time when you will be able to work with the spirits.
2. Prepare yourself and all the materials you require.
3. Call your power animal to you to support you during this ritual.
4. Begin by facing the North.
5. Toss a few grains of rice in this direction and call aloud to Bhumi Devi and thank her for your life, your body, and for all the ways she makes your life possible.
6. Play the rhythm of the earth element, which is the pattern of one beat and a pause.
7. While facing North, feel the stability and immensity of Earth. Feel the gravity that holds you to her body. As you drum and dance with

your dhyangro, get connected with Earth's raw element. Let your imagination be free. Continue to feel the stability of our planet and internalize it—feeling it in your flesh, your bones, your heart, and your consciousness. Feel and allow it to pervade your experience so that you merge with it. This enfolding by Mother Earth's energy helps make you feel grounded, stable, safe, secure, balanced, and focused. The earth element is a feminine energy.

8. When you feel complete, turn counterclockwise to the West.

9. Toss a few grains of rice in this direction and call aloud to the naga spirits and thank them for the blessings of rain, water to drink, for the water in your body, and for all the ways they make your life possible.

10. Play the rhythm of the water, which is the pattern of two beats and a pause.

11. As you beat the water rhythm, use your imagination to feel yourself at the seaside, by a lake, or under a waterfall. Allow yourself to merge with the spirits of water. Feel yourself being cleansed, purified, and regenerated. Merging with the water element helps in purification, love, psychic awareness, dreams, sleep, peace, marriage, healing, and friendship. The water element is a feminine energy.

12. When you feel complete, turn counterclockwise to the South.

13. Toss a few grains of rice in this direction and call aloud to the fire spirits and thank them for the blessings of heat and light, for the ability to see in ordinary and extraordinary ways. Thank them for your passion, the fire of your heart, and for all the ways they make your life possible.

14. Play the rhythm of the fire, which is the pattern of three beats and a pause.

15. This direction is about action, passion, will, force, creativity, and power. This time, imagine the heat of the strong sun or the heat of a burning fire that brings warmth and relaxation to your skin. Allow the warmth to gradually penetrate you. The fire's warmth augments the circulation of blood, metabolism, heat in the muscles, and nerves firing and supports the burning away of both physical and spiritual toxins. Merging with the fire element slowly brings about emotional warmth, love, joy, creativity, and accomplishment of both substantial and insubstantial bliss. The fire element has the most potential to

connect with the spirit realm. This elemental ritual opens gateways to the worlds of ancestors and dissolves all the spiritual blocks and imbalances. The fire element has a masculine energy.

16. When you feel complete, turn counterclockwise to the East.

17. Toss a few grains of rice in this direction and call aloud to the air and wind spirits and thank them for the blessings of breath, for their power to move the weather, and for the ability to move air from your lungs through your vocal cords to speak, laugh, and sing.

18. Play the drum with joyful energy, transitioning to the journey beat.

19. This time, imagine the feelings of a gentle breeze that carries away discomfort, fear, and negative thoughts. Air lifts the spirit and mood. At the level of transference of consciousness, the air element supports the movement of consciousness from the confusion of ignorance to the clarity of realization. The air can dispel heaviness. Therefore, in this direction you may request a healing from the spirits or ask a significant question about a personal issue. The air element has masculine energy.

20. As you transition into the journey beat and feel yourself shifting into the shamanic state of consciousness, honor your power animal, your spirit helpers, and all the elements in your journey.

21. Move your body and sing your joy as you continue to journey and drum.

22. Face the center of your space and look upward. This is the direction to honor the sky and the fifth element of ether. The sky-ether direction is about transcendence, sound, and communication. Imagine rainbows descending to Earth to connect you to the whole universe. These rainbows bring the energy to open our hearts and give us the power of vision. Life-changing answers may be perceived at this level, or you may become aware of new blessings. The ether element has a neutral character that is both male and female.

23. When you feel complete, continue to drum and face the east again.

24. When you feel complete, slow the drumming to the rhythm of three beats with a pause and face the south.

25. After a few moments, slow the drumming to a rhythm of two beats with a pause while facing the west.

26. After a few more moments, slow the drumming to the rhythm of one with a pause while facing the north again.

27. Finally, turn toward the altar at the center.
28. Drum the callback signal and gently return to ordinary consciousness.
29. When you have fully returned, honor your altar with a few rice kernels.
30. When you feel you have finished with the process, thank the spirits with whom you worked and extinguish the flame of your oil lamp or candle. Then go outside to make an offering to the spirits for their help and support.

Once you have internalized this way of honoring the spirits, you may choose to add this simple offering prayer to chant or sing as a spontaneous song while you make your rice offerings to the spirits. Add your own lines to it to honor the other spiritual entities with whom you work:

> *To the Keepers of the North I offer rice.*
> *To the Keepers of the West I offer rice.*
> *To the Keepers of the South I offer rice.*
> *To the Keepers of the East I offer rice.*
> *To the Keepers of the Lower World realm I offer rice.*
> *To the Keepers of the Middle World realm I offer rice.*
> *To the Keepers of the Upper World realm I offer rice.*
> *To the Keepers of the village I offer rice.*
> *To the Keepers of the house I offer rice.*

⌫ Journey Explorations

Journey to your teacher or power animal to ask: How does honoring the spirits of the elementals change me?

Journey to your teacher or power animal to ask: How does honoring the spirits of the elementals help to bring harmony to my life?

Journey to your teacher or power animal to ask: How often would it be beneficial to honor the elementals in this way?

Record the content of your journeys and your perceptions about what you received.

After each journey, thank your power animal, your teacher, and any other spirits who have revealed themselves to you. Then make an offering to the spirits. This can be an offering of incense smoke, bits of food outdoors, or flower petals.

⌦ Process Questions

In what ways did you experience the elementals?

How did honoring them in this way deepen your experience of them in your daily life?

15

Ritual of Spring and Renewal

The most widespread spring festival on the Indian subcontinent is Holi, the festival of colors. In Nepal this festival is called Fagu Poornima, and it falls on the full moon between the end of March and the beginning of April.

After the long, dark winter months, the returning sun and warmer temperatures signal the perfect time for celebration. To celebrate the growing light, a fire ceremony is performed the night before the official Holi celebrations. A huge pile of wood is constructed in each village, and every household contributes logs to what will become an enormous bonfire. The eldest person of the village or the ceremonial leader, who may be a dhami/jhankri, lights the fire. As the flames lick the wood, the rest of the village community joins together to make traditional music with drums, trumpets, and raised voices to accompany dancing around the fire. This fire celebration provides an opportunity to let go of the darkness and cold and to bring healing springtime energies into the self, family, and community and into all interpersonal relationships.

The next day is a joyful celebration of the defeat of darkness by the righteous forces of the light and the union of Dharti Mata/Mother Earth with Akash/Father Sky, which brings forth nature's fertile season. This powerful time of regeneration is celebrated by using many colors.

In Kathmandu the festival begins with the raising of a ceremo-

Figure 15.1. The lotus is honored as a symbol of purity and the ability we have to transcend the difficulties of life. Its seeds are also used for malas that bring peace and abundance.

nial pole or *chir*. The pole is a freshly cut pine tree harvested in the Bhaktapur district and carried from the Nala forest into Kathmandu with much ceremony. Once in the city, it is erected at Basantapur in Kathmandu's Durbar Square. The pole is topped with colorful cloth strips, and it stands in the square until the end of the festival. Lighted oil lamps are placed on a cow dung base at the bottom of the pole. Celebrants also tie colorful threads around the shaft of the pole. The pole symbolizes the union of male and female energies and also functions as a victory banner to welcome the spring (Basalt Ritu). The cloth strips (*chirs*) represent the clothes of the Gopinis (Krishna-adoring women) whose clothes the naughty god Krishna (also called Gopi) hangs high on a tree while they are bathing in a river. Krishna tells them they can't get back their clothes until they perform lengthy prayers to the sun god while standing submerged in the water.

Next comes the aspect of the ritual that is most familiar to Westerners. It is the tossing of colored powders onto friends, loved ones, and community members. People go around in groups smearing colored powder on each other.

The finale of the Holi celebration is the lowering of the chir pole.

Once the chir pole is lowered the waiting crowd rushes forward to grab the cloth strips, which are considered to be potent protection amulets against malignant spirits. After the pole is stripped of its finery, it is dragged to the Tundikhel grounds (a grass-covered plaza in Kathmandu) where it is burned, resulting in a huge bonfire into which women throw coconut shells. Glowing coals and ash are taken by celebrants to purify their homes and properties.

Holi is definitely the most colorful of all Nepalese festivals, but there are those who cannot wait for it to be over because of the some-times raucous behavior that ensues during the celebration!

PERFORMING YOUR OWN CEREMONY OF RENEWAL

This ceremony can be used at the onset of the spring season or anytime you wish to honor a time of new beginnings. You may have completed a big task or reached a landmark birthday, or you may be celebrating a new relationship, the birth of a child, or recovery from a long illness. Events such as these can be thought of as an individual or personal "springtime" and therefore worthy of renewal celebration.

This ceremony may be done privately, or you may choose to bring together supportive friends and family to celebrate with you.

🖎 Creating a Renewal Ceremony

As you have done before other sacred actions, surround yourself with your golden, silver, and iron spheres. Make an offering to the spirits, sing your sacred songs, make an offering of uncooked rice, and honor all of the helping spirits in the directions.

Please read through the directions carefully and gather all that you'll need before you begin. For this exercise, you will need:

- All of your altar objects and a copper plate (thaal), flat winnowing basket (nanglo), or special cloth on which they are to be arranged (or at the very least a lit candle or oil lamp, a bowl of water, a feather, and a stone) placed in the center of your space

- Your dhyangro and gajo to beat the journey rhythm or another way to produce the rhythm
- Other rhythm instruments for the rest of your participants
- A comfortable place to be seated
- A small handful of uncooked rice kernels
- Your journal or a notebook and a pen
- A quiet time and space
- A cut sapling or large limb from a tree with many branches (This should be harvested in a respectful and honorific manner. Make an offering of gratitude to the tree and let it know exactly where you will be cutting its flesh. You must *only* cut what is absolutely necessary. Ask the tree to remove its spiritual energy from the part you will be harvesting. Then reverently cut the limb or tree.)
- Either a hole in the ground or a group of large stones to place around the pole to hold it vertically in place
- A bowl of milk to bless the tree and ground around it (If you are doing this indoors, a water scented with flower petals can be substituted for the milk.)
- A small special spoon to toss the milk or water
- Any seasonal grains, fruit, or flowers for offerings
- Several long strips of cotton fabric in a variety of colors for each person
- A celebratory meal that includes sweets

☙ Performing the Ceremony

1. Choose a time when you will be able to work with the spirits.
2. Prepare yourself and all the materials you require.
3. Begin playing the journey rhythm softly.
4. Call your power animal to you to support you during this ritual.
5. Offer seasonal grains, fruit, or flowers.
6. Begin by spooning drops of milk or scented water around the space the pole will be erected.
7. As you splash a few drops of the liquid, say aloud prayers of gratitude.
8. Hand the spoon to the next person to follow your lead until each person has had a turn.
9. Now it is time to set up the tree. Either place it into the hole or hold

it vertically and arrange heavy stones at its base to keep it in place.

10. Once this is completed, take a strip of cloth and perform a *fu mantra*. This involves holding the strip in both hands and then touching the forehead (third eye) and heart. After touching these parts of your body, blow prayers into the fabric strip.

11. Tie the blessed strip of fabric to the branches.

12. Have each person do a round, and you can repeat a turn with a fresh piece of fabric if you have other offerings of gratitude that you wish to make.

13. Once you have all completed tying strips to the tree, it is time to sing and dance. Make a joyful noise!

14. When you feel you have finished with the process, thank the spirits with whom you worked and return to ordinary reality by drumming the callback signal.

15. Take time to have a celebratory meal with sweets.

Whenever your work is complete, make an offering to the spirits for their help and support.

◺ Journey Explorations

Journey to your teacher or power animal to ask him or her to show you how the world around you is affected by the ceremony you have performed. Record what you learn.

Journey to your teacher to ask: When is this ceremony appropriate to perform?

Record the content of your journeys and your perceptions about what you received.

After each journey, thank your power animal, your teacher, and any other spirits who have revealed themselves to you. Then make an offering to the spirits. This can be an offering of incense smoke, bits of food outdoors, or flower petals.

◺ Process Questions

How did it feel to perform a ceremony of renewal?

What has changed for you after the ceremony was completed?

16

Using Your Voice as a Shamanic Tool

Although the work you have been doing with journeying, drumming, and gathering together and empowering your shamanic implements is vital, it is also important to bring your voice into your work with the spirits. You have already started this by learning and chanting the mantras in earlier chapters. Nepalese shamans usually sing and dance or twirl while drumming during their journeys and while working in ceremony. Using the voice is one way to manifest spiritual energy in the physical world.

Bhola suggests that there are four types of sacred songs that he uses when he works:

First, a seed word, melody, or mantra given to me by a teacher (ancestor, human teacher, or spirit being) is invoked in my heart-mind. This word or sound pours forth from my heart and through my voice and functions to "switch me on" as a jhankri.

Then, I sing the sacred songs related to my shamanic attire, my malas, and the sacred objects held on the altar.

Next, the sacred chants and songs related to the main and helping teacher-spirits are invoked to bring them into the space and to entreat their support for my work.

Finally, songs related to the place where the ceremony is conducted, elemental spirits, rivers, mountains, and so on are sung to bring their cooperation into the ceremony.

I was given just a few seed words and mantras in a dream and one in the cave. The rest of my songs flow on their own once I put on my costume and start beating my drum. These self-generated songs and melodies (apse ap in Nepali) take me into different realms and help my patients' spirits to accompany me on my journey as part of their healing.

Generally, my songs flow on their own, based on what is to be invoked or honored or what is necessary at that particular time.

Dhami/jhankris also use songs to:

Call the spirits, including declarations of intent and creating sacred space

Awaken the spirits of sacred objects

Raise the shaman's personal power, which includes merging with protective spirits

Release unbeneficial spiritual energy from a person, place, or object

Return beneficial spiritual energy to a person, place, or object

Work directly on a patient's body, mind, and spirit to relax the patient and allow deeper healing

Welcome in a soul at birth

Sing a soul out of this world at death

Work with the weather

Heal the land

Offer gratitude to the helpful, healing spirits who have assisted in the shaman's work

End the work (release the shaman's spirit helpers, put the sacred objects back to sleep, close the space, and return the shaman to an ordinary way of being)

These songs can do many, many other things!

As you can see, developing a strong vocal practice is essential to being a shaman. As you open up to using your voice as a tool, you will discover many fresh, spirit songs for your practice. These won't be songs that have been written down or sung before. Instead, they are songs that you will get directly from the spirits. You will learn them over time and through deepening the relationships you have with your helpful spirits.

Since Western culture does not prepare shamanic practitioners to use their voices with spirits in a spontaneous way, here are a few journeys that can be of assistance to you in growing your powers of shamanic song. Do not try to do them all at once! Instead, allow a few weeks or so in between each one so that you can fully internalize each song.

Free downloads of Bhola chanting are available at www.nepal -shaman.com as well as at www.evelynrysdyk.com.

🕊 *Giving Voice to Your Shamanic Practice*

Journey to your teacher or power animal to ask him or her to give you a song to honor your helping spirits. Sing it for at least half an hour to fully internalize it, then into an audio recorder, and then write down any words you received as well as the feeling the song gives you.

Journey to ask your teacher: When is this song appropriate to perform?

Record the content of your journeys and your perceptions about what you received.

After making notes, remember to make an offering to the spirits. Since the voice and the element of air are so intimately related, speak out loud as you make your offering. You may also wish to toss cornmeal into the breeze, burn incense, shake a rattle, or ring a small bell to accompany your voice.

🕊 Journeys for Other Songs

Journey to your teacher or power animal to ask him or her to give you a song to call the helping spirits into a ceremony.

Journey to your teacher or power animal to ask him or her to give you a song for immediate protection.

Journey to your teacher or power animal to ask him or her to give you a song to invite healing energies.

Journey to your teacher or power animal to ask him or her to give you a song for facilitating harmony, peace, and tranquillity.

Journey to your teacher or power animal to ask him or her to give you a song for thanking the spirits.

After receiving each song, sing it for at least half an hour to fully internalize it, then into an audio recorder, and then write down any words you received as well as the feeling the song gives you.

After you receive a song, journey again to ask when the song is appropriate to perform.

Record the content of your journeys and your perceptions about what you received.

After making notes, remember to make an offering to the spirits. Since the voice and the element of air are so intimately related, speak out loud as you make your offering. You may also wish to toss cornmeal into the breeze, burn incense, shake a rattle, or ring a small bell to accompany your voice.

⟑ Process Questions

How did it feel to get and sing these shamanic songs?

What has changed for you since you have opened up your voice as a shamanic tool?

PART 3

Bountiful
Harvest

17

The Cosmic Plan

You have already experienced the energies of the cardinal directions and begun to work with some of the spiritual energies that a Nepalese dhami/jhankri honors. However, there is even more richness in the world of the dhami/jhankri.

As all other shamans do, the Nepalese shamans engage with land spirits, ghosts, ancestors, animal spirits, natural forces, and local spirits in their work. All of these beings are a part of the spiritual landscape that must be continually attended to so that harmony is maintained. This balancing act is best reflected in the myth of why Earth quivers and shakes. The following story related to earthquake and cosmology was passed down to Bhola by his ancestors.

How the Earth Is Balanced

In the beginning, the deep blue-colored and unending primordial ocean of the cosmos was inhabited by the nagas (serpent spirits). Among them was Vasuki the enormous King Naga or Nag Raja (also known as Ananta Sesha). This great serpent has at least seven hooded heads, but they are truly infinite in number as are his coils. The Naga Raja encompasses the Queen Naga (Nag Rani) and many maiden naginis or naga kanyas (female snake spirits or daughters of the snake), too.

As time passed, the Nag Raja decided that he desired a permanent abode on a huge conch shell. There he could find respite from the constant movement of the waters and enjoy a place to bask and rest.

Figure 17.1. The Divine Pillar (pen-and-ink drawing by the author).

Everything is connected. Just as the ripples of vibration produce physical matter, the enormous undulations of the great snake's body set a new possibility into motion.

As soon as the naga king took residence on the conch shell, a huge turtle sailed through the great cosmic sea and came to rest atop the king's many arched and hooded heads.

The cosmic design next attracted eight huge elephants. These great beasts stood on the back of the turtle creating a complete circle. Their heads facing outward, they indicated the eight directions of this newly forming material plane, creating the form of eight-petal lotus called the Maha Padma.

No sooner had the elephants taken their positions, then the creative energy of Mother Earth (Dharti Mata) manifested into form (Bhumi Devi). She reclined on the backs of the elephants and while she slept, she began giving birth to all the many species. Aquatic beasts, terrestrial animals, and creatures of the sky emerged from her womb in great profusion. She also gave birth to different types of plants and trees to nurture her many children. The universe itself was born from her womb.

This is how a perfect equilibrium, the Divine Pillar, was created in the beginning of time with Mother Earth resting on the back of these mighty elephants.

It is believed that if the Nag Raja moves or a tortoise moves or if any of the eight elephants move, then the surface of Earth and the earthly waters move too. In addition, if any inauspicious action knowingly or unknowingly occurs on Earth, the entire structure is shaken, causing disaster in the earth plane, in our bodies, and in the cosmos. Because of this situation, the dhami/jhankri makes offerings to assist in keeping balance and harmony.

The many aspects of the Divine Pillar also reflect power and aspects of the truth of our existence. The basis of the construction is the great, cosmic ocean (*samundra*), which holds the primordial memories of all creation and of all beings. It is one of the most important sources of our lives.

The conch shell (sankha) represents a collective and individual rhythm or sound of life, which is a nonverbal vibration. The conch represents our will and the capacity to hold or to let go. The sound of the conch helps to clear places with heavy energies, to recover primordial memories, to invite the beneficial spirits, and to accompany the soul essences into the other realms.

Nag Raja serpent represents wisdom, sensibility, contact with reality, and inner change or transformation. It also reminds us that the path of knowledge or learning is not in a direct line but one that sways from side to side as it moves forward.

The huge tortoise (*kachuwa*) resting on Nag Raja reminds us of the rhythm that we have to follow in life and our individual sensations. The tortoise's shell represents the protection and support we need. The tortoise's seasonal hibernation reminds us of renewal and change, as well as a reminder to reflect on the environment where we live.

The eight giant elephants (*asta hati*) bear the signs of auspiciousness, of the inner power to remove obstacles, and of the need for constant efforts to achieve our goals and stability.

Dharti Mata or Mother Earth, whose both hands are open and empty and whose legs are stretched out, is continually giving birth to the universe. Creation is never complete but always occurring.

This cosmology reflects the profound truth of our interconnections. Everything relies on something and someone else. If any aspect is thrown into disharmony, everything suffers the consequences—immediately or at a later date. No being is immune to these shifts. The same interconnectedness is reflected in our spiritual, energetic, emotional, and physical aspects, which must also be kept in a balanced state.

The image of the Divine Pillar can help us to have a new understanding of ourselves, to remember what we are made of and where we stand. In having this new way to understand interconnectedness and the inherent fragility of balance, we can see how individual choices and actions affect the entirety. In that way, we can also see the great merit in performing actions to support peace, harmony, and balance.

Shamans have always been activists, performing rituals as well as taking concrete actions to support health, balance, harmony, and wholeness. There has been no better time to take up the drum, to fill our hearts with passion, and to live our lives with the greater purpose of making the Earth safe, healthy, and harmonious for all beings.

BALANCING THE DIVINE PILLAR

A Mansaune ceremony is done to help create balance in the Divine Pillar. Since everything affects the entirety of the whole, this ceremony may be used to heal an individual, a group of people, or on behalf of all creation—releasing and healing anything that interferes with healthy and life-giving harmony. As with all shamanic healing, the release of disharmonious energies is always balanced by making offerings and through energetic and spiritual renewal.

The name of the ceremony is made of two elements: *man* refers to our mind and/or the emotions and thoughtforms our mind produces; *saune*, an agricultural term, refers to preparing a rice paddy field. To have a healthy rice crop, anything that would not contribute to plant health is removed and the soil is tilled into a perfect consistency to receive the new, tender rice plants. Shamanically, it refers to supporting a person to regain balance by purifying, calming, and releasing anything that interferes with his or her clarity, focus, and productive capacity.

In Nepal this ceremony can be done in many different ways using different methods, objects, and chants based on the problem that is presented and also what might be available to use for the ritual. Dhami/jhankris use variations of this ceremony for breaking a curse, removing a spiritual possession, healing an attack by a malignant spirit, or other purposes. In these cases, an effigy representing the entity, ghost, or force needing to be purged is the central figure or point and is fashioned without a face or limbs. This ensures that the negative entity, once removed from the afflicted person, will not have the ability to physically embody somewhere else. Once the ceremony is complete, all the offerings and the effigy are taken beyond a boundary, such as a river, to further prevent the entity from returning to the person or village until the figure has dissolved back to the earth.

The form of the ceremony presented here has a representation of Mother Earth as the central point. When performed in this way, the Mansaune ceremony is used to regain vitality, restore spiritual energy, and foster a well-grounded state.

The foundation for the ceremony requires drawing a simple mandala (*rekhi*), representing a flower. The drawing is done with flour or finely ground cornmeal, which is divided into three batches. One batch is dyed with powdered red food coloring, a second is dyed yellow, and the third is left white. The first set of boxes are drawn in red flour. These will become the outermost loops of the petals and so should be drawn generously large. The next box is yellow and drawn just outside the red one, with the yellow loops falling inside the red loops. Finally, a box drawn with white flour is positioned outside the yellow box and its loops fall inside the yellow ones. It helps to draw this image a few times in colored pencil to understand how it works.

Rekhi drawn in this fashion are used in several ceremonies that are performed by the dhami/jhankri. These drawings or cosmic diagrams are geometric patterns that are used in healing, clearing, and offering rituals. They often function as maps of the shamanic cosmos that can act as receptacles to receive a patient's malady where it can be transmuted into harmless energy. Some mandala designs are given to the dhami/jhankri by lineage teachers, and some are universal in character. Based on what is necessary at the time, the helping spirits may even provide a unique design for a specific purpose. Based upon the guidance from the spirits, even the offerings on mandalas can change, as well.

Drawing the mandalas can be daunting at first as related below by Bhola. However, with his encouragement, you can feel better supported to tackle this ceremony. Remember, your intent is far more important than getting everything perfect—especially when you perform it for the first time.

In the beginning, holding colored rice flour between my two fingers and letting the flour flow according to the correct pattern was very difficult. I started concentrating and focusing on breathing, which helped me to relax and thus the flow became easier and more fluid.

As the ceremony is to release, renew, and revive balance and harmony, the astamangal mandala is used; astamangal refers to the eight signs of auspiciousness. This ceremony can be done in different ways using different rekhis but as the intention is not only releasing pain and suffering from individuals but re-creating cosmic harmony and balance in all dimensions—from the primal ocean to the conch to the naga to the turtle to the elephants and finally to Mother Earth. Mother Earth holds all that is being created as well as the beings who can take away our suffering and bestow all that is necessary. She is represented at the center of the cosmic design without any form as she is considered to be "all pervading." The ceremony is designed to bring forth auspiciousness from any inauspicious situation.

The mandala for this ceremony is drawn on a dark blue cloth or directly on the ground. It is created as an abstract form of the eight-petal lotus (*asta dal kamal*) with the conch, serpent, tortoise, and elephant around the edges. At the center of the mandala, an oil lamp or a candle is lit, and on each petal and on each image of the conch, serpent, tortoise, and elephant, offerings of flowers, fruits, or colored

Figure 17.2. The astamangal mandala for the ceremony of Mansaune.

cloth are made. A figure of Mother Earth is created from flour dough and placed next to the oil lamp or candle.*

This is a ceremony of liberating participants from mental/emotional clutter or confusion and for re-creating harmony. The ceremony is focused on releasing what is not conducive to harmony and reclaiming enlivening energies. It is either performed five or seven levels/rounds. The instructions for a seven round session follow this section.

After every level of releasing, the participants make an offering to the mandala. The offering is usually a mixture of seven uncooked grains called *sata byu* (seven seeds) or *sapta dhanya* (seven types of grains). These might be black, green, or red lentils, wheat, black gram, barley, paddy rice, and millet. If the above-mentioned grains and seeds are not available, then any whole grain or seed can be used. Anyone can fall sick in any part of the world so a dhami/jhankri has to be flexible to negotiate with the disease-causing spirits. In Maine we use the following seven grains during the ritual: corn, quinoa, millet, rice, white beans, black beans, orange peas, and yellow lentils.

Water is sprinkled on each person using a sweeping away gesture and an offering is made to the center of the mandala. This sprinkling of water and central offering is either done by the dhami/jhankri or by

---

*In Nepal the Mother Earth figure can also be made from the dark clay, wheat flour, or cooked rice paste that is used to make Buddhist offering figures or *tormas*.

the shaman's assistant. At the end the participants or recipients walk around the mandala three times going in a clockwise direction. At the conclusion, the dhami/jhankri blesses the participants with a length of multicolored threads to shield their balanced and renewed energies.

Once the blessing is complete, all the offerings and the central figure are taken in a spiritually clean place, like under a tree, in a cave, or by the bank of the river, so that the figure, flowers, and grains may return to the soil.

A celebration usually follows this healing ceremony, which involves eating ceremonial snacks (*khaja*), which can be pancakes, fruits, or a vegetable fried rice dish that is liberally laced with saffron. Westerners can substitute something sweet or even a potluck-style buffet made from dishes supplied by the participants. In Nepal tea is also served abundantly.

Figure 17.3. A completed mandala with a central figure of Mother Earth (Dharti Mata/Bhumi Devi) made of flour dough (photo: Mariarosa Genitrini).

⚜ *The Mansaune Ceremony*

This ceremony is best done with a group of people but may also be done by an individual.

As you have done before other sacred actions, surround yourself with your golden, silver, and iron spheres. Make an offering to the spirits, sing your sacred songs, make an offering of uncooked rice, and honor all of the helping spirits in the directions.

Please read through the directions carefully several times and gather all that you'll need before you begin. (Note: Some of the materials for this ceremony will need to be prepared well in advance.) For this exercise, you will need:

- Your altar materials to be set up in the center of your room
- White flour dough clay (see recipe on page 159)
- A square of dark blue cotton cloth about 45 inches (114 cm) square (If your ceremonial location will allow drawing the flour mandala, building the altar, and tossing grains of rice directly onto the floor or ground, then the cloth will not be necessary. You may want to draw the mandala *very lightly* on the cloth with a colored pencil before the ceremony. This will function as a guide for sprinkling the flour with your fingers as you draw the mandala during the actual ceremony.)
- Red and yellow powdered food coloring (These powdered colors are readily available at cooking/gourmet shops or online.)
- 12 ounces (339 g) flour or finely ground cornmeal, divided into thirds. One-third (4 oz) of the flour or cornmeal is tinted deep red with the food coloring, one-third is tinted yellow, and the last third is left undyed or white.
- A ball of cotton Nepalese rainbow threads (see page 95 for more information about the thread)
- A spirit umbrella (*chatri*) made from two thin twigs and your rainbow thread (see instructions on page 160)
- A small handful of uncooked white rice kernels (akshyaata)
- 2 to 4 pounds (1–2 kg) of a mixture of seven different uncooked grains (*sata byu*) (These can be any seven whole grains.)

Recipe for Flour Dough Clay

Ingredients

2 level cups plus 4 tablespoons cornstarch

1.5 cups boiling water

1 level cup salt

2 tablespoons vegetable oil

2 tablespoons cream of tartar (optional for improved elasticity)

A few drops of liquid glycerin (not essential but will make the dough smoother)

Instructions

Mix all of the dry ingredients together in a bowl. Add the oil. Then pour in the boiling water and mix thoroughly. Allow the mixture in the bowl to cool before kneading it into a smooth dough. If the dough is too sticky, simply add a bit more cornstarch. Store the finished clay in an airtight container in the refrigerator until you are ready to use it for your ceremony.*

---

*In rural Nepal dark mud, red mud, wheat dough, or other substances can be used to make the figure for this ceremony.

- A large bowl to hold the grains that will be placed near the mandala
- A paper cup for each person to have some grains for an offering
- A quantity of fresh fruits, hard candies, fresh flowers, or strips of cotton cloth about ½ inch (1.5 cm) wide by 5 inches (13 cm) long in many different solid colors, to use as offerings on the mandala
- 10 to 15 large green leaves
- 3 sturdy branches or lengths of bamboo, each about a yard or meter long
- An oil lamp or safe, low candle for the center of the mandala with matches to light it
- A small water container for sprinkling water droplets on the participants during the ceremony
- A feather or small bundle of thin twigs to flick the water

- Your dhyangro and gajo to play the journey rhythm or another way to produce the rhythm
- Your journal or a notebook and a pen
- A celebratory meal with foods provided by all participants to enjoy after the ceremony that includes sweets and nonalcoholic beverages

Have participants bring rattles, drums, or other sound-making objects to play at the procession around the mandala at the conclusion of the ceremony. Choose someone to assist you, and tell your assistant what role he or she will be playing during the ceremony.

Making the Spirit Umbrella

Supplies
2 freshly cut, thin, straight twigs or bamboo skewers, split length-ways and soaked in warm water for an hour, one about 10 inches (25 cm) long, the other 5 inches (12.5 cm) long
1 spool rainbow thread

Instructions
Arrange the sticks in the form of a cross and tie them together at the junction with the thread. Now begin winding the rainbow thread around them widening each course. Do this for nine courses until you have a figure like the image in figure 5.4 (page 55).

✑ Performing the Ceremony
1. Choose a time when you will be able to work with the spirits.
2. Prepare yourself and collect all the materials you will require.
3. Begin playing the journey rhythm softly.
4. Call your power animal to you to support you during this ritual.
5. Begin by honoring the spirits and blessing the place where the man-dala will be created with a song and a few rice kernels.
6. Spread the cloth out on the floor.
7. As you draw the mandala, have participants rattle and drum in unison to help hold the energy.
8. Draw the image of the mandala. Remember that the first set of boxes

drawn in red flour will become the outermost loops of the petals, so draw these loops generously large. The next box is yellow and drawn just outside the red one, with the yellow loops falling inside the red ones. The final box is white and is drawn outside the yellow box with its loops falling inside the yellow ones. It helps to draw this image a few times in colored pencil to understand how it works. Take your time and ask your spirits and ancestors for support.

9. Make a leaf bed in the center of the mandala.

10. Create a simple female figure to represent Dharti Mata from the flour dough clay.

11. Place her on the leaf bed.

12. Now stick the spirit umbrella upright in the goddess figure's head. The spirit umbrella protects the ceremonial space and purifies any energy that needs to be transmuted.

13. Construct a tripod of the three sturdy branches, tying the top together with your rainbow thread.

14. Erect the tripod over the mandala.

15. Decorate the tripod legs and peak with flowers, using the rainbow thread to hold them in place.

16. Place your oil lamp or candle on the leaf bed in front of the goddess figure and light it.

17. Place offerings of fruit, flowers, or strips of colored cloth on the center bed of leaves around the goddess figure and oil lamp or candle.

18. Place flower offerings in each loop of the mandala, and sprinkle a few petals on the serpent, elephant, conch, and turtle images, as well.

19. Place eight leaves in a circle around the edge of the mandala and place a small handful of grains on each leaf.

20. Place the large bowl of the grains near the mandala and have everyone take a cupful back to his or her place in the ceremonial space.

21. The dhami/jhankri drums and sings during the ceremony, asking her or his spiritual helpers to assist the participants in their healing. The shaman may also offer grains to "sweeten" the mandala after each round.

22. Now begins the seven rounds of release that will assist in the healing of the seven levels of human pain or imbalance. After each round is spoken, the participants will place a small amount of the offering grains onto the mandala. After that, the shamanic assistant will sprinkle some water in a brushing away gesture over each person.

23. The assistant will speak the following words at each round, allowing time for each round of offerings and blessing/cleaning with water droplets, while the shaman continues to stay connected with her or his helping spirits.

24. *First Level: Physical Pains or Imbalances.* Take a small bit of your grain and by breathing deeply and quietly speaking, give permission for the release of your physical imbalances and physical disturbances. Do this with an open heart and with great gratitude that the desired result has already been accomplished. Give thanks to Mother Earth and the spirits of nature for the work that has already been completed. Energetically, you are creating a matrix into which reality will form itself. Your wounds and disturbances are absorbed by the mandala, and your offering is the gift that you offer in gratitude.

25. *Second Level: Releasing Spiritual Entities and the Return of Your Power.* Take a small bit of your grain and by breathing deeply and quietly speaking, give permission for the release of any negative entities that have attached themselves to you. Do this with an open heart and with great gratitude that the result has already been accomplished. Give thanks to Mother Earth and the spirits of nature for the work having already been completed. Those spirits and energies that are suffering and strife can find a home in the mandala and through it a place of peace. When you feel that they have left you, invite Mother Earth and the entire Divine Pillar to fill you again with power. Welcome your spiritual power back to your body, and with great joy, place an offering on the mandala.

26. *Third Level: Releasing Fear and Regaining Courage and Vitality.* Take a small bit of your grain and by breathing deeply and quietly speaking, give permission for the release of your fears. Some fears may have been with you since childhood, and some may be newer. Allow all of them to be released so that you can be free from the burden or dampening of your vitality that they have caused. Do this with an open heart and with great gratitude that the release has already been accomplished. Give thanks to Mother Earth and the spirits of nature for the work having already been completed. As your fears fly away from you into the mandala to be transmuted, feel the vitality flowing to you from Mother Earth, filling the spaces that were once filled with fear. Feel the courage of the mighty mountains or sea filling you. Allow

the power of the plants breaking through to the light in springtime to fill you. Breathe the boundless vitality of nature into yourself and make your offering to the mandala.

27. *Fourth Level: Releasing Anger to Restore Peace and Reconciliation.* Take a small bit of your grain and by breathing deeply and quietly speaking, give permission for the release of your anger. Your anger may be toward other people and situations and even directed at yourself. Release your rage, resentment, and indignation from what you have experienced. Allow the anger—those pools of poison in your being that keep you separate from others and yourself—to fall away like leaves dropping from trees in autumn. In the same way that fallen leaves nourish the soil, allow a deep peace to return to your heart. Feel yourself coming back into harmony with the spirits of nature and with Mother Earth. Allow her quiet nurturance to reconcile you with All That Is. Make your offering to the mandala.

28. *Fifth Level: Healing Grief and Loss.* Take a small bit of your grain and by breathing deeply and quietly speaking, give permission for the release of your grief. Each of us experiences the pains of loss. Family members leave us, separations occur, we lose something precious, and death claims those we love. Yet we remain. Allow the tears of your grief to flow, give permission for your heart to open up to allow the pain of loss to be washed away. Nature understands loss and yet prevails through her cycles of growth and renewal. A loss must be honored, and we must remember that each loss allows the possibility for something new to grow. Hearts and spirits heal if we give them permission to do so. Open yourself to the healing that nature can offer. Open to the eternal sky and stars of which you and all that you love are a part. You are never alone. Make your offering to honor that you are a being who loves and through whom eternal love flows into the world.

29. *Sixth Level: Healing Relationships.* Take a small bit of your grain and by breathing deeply and quietly speaking, release any way you may have injured someone in relationship. Let go of the hurts you may have felt and how you may have treated another person or other being with anything less than reverence. Ask the spirits of nature to help you renew your ability to be in right relationship with others. Allow the clarity and harmony of the broad and cloudless blue sky to open your eyes and heart. Feel the sense of possibility filling you and

creating balance. Breathe the harmony and balance of nature into yourself and make your offering to the mandala.

30. *Seventh Level: Restoring the Spirit.* Take a small bit of your grain and by breathing deeply feel a great taproot growing down from the bottom of your body and through the souls of your feet. Feel how it reaches downward into the very core, the pulsing heart of our Mother Earth. Feel the grounding embrace of Mother Earth reconnecting you. This connection allows you to travel freely all over her surface and to reach even higher into the cosmic and spiritual realms. You can grow so much more with this grounding connection to the source of all life. Through this umbilicus, you can receive her nurturance, her life-giving and restorative energy. As you feel this connection, call from your deep heart for any soul essences you may have lost to travel through the mandala and then into your heart. They are cleared, healed, and purified by the mandala and bring a perfect wholeness to your soul. Welcome them back, and with joy place an offering of celebration to the mandala.

31. Once all the rounds are complete, have the entire group drum and dance clockwise around the mandala three times. This procession should be done with an air of celebration.

32. Now go around the circle and tie a length of thread around the wrist of each person. Make sure it is loose enough to be comfortable.

33. When you feel you are finished with the process and with the spirits with whom you have worked, return to ordinary reality by drumming the callback signal.

34. Now it is time for your celebratory meal with sweets.

Whenever your work is complete, make an offering to the spirits for their help and support. Take the offerings, the dough figure, the leaves, and everything outdoors to where it can decay naturally in nature. If you used a cloth, you may use it to carry all the material, but the cloth does not have to remain outdoors. It may be washed for reuse or hung on a tree to honor the spirits.*

---

*In cases of spirit possession, spirit darts, witchcraft, or other intentional spiritual harm, different types of specific ceremonies are performed. These ceremonies are performed during the night, and the offerings are kept at the crossroads. In order to block the path of the disease-causing spirits, the ceremonies are done outdoors.

▷ Journey Explorations

Journey to your teacher or power animal to ask him or her to show you how the world around you is affected by the ceremony you have performed.

Journey to ask your teacher: When is this ceremony appropriate to perform?

Record the content of your journeys and your perceptions about what you received.

After each journey, thank your power animal, your teacher, and any other spirits who have revealed themselves to you. Sing your sacred songs, make an offering of uncooked rice to the spirits, and honor all of the helping spirits in the directions.

▷ Process Questions

How did it feel to perform a ceremony of release and renewal?

What has changed for you after the ceremony was completed?

Primary Feminine Deities

There are literally hundreds of deities that are honored in the Himalayan region. Goddesses and gods are numerous to better express the myriad aspects that these forces represent. There is an understanding that the feminine energy is paramount, having given birth to the masculine; however, the two energies are always working together to keep creation's wheel turning.

The Great Goddess is the one who creates, nurtures, and destroys only to re-create once again. This ever-turning cycle is reflected in the seasons, the cycles of the moon, and the ages of life. It is for this reason that working with the Divine Feminine is vital whether you are a shamanic practitioner who identifies as female or male or expresses your gender in some other fashion. Everything and every being is born from her and is eventually returned to the womb of her endless creativity. She has always and will always reshape the forms of the cosmos. She is the great circle that holds everything.

OUT OF ONE, MANY

Although the kaleidoscopic array of goddesses honored by Himalayan shamans is quite complex, they all seem to originate from the Neolithic supreme Great Mother Goddess. The Proto-Indo-Europeans honored her as Plth₂wih₂, who became Pṛthvī Mātā, meaning "plentiful mother," in the Hindu Rig-Veda.* As such, these goddesses are always seen as facets of the larger and unknowable one.

She is the flower of youth, the fruitfulness of the soil, the supreme nurturer, the bestowal of intelligence, wisdom, beauty, art, music, and poetry, the force that causes change, that which brings inspiration, the one who both gives and takes life, the maintainer of balance, the energy of continuance, and the process of decay. She is sexuality and sensuality. She is a healer and destroyer. She is the light and darkness—this fleeting moment and all eternity.

For most dhami/jhankris, the energies of the Divine Feminine are rarely merged with. Being manifestations of primordial power, they hold the world in balance and help life to continue to manifest itself. That being said, it is clear that some female shamans will merge more readily with wrathful aspects of the Mother Goddess such as Kali or Durga, the Mother Kaalaraatri aspect of the Great Goddess. In all cases, shamans' powers develop through cooperation with the spirits with whom they have developed profound relationships. Each one has a different cadre of helping spirits and will work with them in unique ways that have grown out of the shaman's powerful associations.

THE GODDESS DURGA

The goddess Durga is the supreme, invincible force that creates, shapes, and destroys the universe, and Shakti is the primordial, cosmic, creative energy from which all creation, preservation, and annihilation of form arises. In other words, Durga is an expression of the supreme Great Mother Goddess—the being who continually creates and re-creates All That Is from the substance of her own divine energy. She gives birth to herself in myriad different forms as well as to Shiva, her consort and lover. The worship of Durga assumes special

---

*The Rig-Veda is the oldest of the four canonical sacred texts of Hinduism known as the Vedas. It has been dated to approximately 1,700 BCE. The ten books of the Rig-Veda are so ancient that they, along with the other four Vedas, are referred to as *shruti,* or "what is heard"—as opposed to other Hindu texts (such as the Vedangas and the Mahabharata), which are referred to as *smrti,* or "what is remembered." This designation of the Vedas alludes to their having predated written Sanskrit, which arose approximately 2,000 BCE.

Figure 18.1. The goddess Durga (pen-and-ink drawing by the author).

significance for devotees of feminine or mother energy, for healers, and also for dhami/jhankris.

Bhola honors Durga as both "power and the Mother who makes what is impossible into that which is possible. On special times like the nine-day festival in fall and spring, she visits and empowers. I have felt her profound presence as if in physical reality three times. Her presence, like a visit by Kali, is very strong."

Durga's name means "invincible," as well as "very difficult to acquire or unattainable." In this way, we can see the enormous breadth and depth of her being. She is so vast that she may only begin to be known by experiencing her many aspects. She is depicted as a demon-destroying warrior goddess riding either a tiger or lion and having eight to eighteen arms.

She wields weapons that both destroy and create in each of her hands. Along with a conch trumpet, bow and arrow, long sword, javelin, shield, mace, thunderbolt, and noose, she carries the trishul or trident, which is usually associated with Shiva and represents the three realms and the power to destroy them. She also wields a circular, saw-toothed weapon with 108 sharp teeth called a Sudarshana Chakra, which is associated with Vishnu. This spinning disk is also a solar symbol as it was made from the "dust of the sun."

Durga encompasses all divine forces, and as a supreme expression of the ultimate Great Mother Goddess, she manifests in countless forms.* However, nine specific aspects of this goddess embody primary representations of her powers. The nine manifestations of Durga are: Shailputri, Brahmachaarini, Chandraghantaa, Kushmaandaa, Skandmaataa, Kaatyaayani, Kaalaraatri, Mahagauri, and Siddhidaatri.

Some aspects are peaceful and nurturing. Other manifestations are wrathful deities who use ferocity to protect in the way a mother lion or mother bear would savage any creature that dares to threaten her cubs. In either manifestation, Durga attends to the bountiful continuance of life.

Mother Shailputri

Among the nine Durgas, Mother Shailputri (daughter of the mountain) is considered to be the first manifestation of the goddess Durga.† The importance and powers of Mother Shailputri are unlimited. It is why she is honored on the first day of the nine-day Durga festival, Navaratri, which is discussed in the appendix.

Everything on Earth is a part of Shailputri; she exhorts humans to maintain balance with nature and to live in harmony. In her hands she carries a trident and a lotus. The trident is an active, masculine symbol and refers to Shiva. He is the primary deity for dhami/jhankris; Shiva is considered to be the first shaman. The lotus is a symbol of purity, with its roots beneath the water and deeply grounded in the earth. These two symbols together are reflections that Shailputri and Shiva

---

*Hindus recognize 1,008 names of Durga. A list of these names is chanted in the Sri Durga Sahasranamam.

†Mother Shailputri is also known as Amba in some parts of the Himalayan region.

are not separate but one being. This representation furthermore reveals that Shiva, like all other beings, traces his origins and his power from the supreme Great Mother Goddess.

The narrative regarding her birth has been described in the Hindu scriptures. These mythic stories of the gods and goddesses are set in a divine period that lies outside our linear time stream. As you will see, a primordial goddess can suddenly appear as a later character in a storyline. The fluid quality of these tales parallels the way time is experienced in shamanic realms. Like a shaman's journey, these stories are sometimes quite mysterious and magical. The characters in them exhibit very humanlike qualities, and in this way are similar to the gods and goddesses in myths from Indo-European tribes, such as the Greeks and Norse. The characters' triumphs and mishaps help to preserve cultural morays and to provide life lessons. Here is Bhola's version:

In her previous birth, Mother Shailputri was Sati, the daughter of one of the founding fathers of human beings known as Patriarch Daksha. From her childhood, she was deeply devoted to Lord Shiva. When she grew into a young woman, she won the favor of Lord Shiva by her penance and devotion. She desired to be even closer to him and so became his consort.

Once Patriarch Daksha organized a great sacrifice in which all the gods including Brahma, Vishnu, and Indra, as well as many saints and sages, were invited, but Lord Shiva was not. When Sati came to know of it, she could not tolerate the disgraceful way her father treated her love, Lord Shiva.

She was very angry when she came to speak with Shiva. "O Dear Lord! My father, Patriarch Daksha, is performing a grand sacrifice. All the gods, saints, seers, and sages have been invited to participate in this sacrifice, but he has disgraced you openly by not inviting you. I can never bear your insult, so I will go to my father to speak my mind to him!"

Seeing how infuriated Sati was, Lord Shiva said to her, "O Goddess! It does not behoove you to lose your temper over such a simple thing. Patriarch Daksha is the performer of this great sacrifice. It is his will to invite or ignore whomever he chooses. You must not poke your nose into his affairs. Such trivial steps may cause bitterness to grow in your relationship."

Despite Lord Shiva's admonishment, Sati's anger did not subside. Seeing her unyielding anger, Lord Shiva ultimately granted his lovely consort permission to see her father.

When Goddess Sati reached the site of the sacrifice, she heard everybody denouncing Lord Shiva! Even her father, surrounded by his servants, participated in the denunciation. At the same time, Sati's sisters, who knew she was Shiva's consort, began mocking her. Their hostility fanned the fire of Sati's fury. She could not endure the horrible disgrace of her dear one, and in anger and pain, she threw herself into the sacrificial fire. When Lord Shiva heard of Sati's self-immolation, he was filled with sorrow and rage. He immediately sent his attendants to destroy the sacrifice so it would honor no one.

After Sati immolated herself in the sacrificial fire, she became the daughter of Himalaya, the mountain king, and his queen Maina. Because of her auspicious traits, she was given the name of Parvati. She was also as known Shailputri, which means "mountain daughter." In this life, she continued her adoration of Shiva and through her deep devotion and sacrifice became his wife. As Shailputri, you see Durga's continued connection to Shiva. In this story, the goddess is both consort and wife. In addition, you see her capacity for powerful action and her profound connection to Earth.

Most Hindu deities also have an animal helper or one who functions as their vehicle. This is an example of how looking deeper into any religious tradition often reveals its ancient shamanic roots. Shailputri's animal helper is the bull. This animal is closely associated with general fertility and fertile soil.

When it is time to make an offering to Shailputri, she is given bright, parrot-green cloth and ghee (clarified butter). These gifts express gratitude for and signify her ability to bestow a life of good health.

Mother Brahmchaarini

The second manifestation of the nine aspects of Durga is Mother Brahmchaarini. She is clad in white and carries a long mala in one hand and an oblong water pot (*kamandalu*) in the other.

For the dhami/jhankri, Mother Brahmachaarini represents one who never deviates from the spiritual path. She is the spiritual strength and tenacity of the shaman who increases all that is good in the world through effort and sacrifice.

Bhola's narrative regarding Durga's incarnation as Parvati continues:

Parvati grew up into a beautiful maiden. Around this time, the roaming celestial sage Narada happened to reach the court of King Himalaya, where he was warmly welcomed. Himalaya and Maina prayed to Sage Narada to predict the future of Parvati by reading her palms. Sage Narada agreed to their request. So, Parvati was brought to the court in no time.

Seeing Goddess Parvati, Sage Narada stood up and bowed to her with great reverence. King Himalaya and Queen Maina were amazed at Sage Narada's unusual behavior.

They were curious to know why the sage greeted her this way. Thereupon he spoke with a smile, "O Lord of Mountains! This daughter of yours in her previous birth was Sati, the daughter of Patriarch Daksha and the consort of Lord Shiva. She cast off her body in the sacrificial fire as Daksha hurled disgrace on Lord Shiva. Now she is born again as your daughter Parvati. That is why I bowed to her. By virtue of her merits, she shall again be betrothed to Lord Shiva."

Having listened to the prediction of Sage Narada, Parvati inquired of him how Lord Shiva should become her husband. Thereupon Sage Narade advised her to perform an austere penance.

Acting upon the advice of Sage Narada, Goddess Parvati renounced all the pleasures of the palace and started performing penance so that Lord Shiva would become her betrothed.

She spent the first thousand years of her penance living on fruit and roots. Thereafter, she lived on leaves for another three thousand years of her penance. Next, she survived on water and finally air alone, braving heat and cold, rain and storms, and all kinds of sufferings.

Goddess Parvati meditated on Lord Shiva for thousands of years. This austere penance performed by her reduced her to a mere skeleton. A great cry rose up in the three worlds because of her severe penance. All the gods including Indra and all the saints and sages were terrified by her penance. They approached Brahma in a body and prayed to him to bestow the desired boon on Parvati.

At last Brahma, the great grandfather, appeared before Parvati and said to her, "O Goddess! All the gods bow to you in deep reverence.

Such an austere penance could have only been performed by you! Your cherished desire shall soon be fulfilled. You shall have Lord Shiva as your husband. By virtue of this austere penance you shall be known as Brahmchaarini—a woman of incredible purity." Thereafter, Brahma restored her physical charm and grace.

Thus, Lord Shiva became Parvati's husband by virtue of her penance, and she earned the reputation of being a Brahmchaarini.

The worship of Mother Brahmchaarini is conducive to penance, renunciation, purity, virtue, and nobility. Her devotees are endowed with peace and prosperity. On the second day of the Navaratri, Mother Brahmchaarini is adored and worshipped. She is also worshipped as Tara, Chamunda, and Ashtamukhi.

She is offered yellow- and orange-colored cloth and sugar. In return, she bestows peace and prosperity and increases the longevity of one's family members.

Mother Chandraghantaa

On the third day of the festival, another spiritual power or Shakti of the goddess Durga is worshipped. Mother Chadraghantaa's forehead is bedecked with the crescent moon resembling the shape of a bell or ghanta. She rides a lion and inspires her devotees with fearlessness even as she is the very embodiment of serenity.

She dispels distress, physical suffering, mental tribulation, and ghostly impediments. Those who adore and worship her with their deeds, minds, and speech develop an aura of divine splendor. They easily achieve success in every walk of life. Mother Chandraghantaa is ever ready to destroy the wicked, but to her devotees, she is ever visible as the kind and compassionate Mother showering peace and prosperity.

By removing worldly pains and sufferings, she bestows joy and happiness. For the dhami/jhankri, she epitomizes the benefits shamans receive and bring to their patients by working with their helpful healing spirits.

Mother Chandraghantaa has a golden complexion. She possesses ten arms, each of which wields a weapon, such as a sword, a bow, a mace, arrows, and the like. During the battle between the gods and the demons, the cleansing sounds produced by her magnificent ritual bell (ghanta) sent thousands of wicked demons to their death. She is always vigilant and typically depicted in a warrior's stance. This shows her eagerness to destroy anything that interferes with peace and prosperity. Divine vision may be acquired by her grace, and devotees are said to experience the aroma of divine fragrance and hear etheric sounds.

Mother Chandraghantaa should be adored and worshipped with great purity in mind and heart, observing all the rites properly. Having acquired her grace, we get rid of all worldly turmoil and enjoy supreme bliss. Devotees should always have her gentle form in their minds while meditating on her. She is also worshipped as Bhuvaneshwari (the Mother Goddess).

Sky-blue cloth, milk, and sweets made from milk are offered to Chandraghantaa. It is also suggested that devotees make donations to those who are needy on this day.

Mother Kushmaandaa

The fourth manifestation of Goddess Durga is called Mother Kushmaandaa. She is adored and worshipped on the fourth day of Navaratri. Because she dwells in the abode of the sun god, her skin is as brilliant as the sun itself. It is her splendor that pervades in every creature of this universe. All regions of the universe are illuminated by her divine radiance.

She bestows intelligence and decision-making ability on devotees. She has the capacity to heal and eliminate sorrow. This aspect of her power reflects the role shamans have as healers through their relationship with the spirits, which is to be able to discern which spiritual energies need to be released and those that need to be increased.

Here is Bhola's version of her origin story:

When this universe was nonexistent and darkness prevailed everywhere, it was Mother Kushmaandaa who produced the cosmic egg with her mild smile. From this cosmic egg, all of creation was born.

At the time of the creation of the universe, it was Mother Kushmaandaa who infused her own divine light into the sun and the stars. Since that time, each and every object and creature in this universe has been getting its energy from her.

She possesses eight arms and is called the eight-armed mother. In

*her holy hands, she wields the oblong water pot (*kamandalu*), the bow,*
the arrow, the lotus, the pot of nectar, the discus, the mace, and the
rosary bestowing all perfections and treasures. Mother Kushmaandaa
confers all achievements, powers, and salvation on her devotees. Her true
devotion is instrumental in destroying all ailments, troubles, and hurdles
of devotees.

Mother Kushmaandaa bestows all pleasures. Her regular worship is conducive to prosperity, pleasures, power, and, finally, salvation. Her adoration can deliver a person from all kinds of ailments and lead him or her to the path of prosperity and pleasures. A devotee should adore and worship her with a pure mind and intellect. She is also worshipped as Chinnamasta (maternal self-sacrifice) and Lalita (source of beauty).

She is offered pink color cloth and a special fried pancake (*malpua*), which must be offered in the temple.

Skandamaata

Skandamaata, which means Mother of Skanda, is the fifth manifestion of Goddess Durga. She is worshipped on the fifth day of Navaratri. She has a son Skanda, also called Karttikeya or Kumara. He is the representation of the path of enlightenment, and so this aspect of Durga represents the path or way to higher spiritual attainment. For dhami/ jhankris, she is the radiant protection shamans attain while inspirited by their helping spirits.

She possesses four arms. Two of her hands hold lotus flowers. A third hand is always in the boon-conferring gesture, and with her fourth arm and hand, she holds her son Skanda in her lap. Her complexion is a brilliant white, and she is seated on a lotus. She is also called Padmasana, or goddess with a lotus-seat. Like Mother Chadraghanta, her vehicle is the lion.

Those who are selflessly devoted to Mother Skandamaata attain all the achievements and treasures of life. Worship of Skandamaata purifies the heart of a devotee. Her worship is twice blessed. When devotees worship her, they automatically worship Lord Skanda, her son seated in her lap. Thus devotees enjoy the grace of Skandamaata (illumination) along with the grace of Lord Skanda (the clear path to enlightenment).

Skandamaata is also the protective mother of a child and as such she is capable of being the frighteningly fierce rage of Durga. In her wrathful form, she is worshipped as Bhairavi or the blue-black Mahakali: she who is both creation and destruction.

She is offered gray-colored cloth and bananas. Making this offering bestows physical health.

Mother Kaatyaayani

Mother Kaatyaayani is worshipped as the sixth manifestation of Goddess Durga. She is also worshipped as Dhoomawati (cosmic dissolution) and Jagadamba (goddess of the universe). She grants protection from negativity in the same way that dhami/jhankris are kept safe through the protection of their tutelary spirits and power animals. Her power also destroys that which is disruptive or causes strife so that it may be remade into that which brings health. She is the force of transmutation.

The narrative about her birth has been described by Bhola as follows:

The world-renowned sage Kaatyaayana was born in the dynasty of Sage Kaatya. He was an excellent devotee of Goddess Durga. He performed an austere penance for many years to ingratiate himself to her. Being delighted by his devotion, Goddess Durga appeared before him and asked him to demand the desired boon. Thereupon, the great sage Kaatyaayana demanded that she be born as a daughter to him. Goddess Durga granted his wish.

When the atrocities committed by the monstrous demon Mashisha became intolerable on Earth, Goddess Durga's sixth manifestation was born. She came to be known as Kaatyaayani, as she was the daughter of Sage Kaatyaayana.

As soon as Mother Kaatyaayani was born, she assumed a massive form. Sage Kaatyaayana bowed to her with great reverence and adored and worshipped her for three days. Because the gods and goddesses themselves are increased by our devotion, Mother Kaatyaayani grew in strength through the sage's adoration and she was able to assassinate the terrible demon.

Another version in the Puranas is that the sixth incarnation of Goddess Durga was due to the combined splendor emanating from the

triune forms of the Divine Masculine: Brahma, Vishnu, and Mahesha—
the great destroyer form of Shiva. Since Sage Kaatyaayana was the first
to worship her, she came to be called Kaatyaayani.

The four-armed Mother Kaatyaayani rides a lion. It is easy to win her favor through devotion, and she destroys all the sins of her devotees. Her worship is conducive to universal order, wealth, pleasures, and salvation.

Green-colored cloth and honey are offered to her.

Mother Kaalaraatri

The seventh manifestation of Goddess Durga is Kaalaraatri (night of death). Mother Kaalaraatri is also worshipped as Narayani (demon slayer) and Bagalamukhi (the destroyer of illusions.) She is worshipped on the seventh day of Navaratri. Her person is absolutely black like the densest darkness. She possesses three eyes in her forehead, which are as round as the universe itself.

She is considered the fiercest form of Durga, her appearance itself invoking fear. This form of the goddess Durga is believed to be the destroyer of all demon entities, ghosts, malevolent spirits, and negative energies, who flee upon knowing of her arrival. All planetary interferences are also removed if a devotee chants her name with devotion. She confers the state of fearlessness.

The hair on her head is dense but disheveled. She is bedecked with a glorious garland round her neck, which emits great radiance. She breathes out horrible and terrible flames of fire. Although her person is absolutely black, brilliant rays of light emanate from her.

Mother Kaalaraatri carries an iron khurpa ritual dagger. She destroys evil spirits, protects from wild beasts, and removes fear. She also offers rebirth. This is a manifestation of the dramatic actions that are performed by dhami/jhankris while doing their healing work. When the shaman needs to subdue the spirits of disease, battle demons, break the grip of a patient's addiction, or rescue a soul that was stolen by another, the dhami/jhankri is reflecting the power of Mother Kaalaraatri.

She is a four-armed goddess and rides a donkey. She wields the sword and a pointed weapon in two of her hands while her other two hands can be seen in the boon-conferring gesture and the gesture of fearlessness.

Although the outward form of Mother Kaalaraatri is extremely frightening, she always bestows blessings of prosperity, pleasure, and well-being on her devotees, and so she is also called Shubhankari, "the one who always provides auspicious results to her devotees." She bestows the power to let go of old habits and negative thoughtforms to experience a renewal and rebirth in every aspect of life.

She is offered ink-blue cloth and traditional unrefined cane sugar.

Mother Mahagauri

The eighth emanation of Durga helps to keep the thoughts of her devotees on the virtuous path. She destroys illusion and anything that interrupts the flow of creation. This represents the shaman's task of clearing away anything that interferes with harmony and health. This action allows for primordial balance and good health to be reborn. She is the most fierce and bloodthirsty aspect of Durga and is another form of the goddess that can be related to Kali. Animal sacrifices, especially buffalos, are made to Mother Mahagauri.

In the narrative about her from the Hindu scriptures and Puranas, Parvati is transformed into Mahagauri after she performs the austere penance advised by Sage Narada. Bhola tells the story:

> The goddess Parvati's severe penance continued for many years. She bore the extremes of heat, cold, driving rains, drought, and terrible storms. Her body was covered with dust, caked mud, and the leaves of trees. Through the hardship of exposure to the elements, her skin developed a blackish hue. At last, Lord Shiva appeared before her and gave his solemn word that he would marry her. With the holy waters of the Ganga River that pours forth from his matted hair, he bathed her until she became radiant, white complexioned, and glorious. Thus, by virtue of having acquired the coloring of mountain snows, Parvati came to be known as Mahagauri (extremely fair).

Mother Mahagauri is worshipped on the eighth day of the Navaratri. She has four arms, and her vehicle is the bull. She possesses invincible powers and bestows merits on her devotees. Mother

Mahagauri bestows blessings in this lifetime and also for successive lives. Childless couples who worship her are blessed with children.

Mother Mahagauri fulfills all the desires of her devotees. She enables them to enjoy prosperity and pleasures here in this world and salvation hereafter. She is also worshipped as Matangi and Renuka (serene).

Royal blue cloth and fresh coconut are offered to her.

Mother Siddhidaatri

The final, ninth aspect of Durga is Siddhidaatri (bestower of perfection) who grants supernatural powers or *siddhis*. These are both the otherworldly powers that shamans work with and also the infinite possibilities that are present in the spiritual realms. Some believe that Shiva attained his shamanic abilities through Mother Siddhidaartri. She also represents fulfillment and success—the shaman's victory over negative energies and chaos.

Mother Siddhidaatri is seated on the lotus and her vehicle is the lion. She possesses four arms and carries the mace, the lotus, the conch shell, and the disc in her four hands. She fulfills all the mundane and divine aspirations of her devotees, and her worship destroys all distresses. She is also worshipped as Kamala (a perfect lotus).

The story regarding her emergence runs as follows:

When Durga, the Universal Mother, was gripped with the idea of manifesting the cosmos, she first created Lord Shiva, who prayed to her to endow him with perfections. To grant his desires, Durga created Goddess Siddhidaatri from her own body. As the behest of Durga, Siddhidaatri bestowed eighteen kinds of rare perfections, supernatural powers, and potentialities on Lord Shiva, who developed a divine splendor.

Having acquired these powers from Goddess Siddhidaatri, Lord Shiva created Lord Vishnu, who in turn created Lord Brahma, who was entrusted with the task of creation, whereas Lord Vishnu got the task of protection and Lord Shiva that of destruction to create the new.

Lord Brahma found his task of creation difficult in the absence of man and woman. Thereupon he remembered Mother Siddhidaatri. When she appeared before him, Lord Brahma said to her, "O Great Mother! I cannot carry on with the task of creation in the absence of man and woman. Please solve this problem through your supernatural abilities."

Having heard Lord Brahma's dilemma, Mother Siddidaatri converted half of Lord Shiva into a woman. Thus, Lord Shiva became half male and half female and in this form was known as Ardhanarishwara. With this problem resolved, the task of creation went forward smoothly.

According to the Puranas, Mother Siddhidaatri confers eighteen kinds of supernatural attainments, which in shamanic terms are the abilities a dhami/jhankri is able to wield in the journey state. Hindu scripture refers to these extraordinary abilities as siddhis, from which the goddess gets her name. The abilities are: *anima* (reducing the body to the size of an atom), *laghima* (becoming weightless), *praapti* (having unrestricted access to all places), *praakaamya* (realizing whatever one desires), *mahimaa* (expanding the body to an infinitely large size), *vaashitva* (the power to subjugate all), *sarvakamavasayita* (the ability to obtain anything from anywhere), *sarva gyatva* (being all-knowing), *doorshravana* (to hear all that is spoken everywhere), *parkayapraveshana* (to move your soul into another body), *vaaksiddhi* (to create by speaking), *kalpavrikshtva* (to fulfill any wish), *srishti* (to create what is imagined), *sanharkaranasamarthya* (to unify a group for common good), *amaratva* (immortality), *sarvayayakatva* (to benefit all beings through personal offerings), *bhavana* (the ability to produce manifestations), and *siddhi* (complete understanding, perfection, and enlightenment).

Offerings to this aspect of Durga are red cloth and sesame seeds (*til*). Meditation and fasting are recommended on Mother Siddhidaatri's day. These two practices relieve a person from the fear of death and protect him or her from any unforeseen circumstances or incidents.

All-Encompassing Durga Mantra

As you can see, Durga truly encompasses all aspects of the primordial Mother Goddess, the divine force. As such, her mantra also encompasses all of her powers. This unified Durga mantra is a series of Sanskrit words with great power, with the potential to help solve your issues and relax your mind. It is a mantra of renewal as well as an invitation to Durga to eliminate the imbalances that lead humans into poverty, suffering, famine, disease, injustice, cruelty, laziness, and evil behavior through her powers. In this way, she is invoked as a fierce and loving warrior healer who is a powerful ally of the dhami/jhankri.

Chanting this mantra has the effect of protecting you from negative energies and removes the effects of black magic, curses, and disharmonious planetary influence. The mantra blesses the person who chants it with power, prosperity, and positive energy. It is said to improve intellectual ability, giving you a peaceful, clear, and aware mind; to help you to succeed in academics, relationships, work, and financial arenas; and to support a harmonious family life.

Om Aim Hreem Kleem Chamundye Vichche

This mantra is chanted 108 times or in multiples of 108 times. It is best to use a mala with clear quartz, rudraksha, or wooden beads. Friday is an especially auspicious day to perform this mantra; however, chant this prayer whenever you need it.

Chanting is best done while you are seated facing either East or North. Chant regularly for the best results, and observe the effects that it has on your life.

🪷 Journey to Meet Aspects of the Divine Mother Durga

This is an opportunity to work directly with your helping spirits to meet aspects of the supreme Great Mother Goddess as embodied by Durga. Before you begin, surround yourself with your golden, silver, and iron spheres. Make an offering to the spirits, sing your sacred songs, make an offering of uncooked rice, and honor all of the helping spirits in the directions.

Please read through the directions carefully and gather all that you'll need before you begin. For this exercise, you will need:

- A way to produce the shamanic journey rhythm in the background
- A comfortable place to be seated
- A small handful of uncooked rice kernels

- Your journal or a notebook and a pen
- A quiet time and space

Performing the Journey

1. Choose a time when you will be able to work with the spirits.
2. Prepare yourself and all the materials you require.
3. Begin playing the journey rhythm softly.
4. Make a rice offering to the spirits of place that hold you while you are journeying.
5. Call your power animal to you to support you during this journey.
6. Have your power animal take you to meet aspects of the supreme Great Mother Goddess. You may be led to one or several aspects.
7. As you meet an aspect, greet her and thank her for her role in continually re-creating All That Is.
8. Ask the aspects of the Great Goddess expressed through Durga's many forms to share how you may work in harmony with creation for the good of all beings.
9. Repeat this with all of the aspects you meet.
10. When you feel you have completed your journey work, thank the spirits with whom you worked and return to ordinary reality by drumming the callback signal.

Once the journey is complete, remember to make another offering to the spirits for their help and support.

⌂ Journey Explorations

Journey to your teacher or power animal to ask: How may I work in harmony with the Divine Feminine aspects of life?

Journey to your teacher or power animal to ask: How does the Divine Feminine express itself in my life?

Journey to your teacher or power animal to ask: How can working with the Divine Feminine bring a richer experience of living to my life?

Record the content of your journeys and your perceptions about what you received.

After each journey, thank your power animal, your teacher, and any other spirits who have revealed themselves to you. Then make an offering to the spirits. This can be an offering of incense smoke, bits of food outdoors, or flower petals.

⌑ Process Questions

What are you continuing to feel as you explore the Divine Feminine? How does the Divine Feminine teach you more about yourself?

KALI: THE WRATHFUL ASPECT OF THE GODDESS

As we wrote in the section about Durga, some aspects of the Great Mother Goddess are fierce and wrathful. Rather than being radiantly golden or white, they are depicted as deep blue or black. With wild hair, glaring eyes, and sharp teeth, they are the creatrixes who destroy and consume to bring forth new life. Mother Skandamaataa's wrathful form, Bhairavi, is one such version, as is the black and radiant Mother Kaalaraatri and the bloodthirsty Mother Mahagauri.

All of these forms may be related to the Mother Goddess form known as Kali and Mahakali. Her name means the "the black one" and "beyond time." She is the goddess of time, change, power, creation, preservation, and destruction. She is the great cosmic void or pure unmanifested energy—the eternal darkness from which everything is born and into which all physical matter must eventually return. She is the supreme mistress of the universe and is associated with all of the five elements (earth, water, fire, air, and ether).

In one story of her origin, it is said that she burst forth from the brow of Durga as she was battling a demon. As such, Kali represents the force of destruction in service to life.

She is often depicted in conjunction with Shiva. She is shown either standing with her right foot on his chest or sitting on him in coitus (in her Goddess Chinnamasta aspect). These overt and metaphoric representations of the divine couple represent the conjunction of matter (Shiva) and energy (Kali) that is life itself.

♛ *Journey to Meet Kali*

This is an opportunity to work directly with your helping spirits to meet the wrathful aspect of the supreme Great Mother Goddess as embodied

Figure 18.2. Instantly recognizable to most Westerners by her bulging eyes and lolling tongue, Kali is the Great Goddess in her aspect as the deity of time, change, power, creation, preservation, and destruction (pen-and-ink drawing by the author).

by Kali. Before you begin, surround yourself with your golden, silver, and iron spheres. Make an offering to the spirits, sing your sacred songs, make an offering of uncooked rice, and honor all of the helping spirits in the directions.

Please read through the directions carefully and gather all that you'll need before you begin. For this exercise, you will need:

- A way to produce the shamanic journey rhythm in the background
- A comfortable place to be seated
- A small handful of uncooked rice kernels
- Your journal or a notebook and a pen
- A quiet time and space

☙ Performing the Journey

1. Choose a time when you will be able to work with the spirits.
2. Prepare yourself and all the materials you require.

3. Begin playing the journey rhythm softly.

4. Make a rice offering to the spirits of place that hold you while you are journeying.

5. Call your power animal to you to support you during this journey.

6. Have your power animal take you to meet aspects of the supreme Great Mother Goddess in the form of Kali. You may be led to one or several aspects.

7. As you meet an aspect, greet her and thank her for her role in continually re-creating All That Is.

8. Ask the aspect of the Great Goddess to share how you may work in harmony with creation for the good of all beings.

9. Repeat this with all of the aspects you meet.

10. When you feel you have completed your journey work, thank the spirits with whom you worked and return to ordinary reality by drumming the callback signal.

Once the journey is complete, remember to make another offering to the spirits for their help and support.

⌂ Journey Explorations

Journey to your teacher or power animal to ask: How may I work in harmony with the Divine Feminine aspects of life?

Journey to your teacher or power animal to ask: How does the Divine Feminine express itself in my life?

Journey to your teacher or power animal to ask: How can working with the Divine Feminine bring a richer experience of living to my life?

Record the content of your journeys and your perceptions about what you received.

After each journey, thank your power animal, your teacher, and any other spirits who have revealed themselves to you. Then make an offering to the spirits. This can be an offering of incense smoke, bits of food outdoors, or flower petals.

⌂ Process Questions

What are you continuing to feel as you explore the Divine Feminine?

How does the Divine Feminine teach you more about yourself?

PEACEFUL FORMS OF
THE GODDESS

The more peaceful aspects of the supreme Great Mother Goddess are expressed as those that provide nurturance. These are the goddesses who provide, sustain, and enrich as Earth does for all of her life-forms.

Bhumi Devi

One of the peaceful, nurturing forms of the Great Mother Goddess honored by dhami/jhankris is Bhumi Devi. Her Sanskrit name is Prithvi, meaning "the vast one." Bhumi Devi is also a female parallel to Vishnu the preserver and a form of Lakshmi (see below). Bhumi Devi is the spiritual bounty of the Great Mother Goddess that manifests in the world around us. She is the fruitful Earth and the fertile soil from which we receive all our sustenance. She is the old grandmother who is continually bestowing blessings, abundance, and prosperity on all of her children. She is the version of the Divine Mother who sits atop the Divine Pillar that balances all life (see fig. 17.1, page 151).

Earth is also revered as Dharti Mata, the pregnant, birthing, and nursing mother who is honored in May before the rains. There is a figure of her birthing the world into form in Kirtipur, Nepal, that is honored with offerings of flower petals and red pigment. She is the vulva and fruitful womb, the fertile yoni that gave birth to the physical realm.

As Bhola says:

Bhumi Devi is the spiritual aspect of Dharti Mata who is calm, peaceful, nurturing, and heart melting. Both these aspects are loving and nurturing mothers, and their protective aspects are life giving. I have not only felt them deep in my heart but have danced with them, sung with them, and visited their realms during narrative journeys and journeys to empower sick persons.

Bhumi Devi Mantra

This mantra asks Bhumi Devi permission and honors the bounty and blessings of Mother Earth.

Om Ahg-ya Day-oh Bhoo-mee Devee

By offering our gratitude, we give back to her for all she gives to us. It is typically chanted 108 times on a crystal, wooden, or rudraksha bead mala.

🪷 *Journey to Meet the Divine Mother as Our Earth*

This is an opportunity to work directly with your helping spirits to meet Mother Earth, Bhumi Devi. Before you begin, surround yourself with your golden, silver, and iron spheres. Make an offering to the spirits, sing your sacred songs, make an offering of uncooked rice, and honor all of the helping spirits in the directions.

Please read through the directions carefully and gather all that you'll need before you begin. For this exercise, you will need:

- A way to produce the shamanic journey rhythm in the background
- A comfortable place to be seated
- A small handful of uncooked rice kernels
- Your journal or a notebook and a pen
- A quiet time and space

🪶 Performing the Journey

1. Choose a time when you will be able to work with the spirits.
2. Prepare yourself and all the materials you require.
3. Begin playing the journey rhythm softly.
4. Make a rice offering to the spirits of place that hold you while you are journeying.
5. Call your power animal to you to support you during this journey.
6. Have your power animal take you to meet Mother Earth, Bhumi Devi. You may be led to one or several aspects.
7. As you meet an aspect, greet her and thank her for her role in continually re-creating All That Is.
8. Ask this aspect of the Great Goddess to share how you may work in harmony with creation for the good of all beings.
9. Repeat this with all of the aspects you meet.
10. When you feel you have completed your journey work, thank the spirits with whom you worked and return to ordinary reality by drumming the callback signal.

Figure 18.3. Dharti Mata, Mother Earth, giving birth to all life
(photo: Mariarosa Genitrini). (See also color plate 12)

Once the journey is complete, remember to make another offering to
the spirits for their help and support.

⌦ Journey Explorations

Journey to your teacher or power animal to ask: How may I work in harmony with the Divine Feminine aspects of life?

Journey to your teacher or power animal to ask: How does the Divine Feminine express itself in my life?

Journey to your teacher or power animal to ask: How can working with the Divine Feminine bring a richer experience of living to my life?

Record the content of your journeys and your perceptions about what you received.

After each journey, thank your power animal, your teacher, and any other spirits who have revealed themselves to you. Then make an offering to the spirits. This can be an offering of incense smoke, bits of food outdoors, or flower petals.

⌦ Process Questions

What are you continuing to feel as you explore the Divine Feminine?

How does the Divine Feminine teach you more about yourself?

Lakshmi

The goddess in this aspect helps us to know and understand our goals. She personifies wealth, riches, beauty, happiness, loveliness, grace, charm, and splendor. She is honored for her ability to provide abundance in all its beneficial physical and spiritual forms. She is honored as the mother of all women and all that is auspicious. She also grants gods their powers and is a consort of and active manifestation of Vishnu the preserver. Lakshmi is born with an array of precious objects when the cosmic Ocean of milk was churned to create the water of life. She is also called Padmā, the Sanskrit word for lotus flower, since when she arose from the sacred waters she was holding a lotus blossom.

Saraswati

This aspect of the Divine Feminine is the goddess of learning and is also personified as a perennial source of wisdom's constant, riverlike flow. Her name actually translates to "one who leads to the essence of self-knowledge." This represents the understanding that deeply studying the worlds of nature, in the way that artists do, can ultimately bring us deeper understanding of ourselves, just as a deep spiritual practice can bring us more deeply into relationship with nature.

Saraswati represents intelligence, consciousness, cosmic knowledge, creativity, education, enlightenment, music, the arts, eloquence, and power. As such she is honored in springtime to bless all new beginnings, new ventures, and the birth of new creative projects. On midwinter, the day that sits between the winter solstice and vernal equinox, students bring pens and pencils to her shrine to request better memories for their schoolwork and the ability to grasp their lessons. Artists, poets, musicians, and others honor her on this day as they embark on new creative explorations. On this day, shamans cleanse their drums with incense, adorn them with fresh peacock feathers, paint the drumheads with auspicious symbols or images of their protectors, and add new strips of colored cloth to the drum handle.

THE TARAS

Since Nepal is such a remarkable mix of different religions and spiritual paths, it isn't surprising that there are also Buddhist characters who are understood by dhami/jhankris as goddess images. Tara is venerated in several of her twenty-one aspects. For instance, Green Tara is seen as the primordial goddess in her aspect as rescuer or protector from danger, while White Tara is perceived as a form of Saraswati, the Hindu goddess of knowledge, music, arts, wisdom, and learning.

Ugratara, a wrathful form of this goddess who is black and red, is honored by Nepalese dhami/jhankris as a goddess of fertility, unity, and wisdom and as the one who bestows healing powers to shamans. Because all things come around again when working with the Divine Feminine, Ugratara is also closely related to Blue Tara (Ekajati) or Nila Saraswati, a wrathful form of White Tara.

When all is said and done, the feminine principle is revered in myriad forms. What is of primary importance is that you get to work

Figure 18.4. A thangka painting of White Tara on her lotus blossom throne.

with these energies yourself. The following journeys will assist you in meeting aspects of the Mother Goddess so that you can learn from them firsthand. You will be accompanied by your trusted power animal or teacher who can help you to better understand what you are given.

19

Primary Masculine Deities

The Hindu-related male deities that shamans honor all seem to originate from the earliest Proto-Indo-European god Dyēus Ph2tēr who became Dyauspitṛ, or Father Sky, in the Rig-Veda. As it was with the goddess, the divine masculine is honored in a variety of forms. As stated in the previous chapter, male forms of the divine arose from the supreme Great Mother Goddess—the being who continually creates and re-creates All That Is from the substance of her own divine energy. The male deities work in harmony with the Divine Feminine in her many forms. Appearing as her consort, husband, and son, they are partners in turning the wheel of life and represent the active form of the divine.

In the Nepali tradition everything created has hidden male and female aspects. When a male deity or spirit is honored, it is clear that a female aspect is also present. The reverse is true when honoring female deities or female spirits: a hidden masculine energy is understood to be present.

Mahakala Raja, Mahakala Rani
Mahakala king, Mahakala queen

Bhairung Raja, Bhairung Rani
Bhairung king, Bhairung queen

Matte Raja, Matte Rani
Mud/soil king, Mud/soil queen

Bhumi Raja, Bhumai Rani
Earth king, Earth queen

Khole Raja, Khole Rani
River king, River queen

Hariyali Raja, Hariyali Rani
Greenery king, Greenery queen

Aakash Raja, Aakash Rani
Sky king, Sky queen

Naga Raja, Naga Rani
Naga king, Naga queen

Dadai Raja, Dadai Rani
Mountain king, Mountain queen

Bhola explains a bit about how he understands the masculine deities' energies and provides some general ideas about how he works with them in his own practice.

The Divine Masculine deities pass on the wisdom of protection and of safeguarding family, territory, and community. Shiva and Mahadeva and other masculine characters can be offended easily and also easily mollified through prayerful actions. Most of the time they are honored through invocation (pukara) and through making offerings. When malignant spirits or hungry ghouls possess a person, the wrathful, powerful masculine powers are the ones that are invoked by the shaman. To pacify the disarrayed planets, to cut through the karmic entanglements, to re-create order and harmony, and to help confused and stranded souls transition, Mahakala, Kaal Bhairung, Vajrakilaya, and other wrathful deities are called upon. The divine masculine beings, just like the feminine deities, are invoked by tantrikas and by Hindu and Buddhist priests, monks, or nuns. In my practice I often invoke Mahakala or Kaal Bhairung for depossessions and Hanuman for reconciliation and reconnection and for enlivening herbal plant medicine. For me, Shiva-Mahadeva occupies the highest place as mentor, protector, and life giver.

GANNYAP

The elephant-headed god Gannyap (Ganesha) is a well-known figure in contemporary culture. Nepalese dhami/jhankris consider Gannyap to be the ultimate symbol for shamanic dismemberment and rebirth. He also is the remover of obstacles and the one who can bestow bliss, wisdom, power, grounding, and success.

What follows here is Gannyap's origin story as shared by Bhola.

Gannyap's mother is the peaceful, nurturing form of the supreme Mother Goddess Parvati (the Mother Brahmchaarini aspect of Durga) and her consort/husband, Shiva.

It is said that Parvati and Shiva resided together in Mount Kailash, which is the most sacred mountain in the Himalayan chain. While Shiva was away, Pavrati grew tired of being intruded upon by the servants while she bathed. She decided to create a son to be her protector and guard, whose primary loyalty would be to her. She made a figure of either mud or turmeric paste and breathed life into it. In this way she gave birth to Gannyap, in his human form. She assigned him the task of guarding the door while she retired to her private quarters to bathe.

Later in the day when Shiva returned from his adventures in the world, Gannyap stopped him from entering his own home. Not aware that Gannyap was his own son, Shiva was infuriated and ordered his army of devotees to attack him. However, the powerful Gannyap was able to beat them all, forcing Lord Shiva to fight the young boy himself.

Lord Shiva in his anger was able to defeat Gannyap and in the process severed and destroyed the young boy's head. Moments later Goddess Parvati discovered what had happened. Hurt and angered at the loss of her son, she transformed into her multiarmed form and threatened to bring an end to all of creation.

At this point, Brahma, the creator aspect of the Divine Male triune (Shiva, Brahma, Vishnu), recognized the precarious situation that the universe was in and requested that Parvati give up her anger and refrain from causing harm to All That Is. In response to his request, Parvati laid down two conditions to forgive the wrong that had been done to her and her son.

Her first condition was that Gannyap be immediately brought back to life. Her second condition required that he then be identified as the paramount god who would be worshipped before all other gods in any and every religious ceremony.

By this time, Lord Shiva had recognized his tragic folly, and he asked Brahma to fetch the head of the first living creature that he found facing in the North direction. Dashing from the palace, Brahma first spotted an elephant facing North, and in accordance with Shiva's instructions, he returned with the elephant's head.

Shiva placed the elephant head on Gannyap's headless body and restored him to life. Then keeping with Parvati's second condition, Lord Shiva recognized the young man as his own son, assigned him the status of the foremost god, and declared that Gannyap would be recognized as the leader of all classes of beings and would be worshipped before all other deities.

Because of his remarkable origins of being dismembered and re-created in a new form, Gannyap is always honored first in any ceremony or healing ritual. His story has parallels to shamanic initiation. The greatest obstacle for the shamanic initiate is his or her ordinary way of living and perceiving the world. This must be overcome or obliterated so that a new way of being and understanding can be achieved. For these reasons, it is Gannyap who helps initiates to overcome obstacles in their path to spiritual growth and enlightenment.

Bhola has a special relationship with Gannyap:

In his position as the son of Lord Shiva, protector of the doors to the sacred Mount Kailash, lord of the clan, bestower of healing spirits, and path opener, the first presence I feel when I begin my empowerment for performing shamanic work is Gannyap. In the process of incorporating my helping spirits into my body, Gannyap is the main spirit bridge between Mother Earth and me as she stands on the head of Naga Raja—the Naga King. When the spirits start mounting my body, there is much hullabaloo from the spirits as my drum and the bells of my bandolier sound. In this process, the huge earlobes of Gannyap function like winnowing pans to

Figure 19.1. Gannyap is a powerful shaman who is able to overcome obstacles and defeat death to perform the work of bringing grounding, harmony, and joy (pen-and-ink drawing by the author).

help me to focus as I enter into my journey. In both my personal house altar and also in my shamanic altar, there is always a decisive presence of Gannyap.

Shamans believe that all ultimate grounding, nurturing, and healing flows from Mother Earth. Gannyap helps to facilitate that connection and as such is sometimes shown resting on the hood of a naga that connects to Earth. This image helps us understand that when we are truly grounded, we provide a strong, safe container for the spiritual energy inside us to flow upward. In addition, Gannyap actually assists our spiritual energy and awareness to rise for reunion with Divine Oneness.

Along with the many spontaneous songs and chants a dhami/jhankri may use while inspirited, the chanting of mantras is believed to invoke a connection to the particular powers that are associated with the deity being honored by the chanting. The shamans recite Gannyap's mantra or chant along with other invocations to prepare themselves and to help others in healing or other sacred work.

Gannyap's mantra should be chanted after cleansing the body, or at least washing your hands and face. Allow yourself enough time enough to perform 108 repetitions of the mantra. You will use your mala to help you count each repetition; for Gannyap, the mala should be made of crystal, rudraksha, or wooden beads. The Gannyap mantra is always chanted prior to embarking on shamanic work and always followed immediately by an offering of flowers, fruit, sweets, or "clean" liquid, such as water or fresh milk.

This mantra is always chanted while facing North or East and preferably while you are sitting on a wool rug or blanket on the floor. (If you must sit in a chair, have your bare feet on a wool rug or blanket.) The wool prevents any of the rising spiritual energy from leaking out of your body. Since Gannyap is the deity that helps to boost our wisdom and spiritual knowledge, it is important to hold the intention that this chant is for the benefit of all living beings.

The following mantra honors Gannyap and invokes his aid in removing obstacles on your path. Remember, releasing your obstacles must never produce a burden on another; in your heart, feel them leaving you harmlessly. This mantra is referred to as the *vakratunda* mantra: *vakra* means "curved" and *tund* means "trunk," a reference to the elephant-headed god's trunk.

Vakratunda Mahaakaaya Suryakoti Samaprabhaa
Nirvighnam Kurumedeva Sarvakaaryeshu Sarvadaa

Here is a translation of the mantra's words so that you have a better sense of its meaning:

Salutations to the supreme Lord Gannyap,

whose curved trunk (vakra-tunda) *and massive*
body (maha-kaayaa) *shines like a million*
suns (surya-koti) *and showers his blessings on*
everyone (sama-prabhaa). *Oh, may lord of lords*

Figure 19.2. Gannyap statute depicting the deity with ten arms and two heads (a second smaller head can be seen above his primary head), Kathmandu, Nepal. (See also color plate 13)

Gannyap (kurume-deva), *kindly remove all obstacles* (nir-vighnam), *always* (sarva-) *and forever* (sarvadaa-) *from all my activities and endeavors* (sarva-kaaryeshu).

❧ Journey to Meet Gannyap

This is an opportunity to work directly with your helping spirits to meet Gannyap. Before you begin, surround yourself with your golden, silver, and iron spheres. Make an offering to the spirits: sing your sacred songs, offer uncooked rice, and honor all of the helping spirits in the directions.

Please read through the directions carefully and gather all that you'll need before you begin. For this exercise, you will need:

- All of your altar objects and a copper plate (thaal), flat winnowing basket (nanglo), or special cloth on which they are to be arranged (or at the very least a lit candle or oil lamp, a bowl of water, a feather, and a stone) placed in front of you
- Your dhyangro and gajo or another way to produce the journey rhythm
- A comfortable place to be seated
- A small handful of uncooked rice kernels
- A fruit, flower, or sweets offering for Gannyap
- Your 108-bead mala
- A small picture or figure of Gannyap (Ganesha) for your altar
- Your journal or a notebook and a pen
- A quiet time and space

☙ Performing the Journey

1. Choose a time when you will be able to work with the spirits.
2. Prepare yourself and all the materials you require.
3. Chant Gannyap's vakratunda mantra 108 times.
4. Make an offering with fruit, flowers, or sweets on the altar near to the image of Gannyap.
5. Begin playing the journey rhythm softly.
6. Make a rice offering to the spirits of the place that holds you while you are journeying.
7. Call your power animal to you to support you during this journey.

8. Have your power animal take you to meet Gannyap.
9. As you meet him, greet him and thank him for meeting with you.
10. Share something you would like his help in clearing away.
11. When you feel you have completed your journey work, thank the spirits with whom you worked and return to ordinary reality by drumming the callback signal.

Once the journey is complete, remember to make another offering to the spirits and Gannyap for their help and support.

⬩ Journey Explorations

Journey to Gannyap again to ask: How may I work with you to remove obstacles in my path?

Journey to your teacher or power animal to ask: At what times is it useful to call upon Gannyap for assistance?

Journey to your teacher or power animal to ask: How can working with Gannyap bring a richer experience of living to my life?

Record the content of your journeys and your perceptions about what you received.

After each journey, thank all the spirits who have revealed themselves to you and make an offering to them. This can be an offering of incense smoke, bits of food outdoors, or flower petals.

⬩ Process Questions

What has changed for you after meeting Gannyap?

How does working with Gannyap teach you more about yourself?

LORD SHIVA

The god Shiva is one of the trio of male deities who together represent the masculine manifestations of the Great Goddess's actions of creation, preservation, and destruction. They are the concrete, active representations of formless power. The other two gods are Brahma and Vishnu. Brahma is the manifestation of creation, Vishnu is the manifestation of preservation, and Shiva is the manifestation of destruction that paves the way for rebirth and renewal.

Shiva is depicted as having a blue face and a body that is white or covered in ash. Wound around his neck is the Naga Vasuki, a snake god who was used as a rope to extract the ambrosia of immortality (amrita) from the cosmic ocean.

On his head is a conical topknot of twisted hair. From his topknot the milky source of Mother Ganga, the River Ganges, fountains forth. This symbolism presents Shiva as an anthropomorphic symbol for the erect phallus—a producer of regenerative, creative matter that metaphorically "dies" once the task is complete. This echoes Shiva's role in preserving the cycle of life by attending to destruction as the ultimate pathway to rebirth. Indeed, Shiva is also represented in the form of a *lingam*. This stylized, oblong ovoid form is often shown standing erect as a symbolic phallus in the *yoni* or symbolic vulva of the goddess. This structure represents not only the union of masculine and feminine but also the eternal circular flow of form

Figure 19.3. Lord Shiva (pen-and-ink drawing by the author).

and formlessness. This cycle is a universal constant. It is the dance of continuance of which Shiva is a master.

The shaman's role as one who traverses between the tangible and intangible worlds—being an active intercedent in nature's dance on behalf of nature and all beings—helps to explain why Shiva is the primary deity for most dhami/jhankris. He is the archetype for the shaman's path. He embodies the action of attending the delicate balance of all aspects of creation.

Some Himalayan shamans merge with Shiva to become a physical presence of the god's vibration. This is the same as shamans around the world merging with their primary tutelary spirit and thereby embodying the spirit's energy in the physical world.

🪷 *Journey to Meet Shiva*

This is an opportunity to work directly with your helping spirits to meet Shiva. Before you begin, surround yourself with your golden, silver, and iron spheres. Make an offering to the spirits: sing your sacred songs, offer uncooked rice, and honor all of the helping spirits in the four directions.

Please read through the directions carefully and gather all that you'll need before you begin. For this exercise, you will need:

- All of your altar objects and a copper plate (thaal), flat winnowing basket (nanglo), or special cloth on which they are to be arranged (or at the very least a lit candle or oil lamp, a bowl of water, a feather, a stone, and an image of Shiva) placed in front of you
- Your dhyangro and gajo or another way to produce the journey rhythm
- A comfortable place to be seated
- A small handful of uncooked rice kernels
- A fruit, flower, or sweets offering for Shiva
- Your 108-bead mala
- Your journal or a notebook and a pen
- A quiet time and space

☜ Performing the Journey

1. Choose a time when you will be able to work with the spirits.
2. Prepare yourself and all the materials you require.
3. Make an offering with fruit, flowers, or sweets on the altar near to the image of Shiva.
4. Now continue to make offerings to your other spirit teachers, helpers, and power animals.
5. Begin playing the journey rhythm softly.
6. Make a rice offering to the spirits of place that hold you while you are journeying.
7. Call your power animal to you to support you during this journey.
8. Have your power animal take you to meet Shiva.
9. As you meet him, greet him and thank him for meeting with you.
10. Ask Shiva how you may honor him.
11. Once you have learned how to honor him, ask Shiva how he can assist you in your shamanic practice.
12. When you feel you have completed your journey work, thank the spirits with whom you worked and return to ordinary reality by drumming the callback signal.

Once the journey is complete, remember to make another offering to the spirits and Shiva for their help and support.

☜ Journey Explorations

Journey to Shiva again to ask: How may I work with you to keep balance in my life between the forces of creation and destruction?

Journey to your teacher or power animal to ask: At what times is it useful to call upon Shiva for assistance?

Journey to your teacher or power animal to ask: How can working with Shiva bring a richer experience of living to my life?

Record the content of your journeys and your perceptions about what you received.

After each journey, thank all the spirits who revealed themselves to you and make an offering to them. This can be an offering of incense smoke, bits of food outdoors, or flower petals.

▷ Process Questions

What has changed for you since meeting Shiva?

How does working with Lord Shiva teach you more about yourself?

KAAL BHAIRUNG

Lord Shiva also has a wrathful aspect. This fierce face of Shiva is Kaal Bhairung (also called Kaalo Bhairung, Kaal Bhairab, Bhairav, and Kṣetrapāla). This is the active, moving energy of Shiva. This form of Shiva is a particularly powerful helping spirit for dhami/jhankris in Himalayan Nepal. He is called upon to protect the shaman's body while healing work is being performed and when embodying healing energies.

As Westerners, we can think of Kaal Bhairung as a male version of Kali's energy, and indeed, since all male Nepalese deities are thought to hold the female aspect and vice versa, Kali is present in this ceremony.*

There are eight Maha Bhairavas/Bhairungs controlling the eight directions of this universe. Each Bhairung has his own eight forms under him, making a total of sixty-four Bhairungs. All the Bhairavas are ruled and controlled by one Maha Swarna Kala Bhairava (great golden-black bhairava/rung), who is the supreme ruler of time of this universe.

Asidanga Bhairung: This aspect of Kaal Bhairung bestows creative ability

Ruru Bhairung: Bestows wisdom

Chanda Bhairung: Gives incredible energy for defeating one's enemies and rivals

Krodha Bhairung: Bestows infinite power to take massive action

Unmatha Bhairung: Helps one to control negative ego and helps to raise regenerative power

Kapaala Bhairung: Ends all unrewarding work and action

Bheeshana Bhairung: Obliterates evil spirits and negativity

---

*Another aspect of the Divine Feminine who carries a similar energy is Mother Mahagauri, the eighth emanation of Durga.

Figure 19.4. Shiva's fierce aspect Kaal Bhairung depicted in this carving wearing a flayed human skin and holding a cranium full of blood, Durbar Square, Kathmandu (photo: Mariarosa Genitrini).

Samhaara Bhairung: Supports the process of complete dissolution of old negative karmas and actions

Kaal Bhairung is represented in an active standing position with four hands. Some of his weapons include the khadga (a straight sword that may have a flaming blade), the drum, the noose (*pāśa*), the trident, and either a skull or a garland of skulls draped around his neck.

In some of the sixty-four forms of Bhairung, there are more than four hands. He appears either without clothing or with a loincloth of severed heads and is accompanied by a dog. His weapons, dog, protruding teeth, and terrifying accoutrements give him a very frightening appearance.

Kaal Bhairung can punish wrongdoing and ensure that right action is taken at the appropriate time. To be successful in life, we need to take timely actions to move our process forward, and we need to place ourselves at the right place at the right time. When we mismanage time or waste it on frivolous pursuits, we are actually draining away our own life force.

This deity is helpful when we find ourselves unable to think clearly or concentrate. He is useful when a process becomes circuitous or bogged down. He can cut through our mental or emotional paralysis to help us regain a clear vision of our path and what needs to be done to accomplish it. It is believed that our limited perception of reality can hamper our ability to capture instantaneous manifestation opportunities. Chanting the Shiva sutra Udyamo Bhairava can bring about an upsurge of consciousness that can help widen our focus on possibilities. The syllable *bhai* opens up beneficial physical manifestations such as material wealth, *ra* dissolves negativity and limited consciousness, and *va* keeps creating possibilities.

Kaal Bhairung is also a deity who can help you to keep your ego in check. There is an old expression that suggests each of us is our own worst enemy. Our ego can hold us back by us either being too puffed up about our importance or conversely believing that we are worthless or pitiful. Both of these opposing perceptions have their root in our ego. They are perceptual distortions that interfere with us manifesting our most authentic and splendid selves. They are also the greatest interference to a powerful shamanic practice. If you experience either of these mental limitations, doing a journey in the company of your helping spirits to Kaal Bhairung can provide ways to see beyond the veil that ego has placed over your eyes and heart. In addition, chanting the following Kaal Bhairung mantra can be very beneficial in supporting you to realize and manifest your authentic nature.

Living from our true, radiant, and authentic nature is a pathway to opening up the blessings and infinite abundance of the universe. In this way, Bhairung's power assists in fulfilling the spiritual and mundane wishes of his devotees.

Eight Bhairung Mantra

The recitation and invocation of this eight Bhairung mantra is important for protecting the shaman's body while she or he is performing healing duties and for protecting shamanic ritual space. The same mantra can also protect personal assets, which in rural Nepal would be one's animals, fields, house, and property. In this way, it is a perfect mantra to use daily for protecting one's self and surroundings.

Invocation of these eight Bhairungs from eight different directions creates a safe space for the shaman to work at the center. Any obstacles or potential attacks from malignant spirits are negated by the Bhairungs who protect different directions as *kshetrapalas* (guardians of place or direction) and *dwarapalas* (guardians of doors or portals).

This fourteen-line mantra is also used while performing a healing or cleansing, while using the conch shell, while using sacred plants such as mugwort, and while charging food or drink so that it becomes a healing substance that is then offered to a patient. As you can see in the line-by-line translation, this long mantra provides an all-encompassing blessing and protection from all manner of worrisome spirits.

This mantra should be chanted 5, 7, 21, or 108 times. A rudraksha or clear crystal mala is used to count the repetitions.

> *Ehai Guru Raja Guru Rani*
> Honor Teacher King and Queen
>
> *Jala masani, Thala masani, Bira masani*
> Protect from water-wandering, earth-wandering, and
>   funeral-ground-wandering, prematurely dead
>   spirits
>
> *Narsingha masanile Rakshye gari lyauta Guru bacha*
>   *namaha!*
> Honorable Narsingh and teacher please protect!
>
> *Kala Bhairung ta Bala Bhairung, Batu Bhairung ta*
> Time-guarding, power-bestowing young Bhairung

Narsingha Bhairung ta Jage masantaro masantara
Narsingha Bhairung, awaken and dispel the spirits of
the charnal grounds

Jala badhu Thala badhu, Bhuta maru, Preta maru
Bind the water and earth, suppress demons and
wandering human spirits

Chheda maru taha Guru bacha namaha
Suppress the attacking spirits with the oath of my
teacher

Kan base Kundal Bhairung
I welcome ear-dwelling Kundal [earring] Bhairung

Mukha base Saraswati Bhairing
I welcome mouth-dwelling Saraswati Bhairung

Taha Naka base Thingala Bhairung Taho Guru bacha
   namaha
I welcome nose-dwelling Thingala Bhairung,
honorable Guru Taho

Jala dankini, Thala dankini
Bind all water- and earth-infesting malignant spirits

Jala masani, Thala masani taha
Suppress the water- and earth-wandering restless
spirits

Thingala Bhairung, Jala badhu, Thala maru
With the power of Thingala Bhairung, bind the
water and subdue the malignant earth spirits

Taho Guru bacha namaha
To you Great Teacher, I offer my honor.

VAJRAKILAYA: THE LIVING KHURPA

The wrathful deity Vajrakilaya (or Dorje Phurba in Tibetan) is dark
blue and has six arms, a pair of wings, and three faces, each with

three eyes. He is sometimes depicted with the bottom half of his body replaced by the triune blade of the khurpa dagger. Other deities who also sometimes embody this more overt symbol of action and power include Guru Dragpur, the black and red forms of Hayagriva, Yamantaka, the Bön deity, Purba Drugse Chempa, Simhamukha the lion-headed dakini, and Garuda, who is fully explained in chapter 22.

Vajrakilaya embodies the action of the khurpa and its ability to

Figure 19.5. Vajrakilaya, the embodiment of the khurpa's action
(pen-and-ink drawing by the author).

subjugate demons, purify beings and places of spiritual pollution, destroy ignorance, and pierce through illusions, negative attachments, or obstacles. Despite his fearsome appearance, he transcends and transmutes all negative influences that burden our lives. He is the deity that is called upon to subdue and destroy the most malevolent of entities that contribute to the gravest illnesses.

The action of Vajrakilaya can also cut through mental delusions, imbalances of the ego, damaging thought patterns, and stuck emotions that create disruptions in a person as well as clear damaging thoughtforms and troubling entities from homes, businesses, and other places.

As his name suggests, he also embodies the vajra's diamond-like indestructibility and the irresistible force of the lightning bolt. As such, Vajrakilaya can simultaneously replace the negative influences he slays in a flash with the brilliant radiance of illumination, spiritual health, mental clarity, and wisdom. When a dhami/jhankri is working, he or she becomes an embodiment of Vajrakilaya. The shaman becomes the physical manifestation of both aspects of the deity to accomplish his or her work of clearing away whatever sickens or impedes and returning whatever heals and improves the situation.

Vajrakilaya is called upon to subdue the most dreaded products of imbalance with the snake deities or nagas. These include drought and famine and the plagues that often arrive in their wake. His ability to subdue these kinds of disruptions are depicted in his adornments of naga earrings, naga bracelets, naga anklets, a naga cord over his chest, and a naga hair ornament.

Vajrakilaya Mantra

Chanting the Vajrakilaya mantra is a very powerful practice for removing hindrances. According to the mythic stories, the mantra was discovered by Guru Padmasambhava in a cave in Nepal, who then secreted it away as a sacred treasure.

Known for its ability to remove obstacles, this powerful mantra is performed to transform sickness and negativity, slay negative entities, and dispel mental illusions. In removing these obstacles, Vajrakilaya bestows well-being, happiness, clarity, mindfulness, and ultimate enlightenment. This practice is particularly helpful and suitable during these times, both for individual practitioners and for the well-being of our world community.

Om Vajra KilikIlaya Sarwa Bignan Bam Hung Phat

This mantra is said to invoke the spirit, wisdom, and power of Vajrakilaya. It is best chanted 108 times on a rudraksha mala. This translation of the syllables of the mantra can help you to better understand the meaning of the prayer.

Om: Om is actually made up of three syllables, *aaah, oooh,* and *mmm.* This Sanskrit seed syllable is the vibration of the eternal, unified consciousness of the universe. In chanting it, we unite our individual conscious with the divine consciousness and embody it here in physical form.

Vajra: The nature of three cycles of time: past, present, and future

Kili: The awakening of the deity and the dagger

Kilaya: Piercing all phenomenal experience with the dagger

Sarwa: The destruction of all obstacles and destructive forces

Bignan: The subjugating of negative forces

Bam-hum: *Bam* combined with *hum* means to bring order

Phat: The liberation from negative forces

☸ *Journey to Meet Vajrakilaya*

This is an opportunity to work directly with your helping spirits to meet Vajrakilaya. Before you begin, surround yourself with your golden, silver, and iron spheres. Make an offering to the spirits: sing your sacred songs, offer uncooked rice, and honor all of the helping spirits in the four directions.

Please read through the directions carefully and gather all that you'll need before you begin. For this exercise, you will need:

- All of your altar objects and a copper plate (thaal), flat winnowing basket (nanglo), or special cloth on which they are to be arranged (or at the very least a lit candle or oil lamp, a bowl of water, a feather, and a stone) placed in front of you

- Your dhyangro and gajo or another way to produce the journey rhythm
- A comfortable place to be seated
- Your mala
- A copy of the Vajrakilaya-honoring mantra
- A small handful of uncooked rice kernels
- A few slices of fruit and sesame seeds to use as an offering
- Your journal or a notebook and a pen
- A quiet time and space

☙ Performing the Journey

1. Choose a time when you will be able to work with the spirits.
2. Prepare yourself and all the materials you require.
3. Make an offering of fruit and sesame seeds on your altar space in front of you.
4. Make an offering of rice kernels to the spirits of place that hold you while you are journeying.
5. Begin playing the journey rhythm softly.
6. Call your power animal to you to support you during this journey.
7. Have your power animal take you to meet Vajrakilaya.
8. Upon meeting this powerful being, thank him for agreeing to meet with you.
9. Ask Vajrakilaya to share how he affects your world.
10. Ask Vajrakilaya to share how you may work in harmony with him for the good of all beings.
11. Chant the Vajrakilaya-honoring mantra 108 times as an offering to him.
12. When you feel you have completed your journey work, thank Vajrakilaya and the spirits with whom you worked and return to ordinary reality by drumming the callback signal.

Once the journey is complete, remember to make another offering to the spirits for their help and support.

☙ Journey Explorations

Journey to your teacher or power animal to ask: Please give me my own ritual to stay in balance during difficult times.

Journey to your teacher or power animal to ask: What can I do to help regain balance in the world? (Do this journey twice: once for spiritual actions you can do and a second time to find out what physical actions you can do.)

Record the content of your journeys and your perceptions about what you received.

Journey Explorations Specifically Regarding the Khurpa

Journey with your power animal or teacher to Vajrakilaya to ask: Help me to understand how the khurpa can assist me in keeping beneficial balance in my life.

Journey with your power animal or teacher to Vajrakilaya to ask: Please give me an experience of how you embody the khurpa's spirit.

Journey with your power animal or teacher to Vajrakilaya to ask: Please show me how to use the khurpa to dispel unwanted energies.

Journey with your power animal or teacher to Vajrakilaya to ask: Please show me how to use the khurpa to draw in beneficial energies.

After each journey, thank your power animal, your teacher, and any other spirits who have revealed themselves to you and make an offering to the spirits. This can be an offering of incense smoke, bits of food outdoors, or flower petals.

Process Questions

What do you notice in your work with Vajrakilaya?

How does it feel to work with the embodiment of the khurpa energy?

What are you learning about yourself in this work?

20

Hanuman the Monkey God

Lord Hanuman was originally a proto-Dravidian deity who predates Vedic Hinduism. By the tenth century he was recognized as an avatar of Shiva. Hanuman resembles a strong man with a monkey face and long tail. He is an immortal figure who is a demon slayer. He is strong, fearless, determined, devoted, humble, and valorous. He is also known as a fine and eloquent speaker. In Nepali shamanic terms, Hanuman is called bandar deo, the spirit of monkey. Hanuman also represents the air or wind element, like the white horse. Indeed, one of Hanuman's names is Pawan Putra, which means "son of the wind." Known as an example of honesty, respect toward Rama,* fidelity, and clarity of purpose, he is often depicted with an open chest, showing his powerful heart and faithful nature.

Lord Hanuman is called Bajrang Bali due to his immense strength. The word *bali* in Sanskrit means "full of strength." Usually great heroes are called *mahabali*. The word *bajrang* might be a Nepali dialectic corruption of a Hindi word meaning orange or saffron color. (Certainly, the hundreds of sacred rhesus macaque monkeys who inhabit the famous Swayambhunath, Monkey Temple complex in Kathmandu have a decidedly yellow-orange cast to their fur!)

His devotees also address Lord Hanuman as Baba Hanuman. *Baba*

---

*Rama is the seventh avatar of Vishnu and one of the many faces of the Divine Masculine in Hinduism.

Figure 20.1. A mask-wearing, ascetic devotee of Hanuman dancing at the Pashupatinath temple complex in Kathmandu. (See also color plate 14)

means "guru" or "teacher." Hanuman is addressed with this honorific because of his many positive traits, which provide us with a role model for our behavior and for the focus of our spiritual practice.

Hanuman represents highly evolved consciousness and strong, light *prana* or life force. He is simple, direct, compassionate, and courageous. Hanuman's acts of bravery, strength, and devotion are recorded in Hindu religious texts such as the Ramayan, the Mahabharata, and the Agni Puran. In the Ramayan he is called Mahaabeer or Mahaveer, which means "great hero." Described as a great yogi, Hanuman has the shamanic ability to shape-shift his appearance. He can expand his body to become as large as a mountain (Garima siddhi) or shrink himself to the size of a fly (Anima siddhi). Hanuman is considered to be an adept in the science of yoga and has attained spiritual perfection or siddhi as well as remarkable spiritual powers, also called siddhis. It is said that because of those powers, he can transform himself into different forms and sizes and fly (Akashagama) in the air. Of course, these are all feats that shamans perform in their journeys while entranced. It is easy to see why dhami/jhankris honor this deity as one of their own.

HANUMAN MANTRA

Chanting the Hanuman mantra is a very powerful practice for infusing you with energy and life force. His spirit helps to boost courage, erase fear, and dispel malevolent spirits.

He is an approachable aspect of the Divine Masculine who answers all prayers. He is quick in his actions and working with his spirit bestows bravery and fearlessness to his devotees. He is especially useful in giving one the stamina, resilience, and confidence to keep moving forward on your path.

If you are facing a challenging situation, Hanuman can help carry you through the process with a strong heart. It will also help in solving problems by assisting you to have Hanuman's quick mind and physical prowess.

Om Hanumate Namah

This mantra is said to invoke the spirit, wisdom, and power of Hanuman. It is best chanted 108 times on a sandalwood or red coral mala. A quartz crystal mala may also be used. The number of daily repetitions is a minimum of 108; however as many as 11,000, 21,000, or 31,000 repetitions are recommended. Offerings of fresh, fragrant flowers and ripe fruits to Hanuman's spirit can also be made in the direction of the East.

◈ *Journey to Meet Hanuman*

This is an opportunity to work directly with your helping spirits to meet Hanuman. Before you begin, surround yourself with your golden, silver, and iron spheres. Make an offering to the spirits, sing your sacred songs, make an offering of uncooked rice, and honor all of the helping spirits in the directions.

Please read through the directions carefully and gather all that you'll need before you begin. For this exercise, you will need:

- All of your altar objects and a copper plate (thaal), flat winnowing basket (nanglo), or special cloth on which they are to be arranged (or at the very least a lit candle or oil lamp, a bowl of water, a feather, and a stone) placed in front of you
- Your dhyangro and gajo or another way to produce the journey rhythm
- A comfortable place to be seated
- Your mala
- A copy of the Hanuman-honoring mantra
- A small handful of uncooked rice kernels
- A few slices of fruit and flowers to use as an offering
- Your journal or a notebook and a pen
- A quiet time and space

▷ Performing the Journey

1. Choose a time when you will be able to work with the spirits.
2. Prepare yourself and all the materials you require.
3. Make an offering of fruit and flowers on your altar space in front of you
4. Make an offering of rice kernels to the spirits of place that hold you while you are journeying.
5. Begin playing the journey rhythm softly.
6. Call your power animal to you to support you during this journey.
7. Have your power animal take you to meet Hanuman.
8. Upon meeting this powerful being, thank him for agreeing to meet with you.
9. Ask Hanuman to share how he affects your world.
10. Ask Hanuman to share how you may work in harmony with him for the good of all beings.
11. Chant the Hanuman-honoring mantra 108 times as an offering to him.

12. When you feel you have completed your journey work, thank Hanuman and spirits with whom you worked and return to ordinary reality by drumming the callback signal.

Once the journey is complete, remember to make another offering to the spirits for their help and support.

⌦ Journey Explorations

Journey to your teacher or power animal to ask: Please give me my own ritual to honor Lord Hanuman.

Journey to your teacher or power animal to ask: When and under what circumstances is it best for me to work with Hanuman?

Journey to your teacher or power animal to ask: How does working with Hanuman change my shamanic work?

Journey to your teacher or power animal to ask: What can I do to strengthen my own courage?

Journey to your teacher or power animal to ask: What aspect of my personal power/life force needs bolstering? (Follow up with a second journey and ask: How can that aspect of my personal power/life force be strengthened?)

Record the content of your journeys and your perceptions about what you received.

After each journey, thank your power animal, your teacher, and any other spirits who have revealed themselves to you. Sing your sacred songs; make an offering of uncooked rice, incense smoke, or flower petals to honor all of the helping spirits in the directions.

⌦ Process Questions

What are you continuing to feel as you work with the the monkey god?

Under what circumstances do you find you are weakest?

Under what circumstances do you find you are the most courageous?

What are you learning about yourself in this work?

21

The Nagas

The nagas or sacred serpents are the most primordial shamanic animals and deities. Honored across the globe and in many different cultures, their abodes are the oceans, lakes, swamps, rivers, and wells, as well as the surfaces of Earth. They play an important role in shamanic practices, mythologies, folktales, and religions. They are considered to have very strong magical healing powers, vast knowledge, and deep wisdom and yet are also capricious by nature. In other words, they can quickly change from friendly and helpful to angry and malicious. Their bodies are regarded as rainbows and bridges, as they connect this world to other spheres of existence and to the shamanic realms.

Nagas bring health as well as death. They are ladders to the upper and lower realms. They are symbols of renewal of life or the shedding of unhealthy debris or habits. In Nepal it is also believed that the nagas control and maintain the psychic power of all living beings. They are helpful and dangerous as they deliver poison and also a life-giving elixir of immortality (amrita).

The nagas play one of the most important roles in the healing practices of shamans and spiritual practitioners of the Himalayas. Honored by Hindus, Buddhists, Jains, and Bön practitioners alike, they represent primordial time, memory, and life in the underworld. They bring rain, fertility, and wealth; hold sacred knowledge; and bring harmony among the walking beings and the elements of creation. Though they are considered to be immortal, they also suffer greatly due to carelessness, ignorance, and lack of respect from human beings. The naga spirits and their earthly kin suffer through deforestation, the use of chemical agents in agriculture, and our overall disharmony with nature. Because of our destructiveness, Mother Nature is changing in conjunction with the nagas by not bringing rain in the right seasons. Both drought-causing famines and disease-causing floods are becoming much more prevalent in an effort to show us the error of our ways. Like other powerful spirits, the nagas are endeavoring to have us change our ways and remember our place as just one small part of the natural world.

As the nagas are the keepers of the lowest levels of the Lower World realms and also hold up Mother Earth (Bhumi Devi/Dharti Mata), they are honored by the dhami/jhankri. The shamans make offerings to the nagas in good faith, along with engaging in physical actions to help bring about harmony, calmness, and peace. As we have said before in this book, shamans have always been activists, working tirelessly to bring about harmony, healing, and balance by educating people about the sanctity of nature and of our place in it.

The nagas are a potent part of Bhola's retinue of helping spirits.

Nagas, as the rulers of the subterranean realms, Earth, and in-between realms, play a very important role in my personal spiritual life. They work

Figure 21.1. The Royal Bath or Naga Pokhari (Snake Pond) at the Palace of Fifty-Five Windows in Bhaktapur's Durbar Square.

with me in healing others and in understanding the deeper mysteries of life and death. They are one of my very important helping spirits.

They also present themselves in my dreams to provide information on healing if the problems are related to water and Lower World spirits and also to signal an imminent change. One of these vivid dreams came to me in 1997 after I was stung by a white snake on my left palm while crossing a river. When I recollect it, the images are still so vivid that cold waves vibrate up and down my body. Within three months after that dream, I came to meet my wife, Mimi. I also at that time started working with a very well-known and powerful shaman in the Okhaldhunga District.

Besides the annual honoring ceremony during Naag Panchami, I honor the nagas each time I start my preparation for spirit embodiment. The nagas are one of the first spirits invoked for protection and help. Even during healing sessions when the cause of a disease or spiritual disharmony is a naga spirit, they are still invoked, and special offerings are made to request their protection.

As you can see from Bhola's last few words here, the nagas are honored even in those cases where their imbalance has caused illness. In the dhami/jhankri's world, there is no automatic demonization of a spirit even if it has caused disease. Duality has no place, as *all* life is sacred. The shaman's focus is always on how harmony has been lost and what must be done to bring all spiritual energies back into balance.

NAGAS AND CREATION

In the Himalayan creation story, it is the many-headed divine nagas that form the first living foundation for the cosmos. They also represent the energies of change, offer protection, and represent the transitions of death and rebirth, as well as offering the blessings of abundance and wisdom. Shamans may put them around their neck either as live snakes in the manner of Lord Shiva or in the form of snake vertebrae malas to assist in accessing their immense power for healing diseases caused by the spirits of the disrupted earth and waters.

A male naga is called a *nag* and a female Naga is referred to as a *nagini*. There are several Hindu myths that have nagas as featured characters, including one with Lord Vishnu. Here is Bhola's version.

In the pole star, there is a great Ocean of Milk. This ocean (Kshir Sagar in Hindi) is one of the seven cosmic oceans that separate loka, *ordinary reality physical space, from* aloka, *the spiritual realms of noordinary, nondirectional space.*

For the gods to attain immortality—an attribute the Great Goddess already had—they needed the magical elixir amrita. (This is correlated with the ritual water used by the dhami/jhankri that is inspirited and sanctified by her or his helping spirits.) To attain this elixir, the gods determined that the great Ocean of Milk must be churned.

This act was accomplished by using the great Naga King, Vasuki, as a churning rope and the Mount Mandara, the tallest mountain on the back of the cosmic turtle, as the churning post.* Vishnu played the role of an arbiter, and the other gods churned the Ocean of Milk from one side and the demons from the other end. They got more than they bargained for!

The first substance that arose from the waters was a terrible poison that threatened to devour the entire universe. Lord Shiva took the poison into his mouth in an effort to save the day, but his partner, the goddess Parvati, was so horrified that she grabbed Shiva by the neck as if to strangle him and stopped him from swallowing it. As a result, the poison was only able to affect his throat, turning it a vivid blue.

As Vishnu continued to churn the sea, amrita finally boiled up from the milky depths along with several other treasures. Chaos then ensued as all the gods and demons immediately tried to claim the elixir as their own. Vishnu defeated the demons and kept the elixir for the gods. It is kept safe by a ring of terrible fire, a great circle of flashing, rotating blades, and, coming full circle, by two enormous venomous nagas!

This mythic event of Lord Shiva drinking the kalkut poison to protect the universe from destruction is one of the main chants invoked by shamans during healing sessions. It reflects the way shamans extract disease-causing spirits and temporarily hold them in their bodies and then transmute them into positive energy released into the universe. The myth says that

---

*In a traditional Vedic churn, milk is placed in a pot with a post in its center, which is supported to stand upright with a cord. A long rope with a loop at either end is coiled around the post. The person who is churning takes the loops into his or her hands and alternately pulls on the left and right side of the rope. This causes the post to spin and so churn the milk that is in the pot.

after having drunk this poison, Lord Shiva felt a burning sensation in his whole body. In order to refresh himself, he went to the Himalayas, struck the valley with his trishul (trident) in the lap of the Langtang chain of Himalayas, and created the sacred lake Gosainkunda* and submerged in its waters. On a very clear day, it is possible to see a petrified rock in human form sleeping on the bed of this sacred lake, which is why shamans make an annual pilgrimage to Gosainkunda to honor the healing powers of Lord Shiva and and to reactivate their own healing capabilities. In the same way, the Khaas Brahmins and Chettris also make pilgrimages to this sacred lake on the same day to change their sacred initiation thread called a janai, *as a ceremony of renewal and spiritual rebirth.*

🐚 Journey to Meet the Nagas

This is an opportunity to work directly with your helping spirits to meet the naga spirits. Before you begin, surround yourself with your golden, silver, and iron spheres. Make an offering to the spirits, sing your sacred songs, make an offering of uncooked rice, and honor all of the helping spirits in the directions.

Please read through the directions carefully and gather all that you'll need before you begin. For this exercise, you will need:

- All of your altar objects and a copper plate (thaal), flat winnowing basket (nanglo), or special cloth on which they are to be arranged (or at the very least a lit candle or oil lamp, a bowl of water, a feather, and a stone) placed in front of you
- Your dhyangro and gajo or another way to produce the journey rhythm
- A comfortable place to be seated
- A small handful of uncooked rice kernels
- Your journal or a notebook and a pen
- A quiet time and space

🐚 Performing the Journey
1. Choose a time when you will be able to work with the spirits.
2. Prepare yourself and all the materials you require.

---

*Gosain refers to Lord Shiva and *kunda* is the word for lake.

3. Begin playing the journey rhythm softly.

4. Make an offering of rice kernels to the spirits of place that hold you while you are journeying.

5. Call your power animal to you to support you during this journey.

6. Have your power animal take you to meet the nagas.

7. Upon meeting these powerful beings, thank them for the blessings of rain, of the special places that you love near water, and anything else that your heart wishes to say.

8. Ask the nagas to share how they affect the world.

9. Ask the nagas to share how you may work in harmony with them for the good of all beings.

10. Ask them for a song or mantra that you can use as an offering to them.

11. When you feel you have completed your journey work, thank the nagas and spirits with whom you worked and return to ordinary reality by drumming the callback signal.

Once the journey is complete, remember to make another offering to the spirits for their help and support.

⌂ Journey Explorations

Journey to your teacher or power animal to ask: Please give me my own ritual to stay in harmony with the nagas.

Journey to your teacher or power animal to ask: What can I do to help preserve the waters of the world?

Journey to your teacher or power animal to ask: How can I work with the nagas to maintain personal balance?

Record the content of your journeys and your perceptions about what you received.

After each journey, thank your power animal, your teacher, and any other spirits who have revealed themselves to you. Then make an offering to the spirits. This can be an offering of incense smoke, bits of food outdoors, or flower petals.

⌂ Process Questions

What are you continuing to feel as you work with the nagas?

What are you learning about yourself in this work?

HONORING THE NAGAS

During the end of the monsoon season, on the fifth day after the new moon in the fourth month of the Nepalese calendar, the celebration of Nag Panchami is observed. This ceremony honors the primordial naga spirits who hold up Mother Earth: Ananta, Vashuki, Padhmanavha, Kambala, Shankhapala, Dhartarashtra, Takshaka, and Kaliya; those other powerful nagas that live in and around Earth and bring the rains and bounty and bless all beings with fertility; and the physical snakes that rid the fields of destructive rodents.

A story is told in Nepal about the origin of Nag Panchami. It is said that the Kathmandu Valley was once an enormous lake. When humans drained the lake to make a place for their villages, the water-loving nagas became very angry. When they realized what they had done, the human beings sought to make amends. It was necessary to do something to soothe the anger of the nagas to keep the blessings that they provide flowing into the world. To accomplish this, people devoted areas around the valley as sacred pilgrimage destinations. The people also promised to honor the nagas on their own special day. Upon seeing that the human beings kept their word, the nagas agreed to continue their blessings. It is said that as long as we respect the nagas and the honoring rituals continue, balance in nature will be maintained.

On the day of Nag Panchami, the nagas and naginis are worshipped for physical and spiritual healing. People visit temples dedicated to nagas and Shiva shrines to offer prayers. In many places, people honor live cobras as well as pictures and statues of the nagas by offering milk, turmeric, powdered pigments, colorful strips of cloth or colored threads, flowers, and sweets.

People paste small, colorful naga posters above the main doors to their houses for protection from thunderbolts, malignant spirits, and natural calamities. People not only flock to the naga shrines and temples but also to local lakes, ponds, springs and swamps to make offerings to the serpents. No farmer works in the field on Nag Panchami so that these powerful Earth Keepers may have a day of rest.

अगस्त्यश्च पुलस्त्यश्च वैशम्पायन एवच्च सुमन्तु जेमिनिश्चय पश्चैते वज्रबारका: । मुने: कन्याणमिश्रस्य जैमिनेश्चमि कीर्यनात
विध्वरणिमय मासित लिखित गृहमराङ्गले ॥ अनन्तो वासुकि: पद्मो महापद्मश्च मलक: । कुलीर: कर्कत शङ्खवटी नागा: प्रकिलित

Figure 21.2. On Nag Panchami small posters like this one are hung over doorways and blessed with milk to honor the nagas for their blessings and protection. (See also color plate 15)

Other Naga Ceremonies

Honoring ceremonies for the nagas are also done when it is believed that their energies have become unbalanced due to human actions. When the nagas have been made unhappy, they can cause great harm. They can create negative effects called *nāga doṣa* or produce terrible obstacles in our life called *sarpa-bādhaka*. The later is considered to be more severe.

When a shaman is consulted for illnesses such as tumors or cancers, they immediately journey to find a spiritual reason that contributed to the disease. These diseases are said to be sarpa-bādhaka, and so the afflicted person is expected to honor the nagas, Earth, and the water-related spirits to regain his or her health. Honoring ceremonies are considered necessary because in some way the person or his or her family may have disrupted nature, such as using poisons, felling sacred trees, killing snakes, or anything else that is considered an affront to Mother Nature and the nagas.*

Other diseases that have connections to the nagas are skin diseases like eczema, psoriasis, dermatitis, lupus, rosacea, and melanoma; fungal infections; inflammations; urinary infections; and all forms of nervous conditions and psychic problems. In all cases, the spiritual support to assist in healing is often the need to create a right relationship with the nagas.

In these cases, the parties who are affected must make regular offerings, make places for snakes to live on their land, chant mantras that honor the nagas, waters, and Mother Earth spirits, and generally attend to treating Earth in a more reverent manner.

Creating Your Own Ceremony of Honoring the Nagas

In the dhami/jhankri's worldview, working with the snake spirits is very important for mental, spiritual, emotional, and physical health, as well as for assuring an abundant life. Since the Western calendar differs from the traditional Nepalese one, your Nag Panchami ceremony can be done during the new moon that falls closest to August 1. Journeys with your drum or rattle can be done this day with any intentions you have for your life that are in harmony with All That Is. Ceremonies, rituals, or prayers are recommended early in the morning after a shower and on an empty stomach. It is best to fast for the whole day but not required. Here is a simple version of a Nag Panchami ceremony.

Of course, there are other times of the year when the nagas can be honored. Some key times would be at the beginning of January to assist in having a healthy and prosperous New Year. Another time would be at the start of spring when adequate rain is so vital for the plants. During summer the nagas can be honored to help storms be gentler, while autumn is an excellent time to thank them for their role in the

---

*Although we Westerners may find this idea naive, it is true that the degradation of our environment and wide-scale chemical pollution of our air, water, food, and soil all affect our epigenetic field. This is the internal context that can alter how our genes are expressed. Alterations of the DNA can contribute to cellular disruption and so make cancers more possible.

harvest. Honoring the nagas in winter can help the household stay well during the time when illnesses are prevalent. Finally, at the end of wintertime, they can be honored to keep floods from occurring as the snows melt and river ice breaks up. These are suggestions. It is always best to for you to work with your own helping spirits to learn the best ways for you to honor the nagas.

As a part of your naga-honoring ritual, you may wish to chant a mantra to invoke their presence for blessings. If these mantras are recited every day, especially in the morning, the nagas can become close allies and helpful in every aspect of life. They can protect from unforeseen circumstances, premature deaths, and diseases and help to protect property. Each mantra is typically chanted 108 times. Ideally, a mala of clear quartz crystal, precious gems, or snake vertebrae should be used as you chant.

The nine naga mantra is:

Anantam Vasukim Shesham Padmanabham Cha Kambalam
Shankhapalam Dhartarashtram Taxakam Kaliyam Tatha

The eight nagini mantra is:

Vasuki Padma mahapadma Kulir Karkata takshak Sesha

NAGAKANYA

Since Nepal is a cultural crossroads, other forms of the nagas that are familiar to practitioners of Hinduism and the Tibetan Buddhist tradition are honored by dhami/jhankris. One of these is Nagakanya, whose name means "daughter of the naga." She is a hybridized being with the upper body of a beautiful young maiden and the lower body of an enormous snake. She wears a crown made of gold and silver set with many precious gems and growing out of her neck are five cobras that rise up and arch over her forming an even higher, living crown.

Nagakanya shares some physical characteristics with Medusa but none of her negative connotations. Rather than turning people into stone, Nagakanya is honored as a goddess of the three realms (the Upper, Middle, and Lower Worlds) that are traversed by shamans.

As such, she is able to bestow blessings on our path, not only as we travel through the spiritual realms but also on our life journey. She is the deity that supports the generous flow of health, wealth, and well-being.

Nagakanya Mantras

Chanting a mantra that thanks her for bestowing perfection or success on your path honors Nagakanya. This mantra is also chanted 108 times as you have done with other naga-honoring mantras and on the same malas.

Nagakanya honoring mantra:

Om Nagakanya Sarva Siddhi Hung

There is also a way that dhami/jhankris use a mantra to invoke the aid of Nagakanya for healing. In this case, the following mantra is chanted over the sick person. The mantra states that her power is brought forth to clear away any obstacles in the way so that healing is achieved. In this way, Nagakanya is being asked to open the path to health. This mantra is also chanted in circuits of 108 repetitions. However, these circuits may be repeated as often as your helper spirits deem is necessary.

Nagakanya healing mantra:

Om Nagakanya sarva siddhi hung phat swaha

As with all other spirits, having a firsthand meeting with Nagakanya is the best way to learn how you can work with her.

🪷 Journey to Meet Nagakanya

This is an opportunity to work directly with your helping spirits to meet the spirit of Nagakanya. Before you begin, surround yourself with your golden, silver, and iron spheres. Make an offering to the spirits, sing your sacred songs, make an offering of uncooked rice, and honor all of the helping spirits in the directions.

Please read through the directions carefully and gather all that you'll need before you begin. For this exercise, you will need:

- All of your altar objects and a copper plate (thaal), flat winnowing basket (nanglo), or special cloth on which they are to be arranged (or at the very least a lit candle or oil lamp, a bowl of water, a feather, and a stone) placed in front of you
- Your dhyangro and gajo or another way to produce the journey rhythm
- A comfortable place to be seated
- Your mala
- A copy of the Nagakanya-honoring mantra
- A small handful of uncooked rice kernels
- Your journal or a notebook and a pen
- A quiet time and space

Performing the Journey

1. Choose a time when you will be able to work with the spirits.
2. Prepare yourself and all the materials you require.
3. Begin playing the journey rhythm softly.
4. Make an offering of rice kernels to the spirits of place that hold you while you are journeying.
5. Call your power animal to you to support you during this journey.
6. Have your power animal take you to meet Nagakanya.
7. Upon meeting this powerful being, thank her for agreeing to meet with you.
8. Ask the Nagakanya to share how she affects your world.
9. Ask the Nagakanya to share how you may work in harmony with her for the good of all beings.
10. Chant the Nagakanya-honoring mantra 108 times as an offering to her.
11. When you feel you have completed your journey work, thank the Nagakanya and spirits with whom you worked and return to ordinary reality by drumming the callback signal.

Once the journey is complete, remember to make another offering to the spirits for their help and support.

Journey Explorations

Journey to your teacher or power animal to ask: How can working with Nagakanya support the flow of my life?

Journey to your teacher or power animal to ask: What are the best
times to honor Nagakanya?

Journey to your teacher or power animal to ask: Under what circumstances do I ask Nagakanya for her help?

Record the content of your journeys and your perceptions about
what you received.

After each journey, thank your power animal, your teacher, and any
other spirits who have revealed themselves to you. Then make an offering
to the spirits. This can be an offering of incense smoke, of bits of food
outdoors, or flower petals.

⌦ Process Questions

What are you continuing to feel as you add Nagakanya to your work
with the nagas?

What are you learning about yourself in this work?

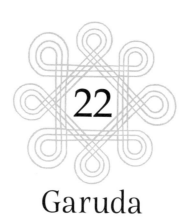

22

Garuda

When issues that have their root with the nagas are not solved through honoring and healing rituals, then the power of Garuda is invoked.

Garuda is a large, mythical birdlike creature or humanoid bird that appears across many Asian cultures. Since Garuda's name is also a Vedic-Sanskrit word for the eagle constellation Aquila, eagles and other raptors, as well as the mythical phoenix, are associated with Garuda.

Honored as a divinity, usually the vehicle (*vahana*) of Lord Vishnu, Garuda is depicted as having the golden body of a strong man with a white face, red wings, an eagle's beak, and a crown on his head. This ancient deity is considered to be massive, large enough to block out the sun while flying.

Garuda is known as the "devourer of serpents" and is called upon to maintain balance when the nagas have created diseases, floods, or famines.

As further proof of his mastery over the nagas, Garuda is depicted wearing the primordial serpents who hold up Mother Earth. The naga Adishesha is on his left wrist, and the serpent Gulika is on his right wrist. The serpent Vasuki forms his sacred thread. The cobra Takshaka forms his belt on his hips. The snake Karkotaka is worn as his necklace. The snakes Padma and Mahapadma are his earrings, and the snake Shankachuda adorns his hair.

Here is the story of how Garuda became the nemesis of the nagas:

Garuda became an enemy of the nagas when he called upon them for help in rescuing his mother who had become enslaved. When Garuda called upon the nagas for help, they demanded that he steal the elixir of immortality (amrita) and bring it to them. This was a nearly impossible task. The deities jealously guarded amrita and wanted to keep it for themselves.

Garuda managed to get through the deities' defenses and stole the elixir. On his flight back, he met Vishnu. Rather than fight Garuda, Vishu exchanged promises with Garuda. Vishnu gave Garuda immortality without needing to drink the elixir, and in turn Garuda promised to become Vishnu's vehicle. As Garuda continued his flight, he met Indra the god of weather. Garuda told Indra that once he had fulfilled his promise to the nagas he would make it possible for Indra to regain possession of the amrita and take it back to the gods. In return, Indra promised Garuda the nagas as food.

Upon reaching his final destination, Garuda placed the elixir on the grass, encouraging the serpents to prepare themselves to partake in this ritual drink. Once his mother was freed, Garuda snatched back the elixir, spilling a few drops on the grass. The enraged nagas realized they

Figure 22.1. Garuda controlling the naga spirits over a doorway in Patan, Nepal.

had been tricked and hurriedly lapped the remaining drops of amrita. The powerful elixir gave them split tongues and partial immortality so they could renew themselves through shedding their skins. From that day onward, Garuda was the ally of the gods, the trusty mount of Vishnu, and the implacable nemesis of snakes.

Nepalese dhami/jhankris honor Garuda as a powerful warrior who can combat diseases—especially those that are caused by the nagas—and as a protector from all forms of poison. They often wear symbols of Garuda as talismans of protection. Some of these depict Garuda with a khurpa ritual dagger replacing the bottom half of his body and legs. This is an overt representation of his ability to assist the shaman in slaying the spirits of illness.

Garuda is also the revealer of the secrets of the "fate of the soul after death." Garuda Purana is a Hindu "Book of the Dead," in which Garuda asks questions of Lord Vishnu about the fate of the soul after death, the journey of the soul, reincarnations, and so on. This is one of the most detailed books on death and dying processes ever written.

Bhola works with Garuda in several ways:

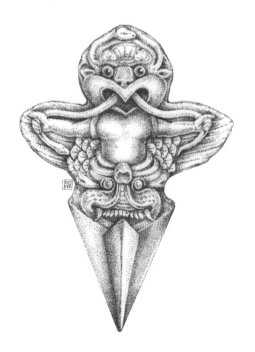

Figure 22.2. A Garuda amulet in bronze with a khurpa blade replacing his lower body (pen-and-ink drawing by the author).

When a sick person has difficulties being present in the moment or looking into him- or herself for understanding, Garuda helps by supporting the person to become a compassionate observer. In this way, the sick person can more easily understand his or her difficulties and obstacles that need to be addressed. He also carries away spiritual poisons. In traveling to the upper realms of the spirits, Garuda offers his wings to lift us up.

Garuda is one of my principal healing powers. He has helped me many times to heal peoples' naga or serpent afflictions.

To gain Garuda's protection and assistance, devotees chant his mantra. Chanting Garuda's mantra ensures safe travel, provides relief from viral fevers and infections, and assists in neutralizing poisonous bites and stings. His spirit is also invoked to assist in healing those diseases that are caused by nagas, such as cancer or tumors. Autoimmune diseases of the skin or fascia such as lupus, eczema, and psoriasis are thought to be related to nagas and are also assisted by working with Garuda.

THE GARUDA MANTRA

Garuda's mantra can also be chanted before starting new ventures such as launching a business, building or renovating a house, and other creative efforts. Honoring Garuda is said to bestow a courageous, confident, and contented life on his devotees, as well as protection from all kinds of negative energies.

You can recite or chant, pray, and honor Garuda on any day and at any time during the day and night. The best day is Saturday, and it is recommended that you can chant either 54, 108, or 1,008 times and use a mala with beads of tulsi (holy basil) wood or of clear quartz.

It is best to sit on a wool blanket with your spine erect to keep the energy of the mantra inside your body. Light your lamp or candle, and make an offering of sesame seeds and fruit before you begin.

Om Eem Om Namo Bhagavathey
Om, Honorable Vishnu in your Bhagavathey–
Krishna emanation

Mahaa Garudaaya Paksha Raajaaya
Great Garuda Bird King!

Vishnu Vallabhaaya Trailogya Paripoojitaa
Garuda who is honored and respected by Vishnu in
    all the three realms

Ugra Bhayangara Kaalaa-nalaroobhaaya
Fearless, thrilling, tribulation dispeller!

Vajra Nahaaya Vajra Tundaaya
May your vajra radiance drive this adversity to
    another place

*Vajra Tantaaya Vajra Thamshadraaya Vajra
    Puchchaaya*
May it be tamed, subdued, and overcome by the
    power of the vajra!

Sakala Naaga Dosha Rakshayaaya
Protect from any harm the Nagas may cause

Sarva Visham Naasaya Naasaya
May all poisons be destroyed!

*Hana Hana Daha Daha Pacha Pacha Pasmee Guru
    Pasmee Guru Hoom Phat Swaaha*
In this auspicious time, I invoke you, my honorable
    teacher, to generate healing. May it be so!

🪷 *Journey to Meet Garuda*

This journey is an opportunity to work directly with your helping spirits to meet the spirit of Garuda. Before you begin, surround yourself with your golden, silver, and iron spheres. Make an offering to the spirits, sing your sacred songs, make an offering of uncooked rice, and honor all of the helping spirits in the directions.

Please read through the directions carefully and gather all that you'll need before you begin. For this exercise, you will need:

- All of your altar objects and a copper plate (thaal), flat winnowing basket (nanglo), or special cloth on which they are to be arranged (or at the very least a lit candle/oil lamp, a bowl of water, a feather, and a stone) placed in front of you

- Your dhyangro and gajo or another way to produce the journey rhythm
- A comfortable place to be seated
- Your mala
- A copy of the Garuda-honoring mantra
- A small handful of uncooked rice kernels
- A few slices of fruit and sesame seeds to use as an offering
- Your journal or a notebook and a pen
- A quiet time and space

⋏ Performing the Journey

1. Choose a time when you will be able to work with the spirits.
2. Prepare yourself and all the materials you require.
3. Make an offering of fruit and sesame seeds on your altar space in front of you.
4. Make an offering of rice kernels to the spirits of place that hold you while you are journeying.
5. Begin playing the journey rhythm softly.
6. Call your power animal to you to support you during this journey.
7. Have your power animal take you to meet Garuda.
8. Upon meeting this powerful being, thank him for agreeing to meet with you.
9. Ask Garuda to share how he affects your world.
10. Ask Garuda to share how you may work in harmony with him for the good of all beings.
11. Chant the Garuda-honoring mantra 54 or 108 times as an offering to him.
12. When you feel you have completed your journey work, thank Garuda and the spirits with whom you worked and return to ordinary reality by drumming the callback signal.

Once the journey is complete, remember to make another offering to the spirits for their help and support.

⋏ Journey Explorations

Journey to your teacher or power animal to ask: How can working with Garuda be beneficial in my life?

Journey to your teacher or power animal to ask: What are the best ways to honor Garuda?

Journey to your teacher or power animal to ask: Under what circumstances do I ask Garuda for his help?

Record the content of your journeys and your perceptions about what you received.

After each journey, thank your power animal, your teacher, and any other spirits who have revealed themselves to you. Then make an offering to the spirits. This can be an offering of incense smoke, bits of food outdoors, or flower petals.

◺ Process Questions

What are you noticing as you work with Garuda?

What are you learning about yourself in this work?

23

Local Deities, Protectors, Ancestral Guardians

Along with all the spirits we have already discussed in these pages, it is important to dedicate a chapter to the local spirits honored by the Nepalese people. From the animist viewpoint, everything is alive and has a spirit, and so these beings must also be negotiated with, honored, and fed to keep everyday life harmonious, fruitful, healthy, and safe.

Some of the nature spirits honored by the people include the already described nagas; the *yaksha* or caretakers of the natural treasures hidden in the earth and tree roots; the *asur* or *danava* who are water-born demonlike spirits; the *gandarva,* male nature spirits who are part bird or horse and are consorts of the female spirits of the clouds and waters known as *aspara;* Kshetrapal, the deity of farmlands; the spirit of the boon-giving peacock (*mayur*); the spirits who protect the valleys and passes (*deurali*); Chandi, the goddess who can bring good fortune or disaster; *bir masan,* the spirits of the dead or graveyard; the spirits of the air (*bayu*) and the clouds (*megha*); tree spirits (*briksha*); spirits of the river (*nadi*), cliffs (*chattan*), and water (*jal*); and spirits of metal (*dhatu*). Bandevi, the goddess of many forms in her forest goddess aspect, is also honored along with her fierce consort Bhairung, the wrathful form of Shiva. In addition, the *shikari,* the hunting spirits of the forests, are honored, as are Sansari Mai, the mistress of the universe; Gaidu, protector of animals and livestock who works along with Mahadeva; *kumaris,* the virgin goddesses; *sime,* the swamp-dwelling spirits who are associated with nagas; *bhume,* the masculine earth spirits; *sarpa deo* or *naag deo,* the serpent spirits; *baag deo* and *singha deo,* the tiger and lion spirits; and *bandar deo,* the monkey spirits.

Deities known as *kul deuta* are honored as protectors of the family lineage. The *grama deuta* protect villages, whereas, the *ishta deuta* are those who safeguard individuals.

In addition, the spirits of local landscape features, such as nearby mountains, rivers, and waterfalls, and revered ancestral spirits are also honored.

All of these beings are routinely fed and honored with ceremonies.

In the rural areas of Nepal, particularly in the western regions, there is a long-standing tradition of carving wooden and sometimes stone figures of praying figures. They adorn rooftops and shrines and are also erected by springs and bridges and at crossroads. These figures, which represent spirits who oversee specific places, become a locus for making offerings and prayers. For instance, a spirit figure at a rustic bridge would be honored so that people could make safe passage over a dangerous gorge. The spirit guardian at a crossroads or intersection of trails in the forest would be fed offerings to dispel the ghosts or malignant spirits who gather there. Other times, shrine figures might represent the spirits of the mountains, forest, and waters who affect the weather, the fertility of the crops, and livestock, as well as the health and safety of the people.

What follows is an exercise to meet a local landscape feature near your home. As with the other exercises you have done, please read through the instructions carefully and have all that you require ready before you begin.

❧ Journey to Meet the Spirit of a Local Landscape Feature

This is an opportunity to work directly with your helping spirits to meet the spirit of a significant or dominant landscape feature near your home. Honoring this spirit can deepen your connections to the land, contribute to increasing the spiritual potency of the landscape, and provide a source of power that you may tap into for your shamanic work. Before you begin, surround yourself with your golden, silver, and iron spheres. Make an offering to the spirits, sing your sacred songs, make an offering of uncooked rice, and honor all of the helping spirits in the directions.

Please read through the directions carefully and gather all that you'll need before you begin. If possible, this journey is best done while outdoors. For this exercise, you will need:

- All of your altar objects and a copper plate (thaal), flat winnowing basket (nanglo), or special cloth on which they are to be arranged (or at the very least a lit candle or oil lamp, a bowl of water, a feather, and a stone) placed in front of you
- Your dhyangro and gajo or another way to produce the journey rhythm
- A comfortable place to be seated
- A small handful of uncooked rice kernels
- A few slices of fruit to use as an offering
- Your journal or a notebook and a pen
- A quiet time and space

▶ Performing the Journey

1. Choose a time when you will be able to work with the spirits.
2. Prepare yourself and all the materials you require.
3. Make an offering of fruit and sesame seeds on your altar space in front of you.
4. Make an offering of rice kernels to the spirits of place that hold you while you are journeying.
5. Begin playing the journey rhythm softly.
6. Call your power animal to you to support you during this journey.
7. Have your power animal take you to meet the spirit of a dominant landscape feature near your home.
8. Upon meeting this being, thank her or him for agreeing to meet with you.
9. Ask the spirit its name and introduce yourself.
10. Ask the spirit to share how she or he affects your home area.
11. Ask the spirit of the landscape feature to share how you may safely work in harmony with her or him for the good of all beings.
12. Ask the spirit what you can do to support her or him. (Make sure

you can follow through with the spirit's request and negotiate a better solution if the spirit suggests something you cannot do.)

13. Make an offering of fruit and rice on the land in gratitude for the spirit's willingness to work with you.

14. When you feel you have completed your journey work, thank all the spirits with whom you worked and return to ordinary reality by drumming the callback signal.

Once the journey is complete, remember to make another offering to the spirits for their help and support.

⟁ Journey Explorations

Journey to your teacher or power animal to ask: Under what circumstances do I work with this spirit?

Journey to your teacher or power animal to ask: How does the spirit of a dominant landscape feature near my home affect my life?

Journey to your teacher or power animal to ask: How often should I make an offering to the spirit of the landscape feature near my home?

Journey to the landscape feature to ask: What can I do to support you to be strong?

Make a series of other journeys to meet other landscape features close to your home so that you can develop a relationship with them.

Record the content of your journeys and your perceptions about what you received.

After each journey, thank your power animal, your teacher, and any other spirits who have revealed themselves to you. Then make an offering to the spirits. This can be an offering of incense smoke, bits of food outdoors, or flower petals.

⟁ Process Questions

How do you feel about the area around your home after meeting the spirit of a dominant landscape feature near it?

What are you learning about yourself in this work?

MASTO GOD

In the west of Nepal, the Khas Bahun and Khas Chhetri people* honor Masto God. This deity is said to be able to relieve pain and suffering, cure illness, remove obstacles, lessen frustration and regrets, and mitigate loss in business, trouble in agriculture, or any kind of discomfort or misfortune. Masto God may have his roots in the original culture of the Khas people, who arrived in Nepal from the area of central Asia lying northwest of the Himalayan chain. These people spoke an Indo-Aryan language derived from Sanskrit, which eventually became the Nepali language.

Those who honor Masto God as their primary deity generally also recognize a wide variety of nature spirits. Like the elemental forces, these spirits are considered to have an untamable nature and so need to be reverently appeased so that they remain benevolent toward humans.

The reason for working with the spirits residing in and enlivening nature is not only to request their assistance and protection but also to appease their more fearsome natures so that no beings will suffer.

Masto God is also said to be a guardian spirit of Mount Kailash, the mountain that is sacred to shamans, Buddhists, Hindus, Jains, and Bön practitioners, in which four major Asian rivers have their source. This mountain is said to be the home of Shiva and Pavarti.

Masto also has connections to the goddess Durga. It is said that there are twelve Masto Gods who each watch over part of the Khas domain. The twelve Masto Gods are brothers to the nine sisters of Durga. These nine Durgas or Durgabhawani are not identical to the aspects honored at Dashain. However, as the goddess Durga expresses herself in 1,008 forms, the sisters of Masto represent a similar cross-section of her attributes. It is clear from this connection that Masto has correlations with Shiva and is perhaps another parallel descendant of the Proto-Indo-European Dyēus Ph2tēr or Father Sky.

Shamans in the Khas areas allow themselves to be possessed by

---

*The modern term Khas Bahun refers to those once identified as Khas Brahmins, and Khas Chhetri is the modern term for the Khas Rajput people. The tribes of Chhetri/Thakuri, Bahun, Badi people, Sarki, Sanyasi, Damai, Kami, and Gaine/Gandharbha were all once collectively refered to as Khas Aryans.

Masto God. When the deity enters their body, they are able to perform remarkable feats and provide their villages direct access to the deity for healing and oracular guidance.

Although Masto God functions as Shiva does for other Nepalese dhami/jhankris, it is also true that he also functions like a kul deuta, protecting their Khas ethnic family lineage. And the individual forms of Masto may be thought of as grama deuta, who protects not simply a village but an entire region.

Meeting your own individual, home, and family lineage protectors is an excellent way to add to your spiritual family. This is especially important as many people in Western societies know very few generations of their family, and if you are adopted, you may not know very much about your lineage.

The following exercises are a series of journeys to meet your kul deuta, who is a family lineage protector; your grama deuta, who safeguards your village or town; and your ishta deuta, who is a personal protector and can complement the work of your power animal.

Here is a mantra you can use for these spirits:

> *Om Kula Devatai Namaha*
> Om honorable lineage protector God
>
> *Pitri Devatai Namaha*
> Om honorable lineage protector spirit

🪷 *Journey to Meet Your Protective Spirits*

This is an opportunity to work directly with your helping spirits to meet the spirits who are willing to stand as protectors. Before you begin, surround yourself with your golden, silver, and iron spheres. Make an offering to the spirits, sing your sacred songs, make an offering of uncooked rice, and honor all of the helping spirits in the directions. Make sure you leave sufficient time for the work, as this will be a three-part journey.

Please read through the directions carefully and gather all that you'll need before you begin. For this exercise, you will need:

- All of your altar objects and a copper plate (thaal), flat winnowing basket (nanglo), or special cloth on which they are to be arranged (or at the very least a lit candle or oil lamp, a bowl of water, a feather, and a stone) placed in front of you

- Your dhyangro and gajo or another way to produce the journey rhythm
- A comfortable place to be seated
- A small handful of uncooked rice kernels
- Your journal or a notebook and a pen
- A quiet time and space

⚘ Performing the Journey

1. Choose a time when you will be able to work with the spirits.
2. Prepare yourself and all the materials you require.
3. Make an offering of fruit and sesame seeds on your altar space in front of you.
4. Make an offering of rice kernels to the spirits of place that hold you while you are journeying.
5. Begin playing the journey rhythm softly.
6. Call your power animal to you to support you during this journey.
7. Have your power animal take you to meet your kul deuta, the spirit that watches over your family lineage.
8. Upon meeting this being, thank her or him for agreeing to meet with you.
9. Ask the spirit its name and introduce yourself.
10. Ask your kul deuta to share how you may safely work in harmony with her or him for the health and well-being of all of your human family, including those who have raised you if you were adopted.
11. Ask how you can step into a working shamanic relationship with her or him.
12. Ask the spirit what you can do to support her or him. (Make sure you can follow through with the spirit's request and negotiate a better solution if the spirit suggests something you cannot do.)
13. Make an offering of rice on the land in gratitude for the spirit's willingness to work with you.
14. When you feel you have completed your journey work, thank your kul deuta and ask your power animal to take you to meet your grama deuta who protects your village or town.

15. Upon meeting this being, thank her or him for agreeing to meet with you.

16. Ask the spirit its name and introduce yourself.

17. Ask your town's grama deuta to share how you may safely work in harmony with her or him for the health and well-being of *all* of the beings who live within the town's area.

18. Ask how you can step into a working shamanic relationship with her or him.

19. Ask the spirit what you can do to support her or him. (Make sure you can follow through with the spirit's request and negotiate a better solution if the spirit suggests something you cannot do.)

20. Make an offering of rice on the land in gratitude for the spirit's willingness to work with you.

21. When you feel you have completed your journey work, thank your town's grama deuta and ask your power animal to take you to meet your ishta deuta who protects you.

22. Upon meeting your ishta deuta, thank her or him for agreeing to meet with you.

23. Ask the spirit her or his name and introduce yourself.

24. Ask your ishta deuta to share how she or he works in concert with your power animals and other protectors, contributing to your safety, health, and well-being.

25. Ask how you can step into a working shamanic relationship with her or him.

26. Ask the spirit what you can do to support her or him. (Make sure you can follow through with the spirit's request and negotiate a better solution if the spirit suggests something you cannot do.)

27. Make an offering of rice on the land in gratitude for the spirit's willingness to work with you.

28. When you feel you have completed your journey work, thank all of the spirits with whom you worked and return to ordinary reality by drumming the callback signal.

Once the journey is complete, remember to make another offering to the spirits for their help and support. Spend some quiet time to allow the depth of connection these beings have for you to sink in.

⊾ Journey Explorations

Journey to your teacher or power animal to ask: Under what circumstances do I work with these spirits?

Journey to your teacher or power animal to ask: "Why do these beings offer their protection?"

Journey to your teacher or power animal to ask: In what way am I changed by knowing these new spirits?

Record the content of your journeys and your perceptions about what you received.

After each journey, thank your power animal, your teacher, and any other spirits who have revealed themselves to you. Then make an offering to the spirits. This can be an offering of incense smoke, bits of food outdoors, or flower petals.

⊾ Process Questions

How do you feel about your life now that you have met these protectors?

How do your responsibilities change now that you realize the precious nature of your being?

What are you learning about yourself as you move forward in these explorations?

Remember to make notes about what you are experiencing and review how these experiences are transforming your perceptions of the world around you and your responsibility to it.

PART 4

Healing through Our Connections to All That Is

24

The Eight Fetters

The Nepalese dhami/jhankri works within the paradigm that all human beings are subject to being bound or hindered by what they refer to as the eight fetters. They believe that these behavioral and perceptual bindings restrict our health and impede our growth and so disturb the harmony of nature as they are the roots of human evildoing.

By reflecting upon these eight fetters, we can discover where we most need healing. This is critical as those called to the shaman's path need to keep clearing any unbeneficial patterns that could cloud the guidance they receive from spirit. The fetters cloud our perceptions of reality, shading all thoughts and all of our interactions. It is important to not succumb to the arrogant idea that we are ever "all cooked"! We must continue to clear away what binds us in this lifetime to better serve the world with our shamanic work. We can do some of that work with our spiritual teachers but that never precludes getting professional assistance.

With a profound compassion and through understanding ourselves better, we have an opportunity to participate in changing the collective's perception of life and become a better stakeholder in the ongoing divine creation on Earth. In this way, we can leave something beautiful for our progeny.

THE EIGHT FETTERS

Fear

Our fears can cause us, and those around us, much pain. In many ways, being fearful is at the root of the other seven fetters. When we are living in fear, we are reacting from our limbic brain—the aspect of us that is purely reactive. It is the fight-flight-freeze state of being that denies us access to our higher, reasoning capacities. Fear keeps us in a never-ending cycle of reacting instead of being able to respond.

Some fears can be legitimately about survival and as such are instinctual and self-protective. However, more often than not, the roots of our current fear lie in an experience from our past, a misperception about who we are, or an illusion about the world around us. When we choose to observe our behavior and feelings, we can notice under what circumstances fear is generated and so begin rooting out its source for healing.

Hate

Hatred causes a person to act horribly toward others thus creating nothing but grief. Hate poisons the mind and is one of the darkest forces. Hate destroys the hater as well—we can be sure about that. Hatred is instinctively brutish and lacking all reason as it has its root in fear. Of course, we hate what we fear! Hate and fear are intertwined. The goal of we humans living on this beautiful planet should be living in harmony and peace. Though we have many differences, we can achieve a sense of unity in diversity, not uniformity. Diversity is the seed of creation: the Divine Mother and Father who created the universe out of their imagination and fertility. As long as some sections of the divine creation feel they are better than others and that their ways are superior, the conflict in the bosom of Mother Earth will continue without end. We humans have to comply with the law of creation.

Pride of Birth

This means the illusionary thought that someone is either superior or inferior on the basis of race, tribe, ethnicity, or geographical location. Also rooted in fear, it is the source of all bigotry, misogyny, xenophobia, and homophobia. When held in the grip of this fetter, we forget that we are the children of the same Divine Mother and Father and so negate true wisdom.

Pride of Family

Like the above fetter, our socioeconomic place in society does not make us more or less precious than any other. The only lineage that should matter to us is the one that teaches we are all brothers and sisters—children of the Divine Mother and Father and carrier of immortal bliss. In recognizing the worth of all people, we have opportunities to learn from others and open up to the wider world through the exchange of thoughts, ideas, the arts, and spiritual traditions.

The Concern about Appearances

Being overly concerned with societal convention and one's appearance is again tied to fear. In this case it is a worry that we aren't enough, don't measure up, or are in some way not worthy. As a result, we focus our attention on making our outward appearance a kind of camouflage so others do not see our true self. It is important to do work to heal from this rather than allow our precious lives be ruled by what others expect or think.

Secrecy

Secrecy consumes a huge amount of energy and is a terrible fetter. It is an enormous waste of one's precious life force to waste it on wondering who knows what about us or our situation. When there is nothing to hide, a natural openness to life awakens automatically. We experience the liberation of spontaneity and of freedom!

Suspicion

We become distrustful when we believe that others harbor secrets. For how long and to what extent can we continue to suspect others? How can we live being suspicious all the time?

Shame

When there is something to hide, it follows that what is being hidden is shameful, and shame is the most dreadful of all the fetters. Shame also dances with blame. Feeling shame can be so terrible that we seek a scapegoat to hold our darkness: we blame others for the same we feel. In this way, individuals and groups of people become persecuted because we have not healed our own shame and other fetters.

If we want our culture to evolve into a more loving, inclusive, and bountiful one, we must attend to healing the fetters that bind us as individuals. Culture is an expression of those living in it. As we transform ourselves, we are participating in transforming the wider world. There is no better path to this destination.

25

Healing and Empowerment through Ceremony

Along with attitudinal or behavioral restrictions, we can be hindered by negative spirits, imbalances between the elemental forces, by actions taken in the past or passed to us through familial or karmic ties, and by imbalances in planetary influences. For these reasons, shamans are always working to release harmful influences, correct perceptions, and harmonize themselves, their patients, and their communities. Some of this work is done through ceremonies that function to release what is impeding or blocking balance and replace it with that which benefits the person or group.

THE KHARDGA PUJA

The Khardga Puja is a ceremony that can support participants to release and be freed from impediments that hold them back in life. This is accomplished through the transference of the obstacles into the mandala where they are neutralized.

Like many other Nepalese ceremonies, a mandala or spiritual diagram drawn in flour is the centerpiece for the ceremony. The mandala for this ceremony functions as an abstract diagram of the cosmos. It usually has several concentric levels that encompass the elements, the realms of spirit, and the levels of human consciousness or experience.

Figure 25.1. The Khardga
Puja diagram.

The Khardga Puja is a communal healing and thanksgiving ritual that is an opportunity for a group to release old wounds and heal relationships while receiving the blessings of a healing from the spirits. The ceremonial mandala becomes a safe container to hold the participants' unwanted energies and a doorway through which they can receive healing.

The Mandala

For this ceremony, a black cloth is used as the foundation. This black fabric represents the universe. The color absorbs and encapsulates negative emotions. This gives them a place to reside away from the participants until a point when they are transmuted into harmless energy at the close of the ceremony.

Here is a key to the symbolism that gets drawn on the cloth with flour or finely ground cornmeal that has been mixed with a bit of red and yellow powdered food coloring to make a peach or salmon color:

The tridents: These represent the fire element that symbolizes the cosmic forces of transformation, change, and rebirth.

The three circles: The outer circle represents the Lower World, our body from the umbilicus down to our feet, our past, and our birth in this lifetime. The second circle represents the Middle World, the center of the body from the heart to the umbilicus, the present time, and our death or mortality. The inner ring represents the Upper World, the upper part of the body above the heart, the future time, and our rebirth.

The four heads: These represent the four cardinal directions.

Figure 25.2. Bhola lighting the oil lamp as a finishing touch to
the Khardga Puja mandala.

The four hands: These represent the cross-quarter directions.

The center of the mandala: The mandala's nine interior spaces
are temporary houses for all the helpful spirits present for the
ceremony. The central house is for the sun and is honored with a
bright yellow flower and a candle.

The Ceremony of Offering to the Mandala

Once the drawing of the mandala is complete, the ceremonial leader
speaks aloud the purpose for each round of the ceremony. After he
has declared the focus for each round, each participant places a small
handful of grain onto the mandala while being filled with feelings
of gratitude that the desired result has already been accomplished.
Energetically, this creates a matrix into which reality will form itself.
Our wounds and disturbances are absorbed by the mandala, and the
offering confirms this.

There are nine rounds of offerings during the ceremony. The first seven provide opportunities to release physical, emotional, and spiritual maladies. The last two are to offer gratitude and welcome healing.

1. *The First Level of Transference and Healing.* This level focuses on internal physical organs such as the heart, liver, kidneys, stomach, and so on.
2. *The Second Level of Transference and Healing.* This level focuses on the external organs such as hair, nails, eyes, ears, and skin.
3. *The Third Level of Transference and Healing.* This level focuses on interpersonal relationships within the family.
4. *The Fourth Level of Transference and Healing.* This level focuses on healing relationships at work and in the community.
5. *The Fifth Level of Transference and Healing.* This level focuses on bringing harmony and balance to the five elements that create our bodies and the universe. At this level it is possible to work on environmental allergies or sensitivities and food allergies.
6. *The Sixth Level of Transference and Healing.* This level focuses on recognizing and diluting the emotions, memories, and suffering of past trauma, such as anger, fear, and sorrow. This is an opportunity to disengage from your identity as a victim or wounded person.
7. *The Seventh Level of Transference and Healing.* This level focuses on realigning planetary problems that may be expressing themselves as issues of the body, mind, emotions, or spirit. The Nepalese people believe that the cosmos can impact our health and well-being. For this reason, attention is paid to supporting balance among Earth's neighbors as well as upon her surface.
8. *The Eighth Level of Transference and Healing.* The eighth level focuses on offering gratitude and thanksgiving to all the helpers, guides, ancestors, family, friends, and community that support us.
9. *The Ninth Level of Transference and Healing.* The final level focuses on receiving blessings and grace. At this level, the participants visualize that they are receiving healing energy from the universe in the form of golden rays of light entering their bodies and expanding out to All That Is.*

---

*Though this ceremony encompasses every aspect of our different levels of health and all that is around us, the participants should only focus on one theme or problem.

Completing the Mandala Ritual

At the closing of the Khardga Puja ceremony, the corners of the cloth are brought together, and the cloth is tied into a bundle with the grain held tightly inside. In this form, the bundle is traditionally carried to a flowing river or to the outgoing tide of the ocean and is placed in water. Today, we simply open the bundle and release its contents into the moving water.

As the contents are released, the dhami/jhankri and participants give heartfelt thanks for the spirits' blessings and the gift of having had a healing.

🪷 The Khardga Puja Ceremony

This ceremony is best done with a group of people but may also be done by an individual. As you have done before other sacred actions, surround yourself with your golden, silver, and iron spheres. Make an offering to the spirits, sing your sacred songs, make an offering of uncooked rice, and honor all of the helping spirits in the directions.

Please read through the directions carefully several times and gather all that you'll need before you begin. (Note: Some of the materials for this ceremony will need to be prepared well in advance.) For this exercise, you will need:

- All of your altar objects and a copper plate (thaal), flat winnowing basket (nanglo), or special cloth on which they are to be arranged (or at the very least a lit candle or oil lamp, a bowl of water, a feather, and a stone) placed in front of you
- Your dhyangro and gajo or another way to produce the journey rhythm
- A comfortable place to be seated
- A square of black cotton cloth about 45 inches (114 cm) square. You may want to draw the mandala *very lightly* on the cloth with a colored pencil before the ceremony. This will function as a guide for sprinkling the flour with your fingers as you draw the mandala during the actual ceremony.
- 8 ounces (225 g) of finely ground cornmeal tinted with red and yellow powdered food coloring (These powdered colors are

readily available at cooking/gourmet shops or online. The final colors of the flour should be a peach or salmon color.)

- Your ball of cotton rainbow threads
- A small handful of uncooked white rice kernels (akshyaata) for your offerings
- 2–4 pounds (1–2 kg) of a mixture of seven different grains (sata byu) If you are unable to procure these, have a similar quantity of uncooked white rice kernels available.
- A large bowl to hold the grains that will be placed near to the mandala
- A paper cup for each person to have some of the grains for making their offerings
- A quantity of fresh fruits, hard candies, or fresh flowers to use as offerings on the mandala
- An oil lamp or safe, low candle for the center of the mandala with matches to light it
- Your drum and beater to play the journey rhythm or another way to produce the rhythm
- Your journal or a notebook and a pen
- A celebratory meal with foods provided by all participants to enjoy after the ceremony that includes sweets and nonalcoholic beverages

Have participants bring rattles, drums, or other sound-making objects to play at the ceremony. Choose someone to assist you and let that person know what role he or she will play during the ceremony.

ᘡ Performing the Ceremony

1. Choose a time when you will be able to work with the spirits.
2. Prepare yourself and collect all the materials you will require.
3. Begin playing the journey rhythm softly.
4. Call your power animal to you to support you during this ritual.
5. Begin by honoring the spirits and blessing the place where the mandala will be created with song and a few rice kernels.
6. Spread the cloth on the floor.
7. As you draw the mandala, have participants rattle and drum in unison to help hold the energy.

8. Place your oil lamp or candle in the center of the mandala. Light the flame.

9. Place offerings of fruit in a circle around the oil lamp or candle.

10. Place the large bowl of the grains near the mandala and have everyone take a cupful back to their place in the ceremonial space.

11. The dhami/jhankri drums and sings during the ceremony asking her or his spiritual helpers to assist the participants in their healing. The shaman may also offer grains to "sweeten" the mandala after each round.

12. Now begin the seven rounds of release that will assist in the healing of the seven levels of human pain or imbalance. After each round is spoken, the participants will place a small amount of the offering grains onto the mandala.

13. The assistant will speak the following words at each round, allowing time for each round of offerings and blessings, while the shaman continues to stay connected with her or his helping spirits.

14. *The First Level of Transference and Healing.* This level focuses on the internal physical organs. Take a small bit of your grain and by breathing deeply and speaking quietly, give permission for the healing and blessing of your internal organs. Give thanks for a healthy heart, lungs, liver, and elimination and digestive systems. Energetically, you are creating a matrix onto which reality will form itself. Make your offering gift in gratitude that the desired results have already been accomplished.

15. *The Second Level of Transference and Healing.* This level focuses on the external organs. Take a small bit of your grain and by breathing deeply and speaking quietly, give permission for the healing and blessing of your external organs. Give thanks for the marvelous envelope of your skin and for your hair, nails, and sensory organs, such as your eyes, ears, and lips. Make your offering gift in gratitude that the desired results have already been accomplished.

16. *The Third Level of Transference and Healing.* This level is focused on interpersonal relationships within the family. Take a small bit of your grain and by breathing deeply and speaking quietly, thank the spirits for healing your familial relationships. Include your ancestors, your parents, your siblings, and your children. Do this with an open heart and with great gratitude so that these relationships can be clear and clean. Give thanks to the spirits and to nature for the work having already been completed. Breathe the feeling of embracing loved

ones into yourself and make your offering into the mandala.

17. *The Fourth Level of Transference and Healing.* This level focuses on healing relationships at work and in the community. Take a small bit of your grain and by breathing deeply and speaking quietly, thank the spirits for healing your community relationships, include schoolmates, your work associates, and your neighbors, both near and far. Do this with an open heart and with great gratitude so that these relationships can be healthy. Give thanks for the work having already been completed. Breathe the feeling of having smooth interpersonal connections with the others in your life. Bring the feeling deeply into yourself and make your offering into the mandala.

18. *The Fifth Level of Transference and Healing.* This level focuses on bringing harmony and balance to the five elements that create our bodies and the universe. Take a small bit of your grain and by breathing deeply and speaking quietly, give thanks to the dance of the elements that made your physicality possible. You and everything on Earth are made of the same stuff of life. You are the fire, the earth, the air, the water, and the spirit made manifest! Release anything that interferes with your deep and profound connections with the body of Earth and the stars. Feel yourself in harmony with all that has made you and that you interact with in the world. The food you eat, the grasses, the flowers and trees, the animals and birds are all part of the same magic that you belong to. Heal anything that interferes with you being in harmony with any of these other beings. Make your offering with deep gratitude.

19. *The Sixth Level of Transference and Healing.* This level focuses on recognizing and diluting the emotions, memories, and suffering of past trauma, such as anger, fear, and sorrow. Take a small bit of your grain and by breathing deeply and speaking quietly, release any way you may have been injured or been made to suffer by another. Let go of the hurts you carry in this life and in lifetimes beyond this one. Pour your memories of trauma and fear from your body into the mandala. Let go of anything that would continue to have you feel like a victim or would make you suffer about your past. Free yourself as you make your offering into the mandala.

20. *The Seventh Level of Transference and Healing.* This level focuses on realigning planetary problems that may be expressing themselves as

issues of the body, mind, emotions, or spirit. Take a small bit of your grain and by breathing deeply and speaking quietly, release any disharmony that may exist on the planetary and cosmic scale. Let go of any way that the planets or stars may be negatively affecting you based upon the circumstances of your birth or from karma. Feel yourself freed from any cosmic burden you may hold as you make your offering into the mandala.

21. *The Eighth Level of Transference and Healing.* The eighth level focuses on offering gratitude and thanksgiving to all the helpers, guides, ancestors, family, friends, and community that support us. We recognize that without our ancestors, we would not have life. Without our helping and guiding spirits, life would be a far more perilous journey. Take a small bit of your grain and by breathing allow yourself to feel grateful for all the beings physical and nonphysical that uphold and support you. Honor the ancestors that gave you life and still continue to transmit those gifts in your DNA. Feel how your power animals, teachers, and guides enable you to reach ever higher into the spiritual realms. Feel their support: the lessons you have been given, the teachings that have healed you and transformed your ways of thinking and feeling. Offer gratitude for all the many gifts the helpers in this world and the spirit worlds have provided. With joy in your heart, place an offering of celebration into the mandala.

22. *The Ninth Level of Transference and Healing.* The final level focuses on receiving blessings and grace. Take a small bit of your grain and by breathing allow yourself to fully receive all the blessings the universe can provide you. Feel golden rays of healing light pouring into you and radiating back out to All That Is. At this point the dhami/jhankri begins to sing songs of harmony, peace, tranquillity, and longevity.

23. Once all the rounds are complete, have the entire group drum and dance clockwise around the mandala, and this dance can widen into a snake dance around the space or from inside to outside and finally back again into a circle. This procession should be led by the dhami/jhankri who is drumming and singing and be done with an air of celebration.

24. Once everyone is back in their places, the dhami/jhankri goes around the circle and ties a length of thread around the wrist of each person. Make it loose enough to be comfortable.

25. When you feel you have finished with the process, thank the spirits with whom you worked and return to ordinary reality by drumming the callback signal.

26. Now it is time for your celebratory meal with sweets.

Whenever your work is complete, make an offering to the spirits for their help and support. Tie up all the grain, flowers, and flour into a bundle and take it to moving water. Untie the bundle and allow the contents to fall into the water to be swept away back to nature. The cloth is then washed for reuse. In some cases, the shaman may be called to bury the entire bundle in the earth as well.

Journey Explorations

Journey to your teacher or power animal to ask him or her to show you how the world around you is affected by the ceremony you have performed.

Journey to your teacher or power animal to ask: When is this ceremony appropriate to perform?

Record the content of your journeys and your perceptions about what you received.

After each journey, thank your power animal, your teacher, and any other spirits who have revealed themselves to you. Then make an offering to the spirits. This can be an offering of incense smoke, bits of food placed outdoors, or flower petals.

Process Questions

How did it feel to perform a ceremony of release and renewal?

What has changed for you after the ceremony was completed?

26

Other Purifying Rituals

THE CHOKHYAUNU/SUDDHA GARNU CEREMONY

A Chokhyaunu or Suddha Garnu ceremony is used to cleanse a building from impurities created by an inauspicious situation that could lead to disease or disharmony for the people residing in it. This ceremony can also be used to cleanse any impurities that may have been created from a difficult birth or death.

One way these ceremonies are usually done is by cleansing the dirt floor of a home by smearing it from the center outward to the door with red clay mixed with cow dung. This functions as a rededication and sanctification of the space. By intentionally reconnecting the house again to Mother Earth (Bhumi Devi/Dharti Mata), it allows the home to once again be blessed by her.

Other forms of cleansing involve smudging the home with mugwort, juniper, sweet-smelling grasses, or resinous incense. Water that has been made precious by adding gold ornaments to it to change the vibration of the fluid may be sprinkled around the home as well. While these cleansing actions are being done, prayers to dispel darkness and to invite auspicious, light energies are chanted. The effect of the latter is to bring harmony, peace, and abundance back to the home.

THE PUCHNU CEREMONY

In Nepali *puchnu* literally means to "wipe away filth or anything that is undesirable." Mopping a floor or even dusting could be thought of as puchnu activities. This simple ritual has parallels to shamanic ceremonies of extraction. In those cases, the dhami/jhankri uses stronger means to remove harmful energies from a person. In shamanic cultures, extractions are done through several methods. The shaman might use a khurpa ritual dagger to "slay" the illness-causing entity, or as a shamanic ceremony, puchnu is done whenever someone feels suddenly nauseous, listless, drained, or overly distracted. In these cases, it is thought that the person could be suffering a spiritual disturbance from a spirit. The puchnu is a method to sweep such an influence away by transferring it to a substance that can be placed outside, away from the home.

Typically, uncooked rice kernels and saffron or turmeric are mixed together. This mixture is then placed on the person's forehead and on down the body. During this action, the healer keeps stating:

Whoever you are, wherever you came from at this time of the day, I offer this rice to you. Maybe this person is spiritually weak; maybe you are hungry. I offer this rice to you. Please accept this as an offering, be happy, and let this person free. When this person feels better, you will be honored and remembered properly. Please leave her or him. Let him or her free.

27

The Shamanic Ransom
Ritual

One of the classic ways shamans use to remove harmful energies from a patient is by transferring the illness to another vessel. What receives the intrusion may be an animal, plant, or object dedicated to this purpose.* In either case, the act of host substitution may be described as a form of ransom ritual.

These ransom rituals are used for healing people and livestock but can also be used to repel the evil eye, to neutralize curses, to arrest the spread of epidemics, to dispel negative energies, and to avert misfortunes of all kinds.

In ancient times, other human beings were used as ransom for another's soul. Rituals using one human being in exchange for the life and well-being of another, or of an entire community, are very archaic indeed. These forms of human sacrifice were practiced in deep prehistory and lingered until the last few centuries in some places. Fortunately, a human figurine or effigy known as an *angsa* or *murti* replaced these barbaric ceremonies in Nepal many millennia ago. Bhola understands this change as a result of the introduction of the law of karma, which declared that the happiness of

---

*Depending on the culture and its beliefs, if an animal or bird is used as a new host, it may either be sacrificed or released into nature. The same is true when plants are used. They are either left in the forest to decay or are burned or buried.

one being cannot be achieved at the expense of another's misery or suffering but, instead, is achieved by increasing the other's well-being.

In this way, the angsa or murti effigy becomes the ransom or substitute offered to alleviate the patient's condition, while also offering the malevolent forces of illness or misfortune a suitable home in return. In other words, even those beings that create disease or disruption do not sustain harm in the process. Those malign forces are simply moved to a vessel where they cannot cause difficulties to other living beings.

The patient agrees to sacrifice any connection or attachment he or she might have to his or her condition. These can include misperceptions of being unworthy, attachments to the perceived benefits of being ill or "stuck," or a belief that they are hopeless. These misperceptions or attachments become "too precious" to the ego to release, and yet that is exactly what is needed for regaining harmony and balance.

The negative aspect of our ego can manifest in obvious ways such as self-importance and boasting, but it also can manifest as feelings of unworthiness or disconnection or wallowing in self-pity. When we let go of these kinds of negative attachments and erroneous perceptions of the self, the effect is like a spontaneous power retrieval. In "sacrificing" what our ego believes is important, we allow realignment with the true self and soul's purposes.

This idea fits in well with the Nepalese ideal of offering something of the self as an act of strength and power. The voluntary sacrifice of one's resources, time, and energy are believed to result in better health, harmonious relations, and deepening of the spiritual path. Precious gifts are given away or sacrificed as an act of self-empowerment. This mystical union of gift giver and gift receiver dissolves the barrier between all. Through giving and the surrender of one's ego to the Divine, the door of consciousness and wisdom is opened. Gifts from the spirits, nature, and other living beings are also received with gratitude. In this way, balance and harmony are nurtured.

Traditionally, the Kalchakra Katne would be used to remove any obstacles in the cycle of time (past/birth, present/life-death, future/rebirth). As a result, issues such as emotional disturbances, troubles in childhood or within a family, fears, traumas, spiritual possession, ancestral burdens, or curses, as well as any issues with the physical body, can be addressed.

Figure 27.1. The flour dough clay ransom effigy. (See also color plate 16)

As a part of the ritual, the dhami/jhankri calls forth the energy of Kaal Bhairung, who is the male deity of time, death, cycles, and destruction. As always, this invocation also recognizes that the energy of Kali, the feminine parallel to Kaal Bhairung, is also present.

In Nepal an experienced shaman performs the Kalchakra ceremony on an individual. If a banana or plantain is available, the sick person is connected to that or to a gourd. The shaman helper does all the preparation, from drawing the rekhi to preparing the ceremonial space, creating the effigy, and so on. The patient collaborates with the shaman by requesting the support of the ancestors, relatives, and householders in his or her healing processes. In cases when the relatives or householders of the patient are not helpful, the patient is taken to another house for healing. If the healing is impeded at that location, then the shaman gives a new name to the patient thus beginning the new phase of life.*

---

*A new name is given to a sick person when multiple healing sessions and ceremonies have not created the desired effects. In some communities when a healing doesn't work, a child is taken to a grocery shop or where rice or other grains are sold, and the child's weight is measured with a scale. A quantity of grain equal to the weight of the child is measured and then given away to many people. This giveaway of grain implies dispersing or giving away the sickness of the child. Afterward, the Kalchakra ceremony is often conducted by an experienced shaman to complete the healing.

The ceremony, described below, is the traditional way of working with Kalchakra, which should not be misunderstood with other religious Kalchakra ceremonies. The group work presented is to help participants to immerse in the Nepalese shamanic world and to learn, in a ceremonial setting, how a sick person's past is reflected into the present. Many shamanic ceremonies are for healing or correcting past events to create a harmonious present and vibrant future.

❦ *The Kalchakra Katne Ceremony*

The Kalchakra Kante ceremony can be done with a large group; however, two people supporting each other in turn can perform the ceremony. The latter method can be incredibly powerful. Read through all the directions and make all the preparations before you begin, including the preparatory journey. This is vital as it is important that you are in alignment and that individuals are in harmony with their intent to release what no longer serves.

As you have done before other sacred actions, surround yourself with your golden, silver, and iron spheres. Make an offering to the spirits, sing your sacred songs, make an offering of uncooked rice and honor all of the helping spirits in the directions.

Please read through the directions carefully several times and gather all that you'll need before you begin. (Note: Some of the materials for this ceremony will need to prepared well in advance.) For this exercise, you will need:

- All of your altar objects and a copper plate (thaal), flat winnowing basket (nanglo), or special cloth on which they are to be arranged (or at the very least a lit candle or oil lamp, a bowl of water, a feather, and a stone) placed in front of you
- Incense or a sweet-smelling bouquet for your altar
- A small handful of uncooked white rice kernels for your offerings on your altar
- A pitcher of healing water (amrita) you have sanctified with your khurpa (Instructions for sanctifying your khurpa are in chapter 7.)
- A small bundle of nine twigs as thin as toothpicks and about 6 inches (15 cm) long that have been tied together with your rainbow threads.

- Your dhyangro and gajo or another way to produce the journey rhythm
- A comfortable place to be seated

Each person who wishes to perform the ritual must also bring the following:

- A ceramic or metal dinner plate
- A circle of dark, solid-colored cotton cloth about 45 inches (114 cm) in diameter
- White flour dough clay (see recipe on page 159)
- 7 types of green leaves of any size
- 3 to 5 large green leaves
- A few ordinary flowers
- A nail clipper
- A small knife
- Clean pieces of your own old clothing
- 1 cup or so of the mixture of seven different grains (sata byu) that you have used in the Khadga Puja ritual (If you are unable to procure these, have a similar quantity of uncooked white rice kernels available.)
- A slim green or dry stick about 12 inches (30 cm) long
- Two matchstick-thin, straight twigs, one about 10 inches (25 cm) long and the other about 5 inches (13 cm) long for creating a spirit umbrella or chatri (see fig. 5.4, page 55) (You can substitute a bamboo skewer that has been split lengthwise. Once split, cut one of the split pieces so it is half as long as the other piece.)
- A few small feathers
- Some pieces of fresh fruit, such as apple slices, orange segments, or grapes
- Small strips of cloth of different solid colors. These are about ½ inch (1 cm) wide by 6 inches (15 cm) long
- One skein each of red, blue, and white cotton embroidery floss. Separate out one thread from the six strands that are in each skein and combine them into one, three-colored strand for use in the ritual. (You could also substitute heavy thread in the same

three colors.) The white strand is for bone, the red strand is for blood, and the blue strand is for the life force or spirit. Together they symbolize the weave of our existence.

- Your ball of cotton rainbow threads
- A small red candle in a safe container
- A small bottle of water from three different, moving sources (preferably from rivers) or from the ocean.
- A bowl large enough to hold a little bit of each person's three-source water
- A cloth to wipe hands and wipe away tears.
- Some sweets or cookies and a nonalcoholic beverage you will use to celebrate
- A new article of clothing that you can put on after the ritual
- Your journal or a notebook and a pen

↳ Preparatory Journey for the Ceremony

Place the bowl in the center of the space and have each participant pour a little of the special water they brought into the bowl. Into that, pour a bit of your healing water (amrita). Using your small twig bundle, lightly sprinkle each person with this water as a form of cleansing.

As you have done before other sacred actions, surround yourself with your golden, silver, and iron spheres. Make an offering to the spirits, sing your sacred songs, make an offering of uncooked rice, and honor all of the helping spirits in the directions. Then begin to play the journey rhythm.

Each person begins his or her journey at a place in nature that feels harmonious and enlivened where the gross elements of creation dance together, such as on a mountain, near a waterfall, where rivers meet, near a huge tree or a big rock outcropping, or a place with clear air and sparkling sunlight.

The participants invite their power animals and spiritual guides to support their hearts to open to the beauty of the nature, allowing the body to resonate with aliveness. When completely filled with the enlivening energies of nature, each person listens for a sound, a word, or a sensation that brings forth a simple song. As soon as the song begins to develop, participants begin singing aloud to the journey rhythm so that the song manifests completely. Sing several times to fully internalize this gift from the spirits.

Play the callback rhythm to bring everyone back to ordinary reality. Take some time to write down the journey, the song, and the overall experience.

Before conducting this ritual, it is important that you are in alignment and that individuals are in harmony with their intent to release what no longer serves.

↳ Performing the Ceremony

1. Choose a time when you will be able to work with the spirits.
2. Prepare yourself and collect all the materials you will require.
3. Place the bowl in the center of the space and have each participant pour a little of the special water they brought into the bowl. Into that, pour a bit of your healing water (amrita). Using your small twig bundle, sprinkle each person lightly with this water as a form of cleansing.
4. Ask participants to clarify their intent for what they are releasing, as you drum and begin playing the journey rhythm softly.
5. While you drum, call your power animal to you to support you during this ritual.
6. Give the callback and then honor your helping spirits and bless the area with song.
7. Ask each person to place a few rice kernels on the area where his or her ceremonial dinner plate will be placed.
8. Each person spreads his or her round cloth out on the floor and places the dinner plate on top of it.
9. Each person covers the plate with large leaves.
10. People begin to quietly hum or sing their personal power songs and will continue to do so during the entire ceremony.
11. Participants now form simple dough figures that represent themselves and place these on top of the leaf-covered plates. (If it is one-on-one, the person who does the healing makes the figure for the recipient.)
12. The figure is now "dressed" with bits of the recipients' fingernails, some saliva, a bit of hair, and tears or perspiration, as well as a piece of fabric from an article of old clothing.
13. The person who will perform the healing then decorates his or her plate around the figure with some of the seven-grain mixture.

14. Each person takes a long thin stick and winds it with the three-colored thread. The number of winds equals the age of the person. In other words, thirty winds around the stick for a thirty-year-old person and so forth.

15. Each person places that stick with the wound thread in the heart of the effigy. This represents Kalchakra: the dark time cycle of the past.

16. Next, the healer makes spirit umbrellas or chatris for each person, using two matchstick-thin sticks and rainbow threads for each chatris. Arrange the sticks in the form of a cross and tie them together at the junction with the thread. Now begin winding the rainbow thread around them widening each course. Do this for seven or nine courses.

17. The healer sticks the chatri in the head of each effigy.

18. Next, each person places feathers in his or her effigy

19. Now, the healing partner uses the three-colored thread to connect the person who is to receive the healing to the effigy.

20. Now, the healing partner makes an offering of strips of colored cloth to the effigy

21. At this point, the ritual of transference begins. There will be seven rounds to release into the effigy any obstacles, attachments, or wounds that have occurred in the cycle of time. At the end of each round, the participant places an offering of grains or rice on the effigy. The shaman or partner of the participant then sprinkles him or her with sacred water.

    The shaman assistant speaks the following words at each round (steps 22–28 for rounds one through seven), allowing time for each round of offerings and blessing and cleaning with water droplets, while the shaman continues to stay connected with her or his helping spirits.

22. *First Round: Transference of Spiritual and Emotional Disconnections or Disturbances.* Taking a small bit of your grain and by breathing deeply and quietly speaking, give permission for any spiritual or emotional imbalances to be transferred to the effigy. With an open heart, give thanks to this stand-in figure who is receiving your pain, your troubles, or your illness. Visualize those imbalances flowing through the threads into the effigy. Make your offering gift in gratitude that the desired results have already been accomplished.

23. *Second Round: Transference of Wounds or Disturbances from Childhood or in Family Relationships.* Take a small bit of your grain and by breathing deeply and quietly speaking, give permission for your past wounds from family or that were otherwise sustained in childhood to be transferred to the effigy. With an open heart, give thanks to this stand-in figure who is receiving your negative experiences from the past so that you can become free. Visualize those wounds and traumas flowing through the threads into the effigy. Make your offering gift in gratitude that the desired results have already been accomplished.

24. *Third Round: Transference of Wounds or Disturbances from Unhealthy Relationships with Intimate Partners, Friends, Coworkers, and Others.* Take a small bit of your grain and by breathing deeply and quietly speaking, give permission for your wounds from your past relationships to be transferred to the effigy. With an open heart, give thanks to this stand-in figure who is receiving your hurt, your troubles, or your feelings of betrayal. Visualize those imbalances flowing through the threads into the effigy. Make your offering gift in gratitude that the desired results have already been accomplished.

25. *Fourth Round: Transference of Fears, Curses, Traumas, or Negative Spiritual Attachments, and Possessions.* Take a small bit of your grain and by breathing deeply and quietly speaking, give permission for entities that resulted from your past emotional and spiritual traumas, your fears, and any negative entities that became attached to you in other ways to be transferred to the effigy. With an open heart, give thanks to this stand-in figure who is receiving your impediments, your fears, or your illness. Visualize those entities leaving your body and flowing through the threads into the effigy. Make your offering gift in gratitude that the desired results have already been accomplished.

26. *Fifth Round: Transference of Any Obstacles to Courage and Creativity.* Take a small bit of your grain and by breathing deeply and quietly speaking, give permission for any blockages, obstacles, misperceptions, or patterns that interfere with your being courageous and creative to be transferred to the effigy. You came into this world as a creative and courageous soul! With an open heart, give thanks to this stand-in figure who is receiving anything that impedes your inherent creativity. Visualize those imbalances flowing through the threads into

the effigy. Make your offering gift in gratitude that the desired results have already been accomplished.

27. *Sixth Round: Transference of Any Ancestral Burdens.* Take a small bit of your grain and by breathing deeply and quietly speaking, give permission for any blockages, obstacles, misperceptions, or negative patterns that you may have inherited from your lineage to be transferred to the effigy. With an open heart, give thanks to this stand-in figure who is receiving your pain, your obstacles, or your illness. See the long line of your ancestors behind you also releasing these patterns and curses. Visualize those imbalances flowing through the threads into the effigy. As you free yourself, all those who have contributed to your manifestation in this life are also made free. Your healing is a gift! Make your offering gift in gratitude that the desired results have already been accomplished.

28. *Seventh Round: Transference of Any Obstacles to Physical Health.* Take a small bit of your grain and by breathing deeply and quietly speaking, give permission for anything that interferes with you being able to attain physical health to be transferred to the effigy. With an open heart, give thanks to this stand-in figure who is receiving your pain, your impediments, or your illness. Visualize those imbalances flowing through the threads into the effigy. Feel your body becoming light, lithe, strong, and vigorous! Make your offering gift in gratitude that the desired results have already been accomplished.

29. Once all the rounds of transference are complete, the thread connecting the person to his or her effigy must be severed with the knife. One half of the thread is draped over the effigy, and the other half is tied loosely around the neck of the patient as a blessing and reminder.

30. Each person's hands are then blessed with water.

31. The plates with the effigies are placed outside, away from the building.

32. Participants now put on their new clothing.

33. The shaman or individual partners each journey to get the patient a new name to honor the new beginning and whispers it into the patient's ear.

34. The shaman or individual partners use drumming and their sacred objects to raise the energy of the participant while holding the intent to create a cocoon of light all around, above, and below the person's

body. This ritual or ceremony is called Siir Uthaune (raising the spirits up and empowerment).

35. The participants observe a period of silence to allow the new experience to become a deeper reality.
36. After this period, sweets and nonalcoholic beverages are shared to feed the new experience of self.
37. The ceremony is closed by releasing the helping spirits
38. When the ceremony is complete, the effigies should be released into flowing water, and if this is not possible, to be allowed to dissolve in the rain in a place away from human beings.

Whenever your work is complete, make an offering to the spirits for their help and support.

⌂ Journey Explorations

Journey to your teacher or power animal to ask him or her to show you how the effigy received the transferred burdens and illnesses.

Journey to your teacher to ask: When is this ceremony appropriate to perform?

Record the content of your journeys and your perceptions about what you received.

After each journey, thank your power animal, your teacher, and any other spirits who have revealed themselves to you. Then make an offering to the spirits. This can be an offering of incense smoke, bits of food placed outdoors, or flower petals.

⌂ Process Questions

How did it feel to perform a healing ceremony of transference?

What changed for you after the ceremony was completed?

28

Honoring Our Relationship with the Cosmos

Just as our planet does not ride the void of space alone, the dhami/jhankri understands that we are connected and influenced by the cosmos. Nepalese culture recognizes three categories of astrological influences. They are the twelve *rashis* (zodiac signs), nine *grahas* (principles of energy that pull or seize, that can include the influence of the planets), and twenty-seven *nakshatras,* which include constellations and lunar houses. The interrelationships of these complex influences create an ocean of information for the astrologer to decode. There is also awareness that the microcosm and the macrocosm reflect each other, as above so below and vice versa.

Nine is a powerful number in Himalayan spirituality. It is believed that nine principles of energy affect everything in the physical universe, including the nine planets in our solar system. These nine can manifest in myriad ways. Seven of the grahas are reflected in the world defined by our senses. For instance, the seven colors in the visible spectrum and the seven major chakras of the physical body. Following these tangible parameters, we structure our weeks with seven days, which correspond to the visible bodies of our solar system.*

---

*Sunday (sun), Monday (moon), Tuesday (Mars), Wednesday (Mercury), Thursday (Jupiter), Friday (Venus), and Saturday (Saturn).

However, there is much that lies beyond the reach of our senses. Beyond the visible spectrum of red, orange, yellow, green, blue, indigo, and violet exist the ultraviolet (Rahu/Dragon's Head or ascending lunar nodes) and infrared areas (Ketu/Dragon's Tail or descending lunar nodes). We also have spiritual chakras that lie beyond our physical body. Although these are not visible to us, they are still very powerful. In the same way, the nine grahas encompass more than simply planets. They are energetic influences that sway the physical world in the way a magnet attracts iron filings and affect how everything works. Every solar system, every celestial dimension, and every plane of existence is acted upon by these nine principles.

Orally transmitted folktales say that Vishnu incarnated as the Navagrahas (nine planets) to bestow on living beings the results of their karmas or actions. He assumed the auspicious form of these nine energies to destroy the strength of the demons (evil forces), to sustain the strength of the devas (the divine beings), and to establish cosmic order. According to Himalayan tradition, the grahas shape the personality of the person, including his or her likes, dislikes, creativity, dreams, friendships, and enmities.

As everything has a spirit, the grahas are also understood as beings with personalities. Here is a story from Bhola where Guru Brihaspati (Jupiter) shares his importance as well as revealing his personality traits:

Once upon a time all nine grahas had a great argument about who was the best among them. They decided to approach Lord Indra's court and describe their powers and characteristics to him.

After Surya (sun), Chandra (moon), and Mangal (Mars) had introduced themselves, it was Budh's (Mercury's) turn to talk about his powers. Hearing Budh logically list his powers, the largest graha, Guru Brihaspati (Jupiter), stepped forward to tell his story.

Guru Brihaspati said: "When I bless a person, I grant him good education, knowledge, and respect from others. If I am happy with someone, I bless the person with good luck and marital bliss.

"My position in a person's birth chart also decides the sex of the child. I fill a person's life with money and good family life, family togetherness, good speech, property, immovable assets, and so on.

"If a person is born on my day [Thursday], he is organized, is an intellectual, has strict principles, is quick to grasp, and will become a king, teacher, poet, writer, advocate, judge, or a politician. He can also be a yogi and earn a lot of respect in society.

"I help keep a check on anger in a person's life. In Kali Yuga [the present era], I represent good knowledge, respect for elders, peace, good behavior, and patience.

"On Brihaspativaar [Thursday], women should worship the pipal tree [Ficus religiosa] or the banana tree. My day can also be marked by wearing yellow-colored clothes, by donating food to those in need, and by offering prasada *[consecrated food] like yellow dals or fruits.*

"It is auspicious to begin an educational course, prepare for exams, observe a fast, pray, or teach on a Thursday.

"I am the lord of Dhanu rashi [Sagittarius people] as well as Meena rashi [Pisces people]. Mangal and Surya are my friends, while Shukra is my enemy.

"A weak Guru Brihaspati in someone's birth chart can cause stomach problems, jaundice, cancer, or cataracts. Wearing a pukhraj *[topaz] set in gold, after proper consultation, or wearing a guru yantra charged by a healer or shaman will allow you to channel my beneficial effects.*

"My mantra to be recited on Thursdays is: Om Gram Greem Graum Sah Guruvayeh Namah.*"*

And having spoken, Guru Brihaspati stood with his hands crossed over his great chest and smiled.

THE NINE GRAHAS

The Sun (Surya)

As the center of our planetary system, the sun represents the central position. It represents the energy of the king or leader, the soul, the masculine principle, and our vital energy.

A strong sun in an individual planetary constellation indicates a person with a leader's personality and someone who has good self-esteem, creativity, and courageousness. People with a strong sun are often spiritually mature as well as physically healthy.

A weak sun can indicate a difficult relationship with one's father, low self-esteem, and low vitality or health problems. An imbalance of sun energy may cause issues of the heart, the blood circulation, the sight (especially the right eye), the head including headaches, and the abdomen and/or stomach, as well as digestive issues, overall dryness, and fevers.

The Moon (Chandra)

The moon represents the mind, the emotions, the vital energy or *prana,* and water and liquids. The moon also represents the mother and one's relationship with her.

A strong moon reflects mental and psychological stability, good concentration, and a capacity for well-being, nurturing, and emotional satisfaction. Strong moon energy allows us to love and be loved in balance as well as have a strong foundation to better deal with life's inevitable challenges.

A weak or disarrayed moon can suggest emotional, mental, or psychological disturbances, issues with female fertility, and disorders of the blood and body fluids, as well as diseases of the lungs, breasts, and chest.

Mars (Mangal)

Mars represents high energy and courage, taking the initiative or action, and, in some situations, war and aggression.

A strong Mars makes a person a spiritual warrior who is fearless in the face of internal and external difficulties or enemies in life. The energy supports control over one's own body and emotions.

A weak Mars can lead to an uncontrolled dissipation or loss of vital energy or physical strength, as well as a tendency to violence and/or aggression. In the physical body, a weak Mars can be expressed in illnesses of the bone marrow, muscles, the head, and testicles and a loss of male sexual virility.

Mercury (Budh)

Mercury represents the intellect or *budh,* the capacity for discernment, communication, language, learning, physical activities, and expansive relationships.

A Mercury dominant person has a constant desire for learning, but it also creates a duality in the mind, always comparing between the pairs of opposites. Mercury represents the pure analytical and rational mind.

A weak Mercury can lead a person to rely more on emotions and instinct rather than on reason and create clouded thinking and memory issues. It can bring difficulties in learning and speech and diseases related to the skin, nervous system, and breathing, including exercise-triggered asthma.

Jupiter (Guru Brihaspati)

Jupiter represents the teacher, the guru, the one who leads us from the darkness of ignorance to the light of knowledge. Jupiter stands for wisdom, knowledge, learning, goodness, good luck, good karma, and expansion. As guru of the devas, the celestial or angelical beings, Jupiter is one of the dominant planets. It is full of wisdom, righteousness, justice, and goodness. Jupiter represents the desire to bless and give prosperity to everyone.

In some cases, an excessively strong Jupiter can lead a person to not make any effort to improve his or her life situation. This can express itself as either an overinflated sense of self or an excessive optimism that can lead to spiritual stagnation.

An afflicted or displaced Jupiter can indicate difficulty in getting a spiritual teacher, or sometimes even getting a wrong, dishonest, or fake teacher or having a difficult relationship with teachers in general. It can bring lack of faith and optimism in life, a more materialistic view of life, or material difficulties that don't allow the mind to expand into a more spiritual awareness.

A weak Jupiter can indicate marital difficulties or difficulties in having children.

In the physical body, a weak Jupiter is related to the accumulation of fluids, obesity, and problems with the liver, pancreas, sugar and fat metabolism, the hips, and the feet. (All the disorders of out-of-balance abundance!)

Venus (Shukra)

Venus is another spiritual teacher, and she is the teacher of the *asuras* or demons—beings who were spiritually evolved at some past time but fell from grace because of strong materialistic or selfish tendencies. Venus helps them find their path of return.

Venus represents feminine energies, beauty, refinement, love, desire and human passions, sexuality, and marital relationships. Venus is also associated with wealth, elegance, finery, music, dance, the fine arts, and creativity.

A strong Venus tends to bestow artistic talents and creativity, physical beauty, a good sense of aesthetics and harmony, prosperity, wealth, and divine grace. A well-located Venus has a spiritual potential of transforming the energy of love and sensuality into devotion, cosmic love, and a feeling of deep connection to All That Is.

A too-strong or dominating Venus aspect can lead to an excessive attachment to sensual pleasure and to the material objects and physical pleasures of the world.

An afflicted or debilitated Venus usually brings difficulties to obtain pleasure or enjoyment in life, which can lead a person to look for exaggerated means of sensual gratification to compensate. Physically, it represents the reproductive organs, urinary tract, and the flow of semen. Weakness of this planet may lead to weakness or diseases of the reproductive organs or sexual disorders.

From a spiritual point of view, a debilitated Venus can lead a person to a sincere spiritual path, developing a strong devotion, looking for God's love alone, and becoming an ascetic or sadhu.

Saturn (Shani)

Saturn represents austerity, discipline, restrictions, and suffering. This planet is also a spiritual teacher that teaches through restriction, hard work, purification, service, and humility, leading the person to face his or her weaknesses and more negative tendencies and to recognize and change them. Saturn represents longevity, old age, concentration, and meditation. It is the planet of spiritual development and evolution.

Saturn makes us face the negative karma we created in the past in the form of restrictions, which will lead us eventually to recognize our negative patterns and develop responsibility and self-discipline to change them. Saturn is a stern but loving shamanic teacher.

A strong and well-located Saturn indicates a good capacity to endure the inevitable hard things of life and to develop the capacity for hard work, a strong sense of responsibility, seriousness, and self-discipline—pulling one's self up by the bootstraps.

An afflicted or misplaced Saturn can cause difficulty in facing responsibilities or trying to evade them, which, in turn, leads to more suffering. It can lead to mental depression, loneliness, feelings of isolation, addictions, and chronic diseases. The more one tries to escape from Saturn's restrictions, the more intense those sufferings become, leading eventually to extremely difficult situations. The best way to relate with Saturn's energy is to understand and accept its restrictions consciously through self-discipline and self-purification.

Saturn moves slowly, an indication that its lessons will have to be learned over a long period of perseverance and hard work. But after that, Saturn can give immense blessings and spiritual strength.

Saturn usually tends to postpone or delay things. Saturn-dominant persons are hard workers, good servants, politicians, yogis, and ascetic people. Saturn's energy can be positively channeled through fasting, selfless service, seclusion, and meditation.

In the physical body, Saturn is associated with the nerves, fascia mobility, and cellular function.

The nonphysical planets Rahu and Ketu don't have a physical mass but are very powerful energetic points in the sky. They are the points of intersection between the path of the sun and the path of the moon, causing the solar and lunar eclipses. They are very important on the spiritual level, as they are related with unconscious material and unresolved karma and conflicts in previous lives. In mythology a snake that was cut into two parts represents these grahas. Rahu is the head and the Ketu is the tail. This inner conflict manifests as two antagonistic, opposite forces in the subconscious mind that generate conflicts, dualities, fears, compulsive desires, rejections or phobias, and karmic situations that are revealed so that we can face them and work them out.

Rahu (the North Node)

Rahu is related with unconscious desires, dissatisfactions, fears, obsessions, ambitions, and unresolved issues from previous lives that need to be experienced in this life. Rahu can stimulate mental restlessness, hypersensitivity, and strong desires to experience what needs to change, but it also stimulates fears about doing so.

Since Rahu stimulates our unconscious to trigger what we need to work on, it can also lead to compulsive behavior, addictions, fantasies, unrealistic imaginations, or suggestions. Rahu represents the unconventional, illegal, dark but desired aspect of our being. Working with these energies requires that we do deep spiritual work, meditation, and self-contemplation to make changes within ourselves.

Ketu (the South Node)

A sadhu or ascetic monk represents Ketu. The sadhu rejects the world and its trappings in his or her quest for essential truth. Ketu indicates areas where detachment has to be developed, areas that will be the source of some suffering until they are illuminated by spirit and healed.

Ketu is considered a very important graha for spiritual evolution because it represents the capacity for renunciation, detachment from the ephemeral, and a search for the truth and the essence of life. It also represents *moksha,* liberation from the cycle of births and deaths and the ultimate attainment of illumination. Ketu dominates the lives of monks, ascetics, and psychic or clairvoyant people.

An adverse Ketu can cause ruptures, breaks, accidents, or diseases, but alternatively it can bestow intuitive knowledge coming from past life experiences.

TABLE 28.1. SIMPLE CHART OF THE NINE GRAHAS

Graha	Attribute When Harmonious	Negative Influence When Imbalanced
Sun (Surya)	Leadership ability, physical health, courage, good self-esteem, mature spiritual energy	Low self-esteem, low vitality, eye problems, heart or circulation issues, headaches, poor digestion, fevers, issues with male fertility, "father issues"
Moon (Chandra)	Balanced emotions, psychological stability, good concentration, capacity for nurturing, emotional satisfaction	Emotional or psychological disturbances, lung and chest issues, fluid imbalances, issues with female fertility, "mother issues"

Graha	Attribute When Harmonious	Negative Influence When Imbalanced
Mars (Mangal)	Energy, fearlessness, initiative, able to face difficulties head-on, self control	Loss of vitality, violence, aggression, headache or head issues, physical weakness, issues with muscles or bone marrow, issues with testicles/virility
Mercury (Budh)	Intellect, discernment, language skills, rational thinking, learning, physical action, expansive relationships	Learning issues, trouble with speech, memory issues, clouded thinking, irrational behavior, skin and nervous system issues, breathing issues, exercise-triggered asthma
Jupiter (Guru Brihaspati)	Wisdom, good karma, good luck, optimism, expansiveness, generosity, righteousness, justice, prosperity, selfless giving, good-heartedness	Trouble discerning a good teacher or guide, lack of faith, pessimism, laziness, hoarding, being emotionally or materially stingy, accumulation of fluids and/or fat, diabetes, hip or foot issues
Venus (Shukra)	Wealth, beauty, love, refinement, sensuality, creativity, artistry, gracefulness, passion, healthy sexuality, good marriage	Narcissism, hedonism, materialism, greed, lustfulness, gaudiness, clumsiness, urinary or reproductive issues, sexual disorders
Saturn (Shani)	Self-discipline, perseverance, patience, responsibility, ability to face life's challenges and overcome them, capacity for hard work	Lack of motivation, stagnation, evading responsibility, impatience, depression, loneliness, addictions, escapism, weak will, chronic diseases
Rahu (Lunar north node)	Dormant spiritual energies, imagination, hidden talents or gifts	Delusions, compulsive behavior, addictions, fears, dissatisfaction, unresolved karmic/past life issues, restless mind, obsessions
Ketu (Lunar south node)	Renunciation, detachment from ephemeral things, spiritual and psychic gifts, attainment of enlightenment, liberation	Accidents, breaks, ruptures, confusion, lack of grounding, mental suffering, anxiety

Figure 28.1. The Graha
Sarne ceremony rekhi
or mandala.

Offering Mantras to the Grahas

These mantras can be used to support balance in the planets. Be sure to journey to find out what mantra would be helpful to you as strengthening one that is already balanced would not be useful. They should be chanted 108 times on a rudraksha mala.

(Sun) Om Guru Suryan Namaha
(Moon) Om Guru Chandran Namaha
(Mars) Om Guru Kuman Namaha
(Mercury) Om Guru Buddhan Namaha
(Jupiter) Om Guru Guru Namaha
(Venus) Om Guru Sukran Namaha
(Saturn) Om Guru Shani Namaha
(Rahu) Om Guru Rahu Namaha
(Ketu) Om Guru Ketu Namaha

There is also a more elaborate shamanic way to balance the grahas for healing. This ceremony is the Graha Sarne. It is also a ceremony of transference that is performed on a rekhi or mandala. Its purpose is to realign and balance the influences of the nine grahas.

HEALING DISHARMONIOUS
PLANETARY EFFECTS

During the ceremony of Graha Sarne, the shaman or her or his assistant prepares a ground mandala or rekhi on a black piece of cloth.* A rekhi with nine petals (lotus) representing the nine planets is made with rice flour that has been colored red, yellow, and white. In the periphery of the rekhi, four tridents drawn in the same colors represent the four cardinal directions. In every one of the nine houses of the planets and the four tridents, different types of flowers, leaves, rice kernels, and seven grains (sata byu) are offered.

At the center of the mandala, a tripod of long green branches or fresh, green bamboo stalks is erected.† The sticks are tied together at the top with red and white strips of cotton cloth. From this tripod, multicolored strips of cotton cloth are hung. This tripod represents the lingam. As noted earlier, this stylized phallus is often used as a symbol of Shiva's divine regenerative energy. The lingam is usually shown sitting within a yoni, representing the Divine Feminine. In this case, the body of Earth herself is used for that purpose.

Sometimes, the shaman discovers during his or her preliminary diagnostic journey that, along with the negative planetary effects, a person has a malignant spirit attached to him or her. In those cases, a small bamboo basket containing a fresh, raw egg is hung from the tripod. If the case is even more serious, or the shaman has been shown that the graha or planet requires a ransom sacrifice, then a rooster would be placed in a similar basket. Fortunately, a raw egg usually suffices.‡

The shaman begins the healing by either beating a dhyangro drum, sounding cymbals, or holding sacred plant leaves in her or his hand and

---

*In the countryside of Nepal, the rekhi would be drawn directly onto an earthen floor that had been sanctified by being smeared with a paste of cow dung or red mud.
†If the mandala is drawn directly in the earth, a single branch, a sacred plant bough, or a green bamboo stalk can be used.
‡If it is necessary to use an egg or a rooster or chick for the ceremony of Graha Sarne, then an additional helper will be needed.

makes an invocation. The first prayer asks the permission of the sick person's ancestors to work on the patient. Next, permission is asked of the spirits of the house and of the land where the ceremony is conducted for the person's support. Finally, the dhami/jhankri calls in her or his helping spirits and merges with one or more of them to support the healing ritual.

The sick person sits facing the ceremonial space and the direction indicated by the shaman. The shaman helper takes a leaf plate or regular plate with the rice kernels and seven types of grains and a container with water collected from five or seven different sources of water. The grain and water is placed near the mandala. Sometimes black sesame barley seeds are added to the water.

When all materials are ready, the shaman sits facing the sick person and the healing rekhi mandala. As the ceremony for healing starts, the first helper touches different parts of the body of the patient with the grains. When the drumming stops, he or she offers the grains to the mandala and then sprinkles the water on the patient with the aid of a flower or a bamboo puki. The shaman concentrates on drumming and singing sacred songs to pacify the effect of the planet and to clear the disease-causing spirits. If the case is life threatening, then an egg,

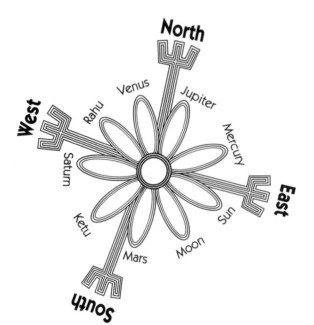

Figure 28.2. The places that each of the planets or grahas holds on the rekhi or mandala.

rooster, or chick is passed over the body of the patient, from the top of the head to the feet, in such a way that the illness is transferred to the egg, rooster, or chick. If the disease is localized to a particular part of the body, then the extraction-transference is concentrated there.

The touching of the body with the grains and the sprinkling of the water are done nine times, while the shaman drums and sings. On the final ninth round of healing, if an egg has been used, it is put in the bamboo container hung in the tripod or lingam. The tripod and the bamboo container are smudged with incense and then taken out of the house and carried to a far-off place, such as the other side of a river or under a distant tree. If the case is associated with a spirit of the dead that has not fully transitioned, then the tripod is erected in the path or road that is closest to the house of the sick person.

If a chick or rooster has been used as the main object of transference, then on the ninth round, the fowl is sacrificed and blood is offered. If an effigy made out of flour or mud is used to represent the malignant spirit, then all the decorations, food, and blood are poured on it, and the head of the rooster is offered to the effigy. All the offerings are then taken to a secluded place in nature. If the patient's condition is very grave (*kaal graha*) or life threatening, then after the blood offering to the effigy, the sacrificial rooster or chick is taken away and left to decay or is buried in the earth.

Having transferred the disarrayed planets and the spirits associated with the ailment, the shaman raises the spirit or soul parts of the patient by using his healing instruments in the ceremony of Siir Uthaune. In this life-prolonging ritual, the sacred water vase (kalasa) is put at the head of the sick person, and after long invocations, the person is given water to drink. Protective talismans or amulets are also made and given to wear on the body.

❦ *The Graha Sarne Ceremony*

This ceremony is best done by the shaman, an assistant, and the person who requires healing. As you have done before with other sacred actions, surround yourself with your golden, silver, and iron spheres. Make an offering to the spirits, sing your sacred songs, make an offering of uncooked rice, and honor all of the helping spirits in the directions.

Please read through the directions carefully several times and gather all that you'll need before you begin. (Note: Some of the materials for this ceremony will need to be prepared in advance.) For this exercise, you will need:

- All of your altar objects and a copper plate (thaal), flat winnowing basket (nanglo), or special cloth on which they are to be arranged (or at the very least a lit candle or oil lamp, a bowl of water, a feather, and a stone) placed in front of you
- Incense for a smoke offering
- Your dhyangro and gajo or another way to produce the journey rhythm
- A comfortable place to be seated
- A square of black cotton cloth about 45 inches (114 cm) on each side (You may want to draw the mandala *very lightly* on the cloth with a colored pencil or chalk before the ceremony. This will function as a guide for sprinkling the flour with your fingers as you draw the mandala during the actual ceremony.)
- A tripod made from three 40-inch-long (1 meter) green branches or fresh bamboo that have been tied together at the top with red and white strips of cotton cloth, to be placed in the center of the mandala
- A small woven basket large enough to contain one egg, which can be suspended from the inside of the tripod (only if deemed necessary in diagnostic journey)
- A raw egg (only if deemed necessary in diagnostic journey)
- 12 ounces (339 g) flour or finely ground cornmeal, divided into thirds, and red and yellow powdered food coloring. One-third (4 ounces) of the flour or cornmeal is tinted red, one-third is tinted yellow, and the last third is left undyed or white. (These powdered colors are readily available at cooking/gourmet shops or online.)
- Your spool of rainbow thread
- A bouquet of flowers for your altar
- A small handful of uncooked white rice kernels for your offerings on your altar
- 2–4 pounds (1–2 kg) of a mixture of seven different uncooked grains (sata byu) (These can be any seven grains; we typically

use a mixture of corn, quinoa, millet, white beans, black beans, orange peas, and yellow lentils.)
- A bowl of flower petals and at least 12 large green leaves for offerings
- Pieces of fruits for offerings (apple slices, orange sections, etc.)
- Strips of solid-colored cotton cloth (red, white, yellow, green, blue, violet, purple, black, etc.) about 1 inch (2.5 cm) wide by 10 inches (25 cm) long
- Your khurpa and other healing instruments
- A pitcher of healing water (amrita) you have sanctified with your khurpa (instructions are found in chapter 7 on page 84)
- A peacock feather or small bundle of thin twigs to flick the healing water over the patient
- A bowl of water from seven different sources (faucets in seven different locations, seven rivers, etc.), into which some black sesame seeds have been added
- Your journal or a notebook and a pen
- A celebratory meal with foods provided by all participants to enjoy after the ceremony, which includes sweets and nonalcoholic beverages

Choose someone to assist you and let this person know what role he or she will be playing during the ceremony.

⮡ Performing the Ceremony
1. Choose a time when you will be able to work with the spirits.
2. Prepare yourself and collect all the materials you will require.
3. Do a diagnostic journey to learn what is needed for the patient. Ask especially what graha needs to be balanced/healed.
4. Once the preparations are complete, set up the cloth and draw the rekhi or mandala in colored flour.
5. Make offerings of leaves and flowers. (Place a large green leaf just beyond the drawn lotus petals, and place offerings of flowers and fruit on top of the leaf. Then make a plate of three overlapping green leaves on the center of the mandala, and make offerings of flowers and fruits there, too.)
6. Erect the tripod over the center offering and tie the sticks together

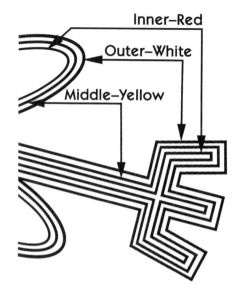

Inner–Red

Outer–White

Middle–Yellow

Figure 28.3. Detail of how the patterns of the rekhi or mandala are colored.

at the top with red and white cloth strips. From this tripod, strips of colored cloth are hung as offerings. If an egg is to be used, the basket to hold it can be suspended inside the tripod.

7. Ask the person to clarify her or his intent for what needs healing, as you drum and begin playing the journey rhythm softly.

8. While you drum, call your power animal to you to support you during this ritual.

9. Invoke the helping ancestors of the patient and ask them permission to work on their progeny.

10. Now invoke the helping spirits of the land and house in which you are working to support the ceremony.

11. Sing and dance with your drum until you feel fully inspirited by your helping spirits.

12. Invite the patient to sit facing the mandala in the direction closest to the imbalanced graha.

13. The shaman also sits facing the mandala on the side opposing the patient.

14. The shaman's assistant now takes the bowl of water, the bundle of small twigs, and the seven-grain mixture.

15. The shaman drums and invites harmony and balance from the graha that is directly in front of the patient. In addition, the shaman has her

or his helping spirits remove any harmful energies from the patient's body and place them into the grains held by the assistant.

16. At the same time, the assistant holds a handful of the seven grains in the right hand and touches the patient over his or her body with the grain-filled hand.

17. The drumming stops, and the assistant offers the grains to the petal of the planet nearest the patient and the center of the mandala.

18. The assistant then sprinkles healing waters over the patient.

19. Going counterclockwise, steps 15–18 are repeated until all nine gra- has have been balanced.

   Optional: If the diagnostic journey suggested that a harmful entity was present in the patient, the egg is passed over the patient by the assistant from the top of the head to the feet. While doing this, the shaman works with her or his helping spirits to transfer the entity to the egg. Immediately after the egg is used, place the egg in the tripod basket and smudge the entire tripod with incense. Then carry the tripod and egg far from the house to a place it won't be disturbed. If no place like this is available, the egg must be buried in the ground.

20. Offerings of incense are now made to the mandala.

21. At this point, the shaman uses drumming, the pommel of her or his khurpa, and other sacred objects to raise the energy of the participant while holding the intent to create a cocoon of light all around, above, and below the person's body. Then the pitcher with sacred water (amrita) is placed on the person's head while prayers for longevity are made by the dhami/jhankri. The patient is then offered sacred water to drink. This is called a Siir Uthaune ceremony.

22. The shaman finishes the ceremony by singing, dancing, and celebrat- ing. The gathered group can join in the celebration with their own drums and rattles.

23. The tripod is removed from the cloth and disassembled.

24. The corners of the mandala cloth are gathered with all of the offer- ings inside. The cloth is then bundled together in preparation for being taken away to a far place. If this is not possible, the offerings are emptied and allowed to dissolve in the rain in a place away from human beings.

25. The shaman releases the helping spirits.
26. A celebratory meal is shared.

Whenever your work is complete, make an offering to the spirits for their help and support.

☜ Journey Explorations

Journey to your teacher or power animal to ask him or her to show you how the grahas were balanced by the ceremony.

Journey to your teacher to ask: What ailments may indicate that this ceremony is appropriate to perform?

Record the content of your journeys and your perceptions about what you received.

After each journey, thank your power animal, your teacher, and any other spirits who have revealed themselves to you. Then make an offering to the spirits. This can be an offering of incense smoke, bits of food placed outdoors, or flower petals.

☜ Process Questions

How did it feel to perform a Graha Sarne ceremony?

What has changed for you after the ceremony was completed?

CONCLUSION

Spiritual and Emotional Unification

Although we have only opened the door on Nepalese shamanism with this book, it is our desire that you continue exploring the realm of these spirits and working with the spiritual technology you find in these pages.

Things in our world are changing very rapidly and not all for the better. Tribal wisdom is being lost as we become more homogenized as a global culture. While the continued movement toward a spiritual and emotional unification of all of the peoples is vital for the preservation of our planet, it should not be necessary that we give up the very things that also make us unique and extraordinary.

Our human diversity is one of our strengths. The precious bundles of truth and wisdom that the many diverse tribes of people have preserved are as important to us as the contribution each individual species makes to the health and well-being of our global environment. We cannot lose any of them without weakening our collective.

In addition, it is clear that the world's shamanic practitioners, with their abilities to grasp the wider view and access hidden resources of knowledge, are the very ones who can contribute to supporting the harmony we require to reconcile our conflicts and find solutions for saving our beautiful planetary home.

We cannot know how long this great work will take, but it is clearly the next and most important step in our evolution. Through prayer, ritual, and healing and by taking direct, positive actions, we can do what needs to be done. May the spirits empower us to do it in time.

EVELYN

Om!
Om!

Hey Daki Lyaiu, Bolai Lyaiu, Chalai Lyaiu, Khelai Lyaiu
We called you, we invited you, we played together

Satai Tala Patal Dekhi, Satai Tala Aakash Dekhi
from seven levels of the Lower World realm and seven levels of the Upper World realm

DashaI Disha, Panchai Mahabhuta
from ten directions and elemental spirits

Mahakal, Kala Chakra, Samaya Chakra
the great time, the period of obstacle, the cycle of time

Kula Guru, Mahadeo Guru, Thani Deo
Lineage teacher, mahadeo teacher, local deities

Yeshai Ghara Mandal Ka Rakhwa Deo
The keeper of this house of this sacred circle

Mula Thamama Basne, Charai Sura Basne
the one who resides in the main pillar, the ones who control the four corners of the house

Mero Aanga Sarirama Chadai Lyaeko
The spirits I invoked and incorporated

Kula Deo, Pitri Deo, Banajhankri Deo
lineage deities, lineage spirits, forest-dwelling shamans

Sir Ko Mukut Ko Majur Deo Shikari Deo
dwelling in my crown peacock and hunting spirits

Pheta, Bhoto, Patuka, Ra Jama, Mala Jala, Deo Jhola
turban, shirt, belt, frock, rosaries, spirit bag

Thana-Bana, Diyo-Dirpa, Naga Mala, Dono Kalasa
The sacred altar, lamp flame, serpent rosary, two
    water vases

Vajra Dhungo, Shila Dhunga, Nali Hada
meteoric stone, fossilized ammonite shell, femur bone

Khurpa/i, Khurungi, Dhupa Deepa, Manne Gunne
ritual dagger, curved sickle, incense, respected and
    honorable

Dhyangro, Gajo, Jhyali Jhyamta
drum, drum beater, cymbals

Naga Raja-Rani, Jimi Raja-Rani
serpent king-queen, earth king-queen

Jaha Dekhi Nimtiyako Thiyo Utai Farki Janu Guru
from where I invited you please go back to your
    abode my teacher

Dakta Aunu Hola, Raksha Gara Tshema Gara
when I invite you please come protect and excuse me

Bidha Bhaye Jam Hai Guru
now I take leave from you my teacher

Galti Bhaye Mapha Pau
if I made any mistakes please pardon me

Rakshya Gara Tshema Gara
Please protect me, excuse me

Satya Guru, Maha Guru
Truthful teacher, great teacher

Figure C.1. Bhola and Evelyn in Kathmandu with their ceremonial tika and jamara decorations, Dashain festival, Kathmandu, 2012.

Tamrai Rakshya, Tamrai Bardan, Tamrai Shakti
Your protection, your blessing, your power

Phata Phata Phata
Release, release, release

Bhola

May all our good works outweigh our missteps.

Acknowledgments

I would like to thank my ancestors, my spirit teachers, and my power animals for their eternal love, protection, and support of my life.

I acknowledge the loving blessings I receive from my shamanic colleagues, my wonderful family, my dear friends, and especially my wife, co-conspirator, and "partner in all things," Allie Knowlton. Allie's tremendous support and her ineffable graciousness when I am deeply engrossed in a creative project is a priceless treasure.

My gratitude goes to Mariarosa "Mimi" Genitrini for her loving spirit and her marvelous photography.

Thanks also go to my fabulous agent Stephany Evans for being a relentless, one-woman cheering section. And to Jon Graham of Inner Traditions for publishing this book!

My incredible friendship with Bhola has enriched my life immeasurably. For over a decade, our times together have been filled with stories, wisdom, and, most precious of all, his warm laughter. It has been my great privilege to present Bhola's native practices to the world so that these shamanic traditions will not only be preserved but will also remain vital for many generations to come as they spread beyond Nepal's borders.

(Bai, I hope this Diddi served you well!)

EVELYN

ॐ

This sacred sharing of my ancestors' gifts is to create a concrete, participatory bridge between ancient wisdom and modern understanding. The introductory foundations, presentation of every chapter, illustrations, step-by-step explanation of rituals, and hand-drawn diagrams by Evelyn are some of the first presentations of Nepalese Himalayan Shamanism for the modern shamanic communities.

Mariarosa Genitrini's shamanic vision that embues her photography is heart opening!

To bring oral transmission and rituals in written form while maintaining the core of old wisdom is not an easy task. The use of shamanic terms and the descriptions may not be as authentic as they could be, but we offer this book as the beginning of bringing ancient knowledge in written form. I invite our Nepalese shamanic communities and local shamans to continue deepening and adding to this unfolding of our cultural treasures.

The dense forest of spirits, gods, goddesses, deities, and ancestors of various levels is only a small relfection of the vast ocean of shamanic wisdom. We will continue our projects in writing, and documenting visuals for years to come.

I thank from my heart my ancestors, lineage keepers, all my shamanic teachers in ordinary realities and nonordinary realities, and all the collaborators.

May your blessings and empowerments reach and touch the hearts of all the living and nonliving beings at all levels of creation.

May the readers and practitioners of this path benefit from this small but authentic book of wisdom.

Namaste!

BHOLA

APPENDIX

Celebrating Durga and the Customs of Dashain

Twice a year the nine manifestations of the goddess Durga are especially adored and worshipped. The springtime festival for Durga is called Chaitra Navaratri, and in autumn, the festival is called Shardiya Navaratri, which is also known as Dashain.

Dashain is the biggest festival in Nepal and is celebrated just before the rice harvest after the monsoon season when the weather cools and the skies clear. This is trekking season when the spectacular panoramic views of the Himalayas take your breath away. The cool breezes make for great weather to fly kites, and as Dashain approaches, the shops blare the ancient instrumental music Dashain Dhun, which signals the arrival of the festival. In the villages great long swings known as *pings* are set up, and the young people line up to get a turn to ride high.

Durga is celebrated with great gaiety and devotion throughout the length and breadth of the country. The festival is fifteen days long, starting on Shukla Paksha (a fortnight before the full moon) and ending on Purnima, the full moon. This is the twenty-seventh day in the month of Ashoj in the Nepali calendar. On Western calendars the festival falls in either September or early October.

The Dashain festival has a strong emphasis on family gatherings and the renewal of family ties. As a result, those Nepalese people who live or work around the world return to their homeland to celebrate with their families. Anyone who chooses to travel to Nepal during this auspicious season can expect to have the plane filled with joyful Nepalese families who are looking forward to being with their relatives.

The festival is a blend of ancient animistic festival traditions and Hindu tantric rituals. All businesses and governmental and educational institutions provide five to ten vacation days for Dashain. This allows people to celebrate the festival with their families and friends, which is one of the essences of Dashain. During the fifteen days of festivities, the most significant days are the first, seventh, eighth, ninth, and tenth. The first nine days of Dashain are called Navaratri, *nava* meaning "nine" and *ratri* meaning "night." Some people also refer to Dashain as Navaratri.

Although people share different mythological tales during the celebration, Dashain has always been regarded as a festival of victory over evil.

On the first day, called Ghatasthapana, the Dashain Ghar, or special worship room, is set up: this room is used to worship the Astha-Matrikas (the eight mother goddesses) as well as the Nava Durgas (the nine goddess manifestations of Durga), to whom the festival is dedicated.

The Ghatasthapana rite begins by setting up a diyo (oil lamp), a kalasa (sacred water vessel), and a figurine of Gannyap and worshipping them. Usually it is done in the prayer room.

The head of the household sows barley seeds on a bed of mud in big earthen pots that have had their interior surfaces prepared with a coating of cow dung. In other situations, the seeds are sown in large, flat circular containers made from woven leaves containing mud. In either case, the seeds are sown and watered and a cover is placed over the container. Thus prepared, the festival participants offer prayers and spray the seeds with water for nine days. By the tenth day of Dashain, known as Vijaya Dasami or Durga's Victory Day, the covered containers are filled with brilliant yellow barley sprouts.

These sprouts, which symbolize a good harvest, will be decoratively placed on the heads of family members later on in the festival as a blessing. The sprouts, known as *jamara,* are placed in women's hair knots if they have long hair or above the left ear if they have short hair. Men wear the jamara over their right ear or just above the forehead tucked into a traditional cap or *topi*.

The barley sprouts have an important significance during Dashain as the sprouts represent Yawannkur—the favorite flower of Durga. It is said that she receives energy or power from this plant. Durga is revered as the one who fought against evil to protect humankind. Worshipping her nine most important emanations with jamara symbolizes the people's desire to give back in sacred reciprocity. Nurturing the barley seeds is seen as helping to create more of what nurtures Durga, and in turn, the jamara is said to contain the blessings of Durga. It is a marvelous circle of blessing and an indispensible aspect of the Dashain festival.

The *tika* is also prepared on the tenth day of Dashain. Combining cooked rice with vermilion-colored powdered pigment and milk curd or yogurt creates a sticky and colorful paste. As a blessing, this paste is then applied to the forehead of festival participants by elders or priests. It is an auspicious symbol that bestows good fortune, health, and long life upon those who wear it. Though it might be a bit messy, the tika not only adds color to the spirit of Dashain but is also a means of showing off how many relatives you have who love you and are offering blessings for your well-being. In fact, the messier and larger the tika becomes, the better it is. It is also believed that the goddess Durga herself fills the tika as well as the jamara with her own Shakti or power.

On the tenth day of the festival, people can be seen moving from one place to another to receive blessings from their elders in the form of tika and jamara. Indeed, sporting a red tika on the forehead and yellow jamara on the head is the distinctive look only seen during Dashain. Dashain without tika and jamara is almost unimaginable!

THE MOST SIGNIFICANT DAYS

To help you make sense of this special festival season, what follows is a guide to the most significant days of Dashain. These are the first, seventh, eighth, and ninth days of the festival.

Day 1: Ghatasthapana

Ghatasthapana marks the beginning of the festival (*ghata* means "pot" and *sthapana* means "establishing"). The barley seeds are sown while prayers are offered. The auspicious time to perform the ritual is determined by astrologers. The room where the kalasa is established is called Dashain Ghar, or Dashain Home.

From this day, people are busy visiting all the temples of Durga, especially in the morning hours. People living away from home return with gifts for their families. Having luxurious feasts and family gatherings, flying kites, and playing cards are the customary ways to celebrate Dashain.

Day 7: Fulpati

During Fulpati, which literally means "flowers, leaves, and plants," the royal family's kalasa, filled with holy water, banana stalks, jamara, and sugarcane tied with red cloth, is carried by Brahmans from Gorkha (the original home of the Shah dynasty) to Tudikhel on a decorated palanquin under a gold-tipped and embroidered umbrella. Hundreds of government officials gather together in national dress to witness the event. There is a splendid parade by the Nepalese army followed by a celebratory firing of weapons lasting for ten to fifteen minutes. After the event, the Fulpati is taken to Basantapur Hanuman Dhoka (also called Dashain Ghar), the ancient seat of Nepal's kings. In the past jamara was brought to the royal family, but since the abolishment of the monarchy in 2008 the offering of Fulpati is taken to the residence of the prime minister.

Day 8: Maha Asthami

On this day, the temples of the goddess Durga are drenched with the blood of sacrificed buffalo, goats, ducks, and pigeons. The sacrifices are performed throughout the country to appease the fierce aspect of Durga. This day is called Kal Ratri (Black Night). At midnight a total of fifty-four buffalo and fifty-four goats are sacrificed in the Dashain Ghar. After the blood has been offered to Durga, the meat is taken home, cooked, offered to the household deities, and distributed among the family members as *prasad* (food blessed by the Divine).

Day 9: *Maha Nawami*

The ninth day of Dashain, Maha Nawami, is also the last day of Navaratri. On this day, official military sacrifices are held in the *kot* (courtyard) of Hanuman Dhoka. Mostly black buffalo are slaughtered to honor and seek blessing from Durga. The Taleju Temple at Hanuman Dhoka is opened for the public only once a year on this day. The temple is therefore crowded with thousands of people coming to pay their respect to the goddess. Even foreigners are allowed to witness this celebration.

On this day, Vishwa Karma, the god of creativity, is also worshipped with the belief that all things responsible for our living should be kept happy. So, all factories, vehicles, machinery, and other tools are honored. All vehicles are washed and lavishly decorated with flowers and auspicious signs written in tika paste on this day. This is believed to hinder accidents throughout the year.

Day 10: *Vijaya Dashami*

On the day of Vijaya Dashami, along with the tika and jamara, the elders also give *dakshina,* a small amount of money, to children, making this one of the exciting parts of Dashain for youngsters. Like all good holidays, the applying of tika and jamara is accompanied by a lavish feast. This gaiety continues to be observed for five days till Purnima, the full moon.

The final, fifteenth day of the festival is Kojagrata Purnima ("who is awake"), which falls on the full moon day. It's the day for rest and revitalization from the hectic activities of the festival. Lakshmi, the Hindu goddess of wealth, is worshipped on this day. It is believed that the goddess Lakshmi descends to Earth and showers wealth and prosperity to everyone who is awake throughout the night. To keep from falling asleep, people busy themselves by playing cards.

Glossary

agni baan—(Nepali) A lightning bolt; literally, fire arrow.

agni deo—(Nepali) Fire spirits and also the umbilicus area where the "fire in our belly" is housed. This is the fire of creativity, passion, courage, rebirth, and renewal.

aina—(Nepali) A bronze, copper, or silver mirror used to reflect away negativity, to function as a portal for deities to enter the human realm, and for "seeing" in a divinatory manner. The Tibetan word is *melong*.

akshyaata—(Nepali) Uncooked rice kernels that are used as offerings.

amliso—(Nepali) The shaman's broom. The flowering stems of the *Thysanalaena agrestis* plant are not only used to clean houses but also to cleanse the spiritual body of an ailing person.

amrita—(Nepali) The elixir or water of immortality from the Sanskrit word *amrit*.

Ananta Sesha—(Sanskrit) The primordial, infinite snake spirit that holds all the other primordial nagas in his body. Rising from the cosmic sea, he rests on a great conch shell and forms part of the foundation on which Mother Earth rests and gives birth to creation.

animism—(English from Latin *anima*, "breath, spirit, life") A belief that all things—animals, plants, rocks, rivers, weather systems, buildings, other artifacts, and even spoken words—are considered to be animate, alive, and inspirited.

apse ap—(Nepali) The spontaneous songs that arise when the dhami/jhankri becomes inspirited by her or his spirits or during a shamanic journey.

Ardhanarishwara—(Sanskrit) A half-male and half-female figure representing the divine union of masculine and feminine energies in Sanatana-Dharma Hinduism and Tantra.

asan—(Nepali) A cushion, low chair, or folded blanket for sitting.

aspara—(Sanskrit) Female spirits of the clouds and waters. Their consorts are the male *gandarva* nature spirits who are a hybrid of human and either bird or horse features.

asta hati—(Hindi) The eight elephants on whom Bhumi Devi rests in the Divine Pillar that holds up the world.

asur—(Sanskrit) Water-born demons who can cause water-related illnesses and are related to and/or may be aspects of the more beneficent *danava*.

baag deo—(Nepali) The tiger spirit.

baar—(Nepali) Banyan tree (*Ficus benghalensis*).

Banaskhandi—(Nepali) A name used in the Nepali hills for Banjhankri.

Banbibi—(Bengali) The name for Bandevi in Muslim areas of eastern Nepal and Bengal.

bandar deo—(Nepali) The monkey spirit.

Bandevi—(Nepali) The forest goddess.

Banjhankri—(Nepali) The primordial forest shaman who kidnaps potential shamanic initiates. He is typically described as a golden, fur-covered dwarf with a conical hairstyle and backward-facing feet but has other forms as well.

Banjhankrini—(Nepali) The female consort of Banjhankri who is described as enormous, dark-furred, and very fierce. She and Banjhankri work together to train shamanic initiates.

bans—(Nepali) Plants of the bamboo or Bambusoideae subfamily.

Basalt Ritu—(Nepali) The spring season.

baya kuma—(Nepali) The left shoulder.

bayu—(Nepali) Spirits of the air.

bhaar—(Nepali) A small bamboo shelter to protect sacred objects.

bhalayo—(Nepali) The marking-nut tree (*Semecarpus anacardium*), used to make the *khurpa* (ritual dagger) or *murro* (drum handle). The *bhalayo* can cause strong allergic reactions in people, and it is said to cause negative spirits to flee.

bhed jhiknu—(Nepali) The shamanic ritual of extraction or removing harmful energies from a person's body.

Bhimsen Deo—(Nepali) Mother Earth's body.

bhoto—(Nepali) The waist-length, white cotton shirt of the dhami/jhankri.

bhume—(Sanskrit) Masculine earth spirits.

Bhumi Devi—(Sanskrit) Mother Earth. This name in particular refers to the physical nature and power of Earth—the soil, stones, and fertile surface we depend upon for life. She is abundance in all its nurturing forms.

bir masan—(Nepali) The spirits of the wandering dead, those who have died unnatural deaths, and malevolent spirits of the graveyard—all of whom may cause illness or calamity. Ancestors who have been forgotten or are not venerated can also become *bir masan*.

Bön—(Tibetan) A Tibetan religion that self-identifies as being distinct from Tibetan Buddhism, although it shares the same overall teachings and terminology. Like Tibetan Buddhism, it has preserved echoes of earlier shamanic concepts.

Brahmachaarini—(Sanskrit) *See* Durga.

Brihaspati—(Sanskrit) Name of the planet Jupiter; also known as Guru Brihaspati.

briksha—(Nepali) Spirits of the trees.

Buddha—(Sanskrit) The founder of the Buddhist religion; also a name for the planet Mercury.

chammar—(Nepali) A yak's tail. The tail is removed from the animal, washed, dried, and used like a whisk broom over a patient to remove negative influences and spiritual intrusions.

Chandra—(Sanskrit) The moon.

Chandraghantaa—(Sanskrit) *See* Durga.

Chandi—(Sanskrit) A ferocious form of the Mother Goddess that slays any evildoer without mercy. She is also able to annihilate obstacles on the path. She can either bring good fortune or disaster if not properly appeased.

chatri (or chata)—(Nepali) A spiritual umbrella or yarn cross. It is used to trap malignant spirits or to hold healing energy and protection.

chattan—(Nepali) Spirits of the cliffs.

chil deo—(Nepali) The eagle spirit.

chirs—(Nepali) Strips of colored cotton cloth used for offerings.

chopshee—(Nepali) Counters for counting rounds on the mala.

chorten—(Tibetan) *See* stupa.

chupshed—(Tibetan) *See* chopsee.

damaru—(Tibetan) A small, two-sided hand drum made of wood with goatskin drumheads or of two human craniums and human skin.

danava—(Sanskrit) Wild, water-born spirits that may be made calm and beneficient through offerings. They are related to *asur* demons who can cause water-related illnesses.

danda ra khola ko rakhwa—(Nepali) Spirit keepers of the mountains and rivers.

dangri—(Hindi from Sanskrit) The shaman's helper; also called *saha-yogi*. A colleague who helps the shaman accomplish her or his work.

daya kuma—(Nepali) The right shoulder.

deurali—(Nepali) The spirits who protect the valleys and mountain passes.

deuta-aunu—(Nepali) Being called to the path of the shaman.

devata—(Nepali) A deity, god.

dhanus *and* **kand**—(Nepali) A bow and arrow. They are the weapon of and symbol for some wrathful deities and spirits and are used as a spiritual antidote for the effects of food poisoning, for repelling spiritual attacks, and for supporting strongly focused concentration.

Dharti Mata—(Sanskrit) Mother Earth. This name in particular refers to the endlessly generative energy of nature, which replenishes and continually gives birth to all aspects and beings in the natural world.

dhatu—(Nepali) The spirits of metal.

dhupauro—(Nepali) An incense burner made of clay or metal for burning sacred plants or incense, which are transformed into a divine purifying smoke.

dhyangro—(Nepali) The most common form of a Nepalese shaman's drum. It has two faces and a handle in the shape of a khurpa or phurba (ritual dagger).

diyo—(Nepali) A bowl-shaped oil lamp.

Diyo-Batti Dinne—(Nepali) Initiation ceremony; literally, "to grant the oil lamp." A ceremony for recognizing and confirming a new shaman.

dorje—(Tibetan) *See* vajra.

DorjePhurba—(Tibetan) A wrathful deity who embodies the actions and powers of the khurpa (dagger). *See also* VajraKilaya.

Dude Jhankri—(Nepali) A one-handed manifestation of Banjhankri who teaches initiates how to drum or beat a brass plate with one hand and how to use medicinal plants and boughs and work with spirits for healing.

dumsiko kanda—(Nepali) Quills from the Himalayan porcupine (*Hystrix brachyuran*).

Durga—(Sanskrit) One form of Mahadevi, the supreme, invincible force that creates, shapes, and destroys the universe, and Shakti, the primordial, cosmic, creative energy from which all creation, preservation, and annihilation of form arises. She has endless forms but there are nine primary aspects: Shailputri, Brahmachaarini, Chandraghantaa, Kushmaandaa, Skandmaataa, Kaatyaayani, Kaalaraatri, Mahagauri, and Siddhidaatri.

dwarapala—(Sanskrit) Guardians of entrances, doors, and portals.

Dyēus Ph2tēr—(Proto-Indo-European) Original name for Dyauṣpitṛ, or Father Sky, in the Hindu Rig-Veda.

Ekajati—(Sanskrit) An emanation of Ugratara, a wrathful deity whose ascribed powers are removing the fear of enemies, spreading joy, and removing personal hindrances on the path to enlightenment. She is depicted with one eye, one sharp tooth, one breast, and one long braid, signifying her single-minded determination on the path.

feta—(Nepali) A floor-length headband fashioned from white and red cotton cloth.

gaanj—(Nepali) In western Nepal, an effigy created from a spirit pole topped with yak tails for "hair."

Gaidu—(Nepali) The spirit protector of animals and livestock who works with Shiva or Mahadeva.

gandarva—(Sanskrit) Male nature spirits who are a hybrid of human and either bird or horse features. They are consorts of the *aspara,* female spirits of the clouds and waters.

gajo—(Nepali) A curved drumstick made from the bent and dried stem of a cane plant. It is used with the *dhyangro* drum.

Gannyap—(Nepali) The elephant-headed Hindu god Ganesha; also known as Ganapati and Vinayaka.

Garuda—(Sanskrit) A protective entity represented in shamanic, Hindu, Buddhist, and Bön traditions. It is a mythical, semidivine man-bird hybrid creature that is the enemy of the serpent spirits or nagas.

ghanti—(Nepali) Metal bells fastened to a dhami/jhankri's chain bandolier.

ghuda—(Nepali) The knee region.

ghunring—(Nepali) A stiff grass (*Neyrandia madagascariensis*) in the bamboo family.

ghunring pukis—(Nepali) Special sticks used on a shaman's altar to represent aspects of the cosmos and their interconnections. Pukis are made from the stems of the ghunring plant. The stems are shaved, producing fuzzy fluffs along the stem. These pukis are then placed upright in piles of rice and connected to each other by unshaven stems of ghunring and cotton thread.

Gosain—(Sanskrit) Another name for Shiva.

grama deuta—(Nepali) Spirits or deities who protect a village.

gufa—(Nepali) A cave.

gundri—(Nepali) A straw mat.

Hariyali ki dhani—(Nepali) Mistress of the green.

hata-pakhura—(Nepali) The hands and arms.

Indra—(Sanskrit) Hindu god of heaven, the weather, lightning, thunder, storms, rain, and river flows. He has similar powers to other Indo-European deities such as Zeus, Jupiter, Perun, Hadad, Thor, and Odinn/Wotan.

ishta deuta—(Nepali) Spirits or deities who protect an individual.

jal—(Nepali) Spirit of the water.

jala basne—(Nepali) Water spirit beings.

jama—(Nepali) The white cotton skirt of the dhami/jhankri worn with the *bhoto*.

janawar ko singh *and* **dara**—(Nepali) Animal horns and teeth used as shamanic talismans or power objects.

jhankri—(Nepali) Shaman.

jhankri kaath—(Nepali) The *Actinodaphne angustifolia* tree. It is used to make the *murro* or handle of the *dhyangro* drum.

jhyamta—(Nepali) A set of cymbals that may be used to accompany the drum.

jokhanna—(Nepali) The ritual of divination used by dhami/jhankris for diagnosing a patient.

jyoti netra—(Nepali) This term refers to both the eyes and to the ability to penetrate the veil of reality.

Kaalaraatri—(Sanskrit) *See* Durga.

Kaal Bhairung—(Nepali) The black, wrathful form of Shiva; also known as Kal Bhairava. This aspect of Shiva is called upon by shamans to defeat witchcraft and sorcery or to return negative energies back to the one who sent them.

Kaatyaayani—(Sanskrit) *See* Durga.

Kachuwa—(Hindi) The tortoise of the Divine Pillar on whom the elephants upholding the goddess Bhumi Devi stand.

kalasa—(Nepali) The sacred water pitcher that is believed to hold the elixir of immortality (*amrita*).

Kalpa Vriksha—(Nepali) The world tree or tree of immortality that unites the realms of existence. In Nepalese tradition, roots of this tree face upward so that it is literally planted in the upper realms.

kamalgatta—(Nepali) Indian or sacred lotus (*Nelumbo nucifera*).

kangling—(Tibetan) A trumpet fashioned from a human femur used in Tibetan Buddhism. It is used in outdoor Chöd rituals when the practitioner, motivated by compassion, plays the *kangling* as a gesture of fearlessness to summon hungry spirits and demons so that she or he may satisfy their hunger and thereby relieve their sufferings. It is also played as a way to cut through the ego.

katu—(Nepali) Evergreen broad-leaf tree (*Castanopsis hystrix*) whose leaves are used for offerings and for clearing negative energies.

kaulo—(Nepali) Evergreen broad-leaf tree (*Machilus odoratissima*) used to make the *khurpa* (ritual dagger).

kera—(Nepali) Banana tree or the fruits (banana or plantain) of these trees (Musaceae family).

keshar—(Nepali) The yellow powdered pigment used for making *rekhis* or mandalas for ceremonies and for ceremonial markings on the forehead.

Ketu—(Sanskrit) The lunar south node in Vedic astrology and a term for infrared light.

khadko/khadga—(Nepali) A sharp ritual knife; also an obstacle on the path.

khaja—(Nepali) Celebratory snacks or treats served after a ritual.

khukuri—(Nepali) The inward-curving short sword or knife of the Gurkha warrior.

khurpa—(Nepali) A triangular ritual dagger; also called *kila, phurba,* *purba, phurbu.* It is used by shamans, lamas, and Buddhist and Bön practitioners.

khurungi—(Nepali) A small, sharp hand sickle used for harvesting plants, typically wielded by female deities.

kila (kilaya)—(Sanskrit) *See* khurpa.

koirala—(Nepali) Flowering deciduous tree (*Bauhinia variegata*). Its wood is used for the hoop-shaped frame of the *dhyangro* drum.

Kshetrapal—(Sanskrit) A deity that protects farmland and is the guardian of a specific place or direction; also known as Kshetrapala.

kul deuta—(Nepali) Ancestral, lineage deities.

kul devata—(Sanskrit) Ancestral, lineage deities.

kumari—(Nepali) Virgin nature goddesses.

Kushmaandaa—(Sanskrit) *See* Durga.

Lakshmi—(Sanskrit) Hindu goddess of wealth, riches, beauty, happiness, loveliness, grace, charm, and splendor.

Langade Jhankri—(Nepali) A manifestation of Banjhankri who is fast, powerful, and also lame. A shaman-to-be possessed by his or her healing spirit would walk like a crippled person.

Lato Jhankri—(Nepali) A manifestation of Banjhankri who doesn't speak but instead uses gestures and signals to communicate.

lokur chuni—(Tibetan) A special form of the *aina* or *melong* (shamanic mirror) that has auspicious symbols or animals on its reverse side.

Mahadeva—(Sanskrit) The god Shiva as the lord of the gods.

Mahagauri—(Sanskrit) *See* Durga.

Makara—(Sanskrit) A sea creature in the Hindu tradition. It is generally depicted as a terrestrial animal in the front (stag, deer, crocodile, or elephant) and an aquatic animal in the hind part, usually having a fish or seal tail—though sometimes a peacock or even a floral tail is depicted. Tradition identifies Makara with water, the source of all existence and fertility.

mala—(Sanskrit) A string of beads used for prayer or to count repetitions of sacred chants or mantras.

Mangal—(Sanskrit) The planet Mars.

Marut—(Sanskrit) The deity of clouds and weather.

Masto God—(Nepali) Primary deity of the Khas people of western Nepal who is an analog to Shiva.

manushya lok—(Nepali) The earthly realm of human existence.

mayur—(Nepali) Peacock.

megha—(Nepali) Spirits of the clouds.

melong—(Tibetan) *See* aina.

meru danda—(Nepali) The spine or vertebral column.

mukh—(Nepali) The mouth.

murro—(Nepali) The *khurpa*-shaped handle of the shaman's *dhyangro* drum.

mutu-chati—(Nepali) The region of the heart, the heart chakra.

nadi—(Nepali) River or spirit of the river.

nag/naag deo—(Nepali) The snake spirit.

naga—(Sanskrit) A snake or divine snake spirit.

nāga do□a—(Sanskrit) Negative effects or diseases caused by the nagas.

nalihar—(Nepali) A human forearm bone (ulna) that is used as a trumpet in a similar fashion as the Tibetan femur trumpet *kangling*.

nali haard—(Nepali) A femur bone from the left leg of a human being or an animal used to gather and subdue the disease-causing, wandering spirits of humans and animals.

nanglo—(Nepali) A winnowing basket made from bamboo that may be used as a sacred space as one would use a *thaal* (ceremonial plate).

nava/aakash udne—(Nepali) Sky-flying spirit beings.

pagari—(Nepali) The dhami/jhankri headdress worn over the *feta*. It is adorned with upright peacock feathers and porcupine quills.

pala-byu—(Nepali) An unspecified flower, leaf, or vegetal offering. Any plant that happens to be in bloom or thriving in the local area can be used as an offering.

palla—(Nepali) A simple earthenware oil lamp used for an offering or for use outdoors.

panas batti—(Nepali) Tall, pillar-like oil lamps.

pancha rangi—(Nepali) A lightweight cord of five-color rainbow threads used in ceremonies.

pani—(Nepali) Water or waters; also can be used to designate a watershed.

para *or* **paru janu**—(Nepali) Shamanic trance state.

parvata—(Nepali) Mountain.

patuka—(Nepali) The wide, red cotton cummerbund wound around the dhami/jhankri's waist where the bhoto shirt and jama skirt meet.

phurba—(Tibetan) Also called *purba, phurbu*. See khurpa.

pipal—(Nepali) The bodhi tree (*Ficus religiosa*).

Plth₂wih₂—(Proto-Indo-European) Original name for Pṛthvī Mātā, meaning "plentiful mother," in the Hindu Rig-Veda (Plth₂wih₂ may have also been refered to as Dg'hom).

pokhari—(Nepali) Lake or pond; also called *taal*.

prasada—(Sanskrit) An offering to a deity, saint, or master/sage; literally "a gracious gift." The offering, typically an edible food, is then distributed to the deity's or saint's followers or others as a blessing.

prakriti—(Sanskrit) Female energy; the counterpart to *purusha,* which is male energy.

puja—(Sanskrit) A ritual form of Hindu worship.

purusha—(Sanskrit) Male energy; the counterpart to *prakriti,* which is female energy.

radi—(Nepali) A sheep-wool blanket or rug used for sitting or sleeping.

Rahu—(Sanskrit) The lunar north node in Vedic astrology and a term for ultraviolet light.

rekhi—(Nepali) A mandala or spiritual diagram drawn for shamanic ritual use.

rittha—(Nepali) The soap nut tree (*Sapindus mukorossi*).

Ritthe Jhankri—(Nepali) A manifestation of Banjhankri who is dark like the *rittha* (soap nut) beads of the shaman's cleansing mala. He whistles, flutters his eyelids, and twitches with the electric effects of spiritual power. The shaman initiated by this aspect of Banjhankri would behave in a similar manner when possessed by her or his healing spirits.

rudraksha—Large, broad-leaved evergreen tree (*Elaeocarpus sphaericus*). The hard, wrinkled seeds produced by several species of this tree are strung for use in malas and used singly as blessing tokens, talismans, or offerings. The name is derived from two Sanskrit words: *rudra* and *aksha*. Together, these refer to "Shiva's tears," which were shed during a deep meditation.

saal—(Nepali) The leaves of this tree (*Shorea robusta*) are used to make plates and offering vessels.

sahayogi—(Hindi) The shaman's helper; also called *dangri*.

samundra—(Nepali) The great cosmic ocean.

sankha—(Sanskrit) Conch shell and the conch shell trumpet.

Sansari Mai—(Nepali) Mistress of the universe.

sapta dhanya—(Nepali) A mixture of seven grains; also called *sata byu*. They are used in offering, healing, and transference rituals.

Sarir Jagaunu Deuta Chadanu—(Nepali) The shaman's ceremony for awakening the body and embodying the spirit.

Saraswati—(Sanskrit) Hindu goddess of learning and wisdom; literally, "one who leads to the essence of self-knowledge."

sarpa—(Nepali) A snake or divine snake spirit; also called *naga*.

sarpa-bādhaka—(Sanskrit) Calamitous obstacles or diseases caused by the *nagas*.

sata byu—(Nepali) A mixture of seven grains; also called *sapta dhanya*. They are used in offering, healing, and transference rituals.

Shailputri—(Sanskrit) *See* Durga.

Shakti—(Sanskrit) Spiritual power or energy. Also the name of the goddess representing the ultimate spiritual power.

shaligram *or* **shila**—(Sanskrit) A black ammonite fossil stone typically found in the Kali Gandaki or Narayani River of Nepal.

shang—(Nepali) A flat handbell played with the left hand.

Shani—(Sanskrit) The planet Saturn.

shila dhunga—(Nepali) Clear quartz crystal.

Shiva—(Sanskrit) The primary god of the Nepali shamans. Shiva is one of a trio of male deities who together represent masculine manifestations of the Great Goddess's actions of creation, preservation, and destruction. They are the concrete, active representations of the Great Goddess's formless power. The other two gods are Brahma and Vishnu.

Shukra—(Sanskrit) The planet Venus.

siddhi—(Sanskrit) An extraordinary or supernatural ability or power; also, a state of complete understanding, perfection, or enlightenment.

Siddhidaatri—(Sanskrit) *See* Durga.

Siir Uthaune—(Nepali) A ceremony for raising the spiritual energy of a person using shamanic implements.

sikhari—(Nepali) Hunting spirits of the forest.

sime—(Nepali) Swamp-dwelling spirits who are associated with the *nagas*.

singha deo—(Nepali) The lion spirit.

sira—(Nepali) The head.

Skandmaataa—(Sanskrit) *See* Durga.

stupa—(Sanskrit) A reliquary for a saint's bones or relics or a Buddhist shrine.

sukul—(Nepali) A straw mat.

sukunda—(Nepali) An oil lamp with a pan-shaped area for the lit wick and a reservoir for additional oil. These are usually decorated with images of deities.

Suna Jhankri—(Nepali) A golden-haired manifestation of Banjhankri who appears to students with a jolly personality and a contented spirit or who can move in and out of the spiritual realms easily and rapidly.

sumicha—(Nepali) A ritual spoon used to refill the oil pan that holds the lit wick on a sukunda oil lamp.

supari—(Nepali) Betel nut, which is the seed of the areca palm tree (*Areaca catechu*).

Surya—(Sanskrit) The sun.

taal—(Nepali) A lake or pond; also called *pokhari*.

tapari—(Nepali) Offering vessels made from the leaves of the saal tree (*Shorea robusta*).

teshro netra—(Nepali) The center of the brow, the region of the third eye.

thaal—(Nepali) A ceremonial plate made of hand-beaten copper with raised, auspicious decorations. It is used to hold rice and for keeping all of a shaman's sacred objects; it serves as the central platform of a dhami/jhankri's altar.

thaan—(Nepali) The dhami/jhankri's altar.

thala basne—(Nepali) Spirit beings of the land.

titepati—(Nepali) Mugwort (*Artemisia vulgaris*); used as an offering, for cleansing the environment, as incense, and as a medicinal plant.

totola ko phul—(Nepali) A flowering plant (*Oroxylum indicum*); literally "most sacred and purest flower." The seeds of this plant and their diaphanous coverings are called soul flowers by dhami/jhankris.

tri-khandi—(Nepali) Having the tripartite power of spiritual or divine, human, and animal aspects in one being. It is also a designation for one who lives in all three realms of existence: our ordinary or base physicality, our divine (enlightened/inspired) physicality, and our noncorporeal state; also the three shamanic realms of the Lower, Middle, and Upper Worlds.

trishula—(Sanskrit) The trident of Shiva, which symbolizes the three moments of birth, death, and rebirth; the three states of creation, preservation, and destruction; and the experience of illumination, as well as the fire elemental.

tulsi—(Sanskrit) Holy basil plant (*Ocimum sanctum*).

Ugratara—(Odia) A wrathful form of the Great Goddess. She is black and red and is honored by Nepalese dhami/jhankris as a goddess of fertility, unity, and wisdom and as the one who bestows healing powers to shamans.

upatyaka—(Nepali) Valley.

vahana—(Sanskrit) A being that functions as deity's vehicle.

vajra—(Sanskrit) A ritual weapon that symbolizes both the properties of a diamond (indestructibility) and a thunderbolt (irresistible force); the word means both "thunderbolt" and "diamond." The vajra represents the undeniable and eternal spiritual power available for the shaman.

vajra dhunga—(Sanskrit-Nepali) An iron meteorite considered to be a thunder or lightning stone.

VajraKilaya—(Sanskrit) A wrathful deity who embodies the action of the *khurpa* (ritual dagger); also called DorjePhurba.

vishva-vajra—(Sanskrit) An object that is formed from two *vajra* crossed at right angles to each other. It represents the stable foundation of Mother Earth and is a protective symbol that cannot be destroyed but itself can destroy all evil.

yaksha—(Sanskrit) A caretaker spirit of natural treasures hidden in the earth or in tree roots.

yantra—(Sanskrit) A mystical diagram that functions as a mechanism producing a specific beneficial vibration and having effects that are equivalent to a spoken mantra and also augmentations of their effectiveness when meditated upon. A yantra functions on the idea that every shape emits a specific frequency and energy pattern.

Index

Numbers in *italics* preceded by *pl.* indicate color insert plate numbers.

abundance-increasing offering, 62, *pl. 8*
aina
  on altar, 94, 110–11, 114
  defined, 54
  use of, 94
  wearing of, 93–94
air element, 132–33
akshyaata, 54
altar
  aina, 94, 110–11, 114
  approach to, 38
  basic structure of, 109–11
  Bhola method for building and
    awakening, 111–14
  Bhola preparation photo, 108
  binding and protecting, 114–15
  ceremony for awakening and
    consecrating, 116–18
  characteristics of, 54
  copper plate or winnowing basket, 110
  copper vase, 110
  diyo, 110
  elements on, 111
  functioning as center of the cosmos, 38
  incense burner, 110
  journey to clear and empower, 94–96
  photo of, 53, *pl. 5*

  pivot point, 107
  plants and seeds used on, 64–66
  porcupine quills, 110
  rice kernels offering, 40
  Shiva, 105, *pl. 9*
  sitting orientation, 109
  space, 109
  trishulas, 105, 112
  water pitchers, 111, 113
amliso, 54
animal spirits, 10
animist tradition, 6
Asidanga Bhairung, 204
atma, 47

baar, 64
balance, Earth, 150–52
Banjhankri
  Bhola and, 20–23
  in calling to the path, 17–20
  defined, 17
  description, 17–18
  Dude Jhankri, 20
  image on dhyangro drum, 18, *pl. 1*
  journey to meet, 25–27
  kidnapping of shaman-to-be, 19
  Langade Jhankri, 20

Lato Jhankri, 20
malignant spirits masquerading as, 28
Ritthe Jhankri, 20
spirit of, honoring, 25
Suna Jhankri, 19–20
taken by, 20–24
wife/consort, 18–19
Banjhankrini
Bhola and, 23
description of, 18–19
as face of power, 19
journey to meet, 25–27
meeting of, 24
painting, 18, *pl. 2*
spirit of, honoring, 25–27
bans, 64
Bheeshana Bhairung, 204
Bhola
chant-song welcoming spirit
participation, 124–29
creation story with vajra told by,
62–63
Diyo-Batti Dinne ceremony, 29–32
drumming photo, 131, *pl. 11*
in early use of the khurpa, 73
father, 33, *pl. 3*
Gannyap and, 194–96
Garuda and, 234–35
grandfather, 31–32
Guru Brihaspati story, 278–79
on how the Earth is balanced, 150–52
journey to meet, 187–89
on masculine deities' energies, 193–94
method for building and awakening
the altar, 111–14
on Mother Kaatyaayani, 176–77
on Mother Kushmaandaa, 174–75
on Mother Mahagauri, 178
on Mother Siddhidaatri, 179–80
on nagas, 220–23

on Parvati, 170–71, 172–73
photo of altar preparation, 108
playing dhyangro, 89
prayer beads, 99
reception of tools, 67–69
ritual attire, 119–21
on sacred songs, 145–46
shaman's body as sacred container
and, 41–42
taken by Banjhankri, 20–23
testing by shaman elders, 28
Bhumi Devi
defined, 129
in drumming to the elements, 129–34
giving birth, 188, *pl. 12*
mantra, 186–87
as peaceful form of Mother Goddess,
186
bird forms, 76
blade (legs), 74, 76–77
blessing ritual, 39–40
blood, calling of, 16–17

calling to the path, 16–17
cave, 24
center of the cosmos, 38, *pl. 4*
ceremonial actions, 5
chammar, 54, 55
Chanda Bhairung, 204
chanting, 98. *See also* mantras
chatri yarn cross, 55–56, *pl. 6*
Chokhyaunu/Suddha Garnu
ceremony, 264
concern about appearances, 252
creating a renewal ceremony, 142–44
creation story, 63

Dashain festival
characteristics of, 302–3
defined, 301

emphasis, 301–2
most significant days, 303–5
dedication ceremony
experience of, 42
performing, 43–44
personal, journey to experience, 42–45
shaman's body as sacred container, 41–42
dhami/jhankri. *See also* shamans
altar, 37–38, 107–18
in balancing spiritual aspects, 6–7
blessing ritual, 39
bodily organs and, 42
body as sacred container, 41–42
defined, 3
deities and, 6
ecstatic dance, 42
mala use, 99
reinforcement of connection through ritual, 37
songs, 112
soul transition and, 47
use of songs, 146
dhami/jhankri costume
Bhola, 119–21
different versions of, 122
feta, 121
journey to receive a vision of ceremonial attire and, 123
overview, 119
pagari, 121
patuka, 121
use of, 122–23
dhanus, 56
dhupauro, 56
dhyangro
charms, beads stones for enlivening, 90
defined, 56, 88
drumheads, 90
handle, 56, 88–90
holding, to receive spiritual energy, 57, *pl. 7*
illustrated, 88
journey to clear and empower, 90
photo of Bhola playing, 89
playing position, 90
Divine Pillar
aspects of, 152
balancing, 153–65
illustrated, 151
Mansaune ceremony and, 153, 158–65
understanding of ourselves and, 153
diyo, 56–58, 110
Diyo-Batti Dinne ceremony
Bhola's, 29–32
defined, 28–29
pukis, 29–30
Dorje Phurba, 73–77
dreams/visions, in shamanic calling, 17
drumming, to honor the elements, 129–34, *pl. 11*
Dude Jhankri, 20
dumsiko kanda, 58
Durga
aspects of, 168–69
celebrating, 301–5
illustrated, 168
journey to meet aspects of, 181–83
mantra, 180–81
Mother Brahmchaarini, 171–73
Mother Chandraghantaa, 173–74
Mother Kaalaraatri, 177–78
Mother Kaatyaayani, 176–77
Mother Kushmaandaa, 174–75
Mother Mahagauri, 178–79
Mother Shailputri, 169–71
Mother Siddhidaatri, 179–80
Skandamaata, 175–76
worship of, 167–68

earth element, 129–30
eight fetters
  concern about appearances, 252
  defined, 250
  fear, 251
  hate, 251
  pride of birth, 251–52
  pride of family, 252
  reflecting upon, 250
  secrecy, 252
  shame, 252–53
  suspicion, 252
ether element, 133–34

fear, 251
feminine deities
  Bhumi Devi, 129–34, 186–89
  goddess Durga, 167–83
  Great Mother Goddess, 166–67
  Kali, 183–85
  Lakshmi, 189
  peaceful forms of the goddess, 186–90
  Saraswati, 189–90
  Taras, 190–91
femur bone, 112–13
fire ash, 113
fire element, 130–32
flour dough clay ransom effigy, 268,
  pl. 16
flour dough clay recipe, 159

gajo, 57, 58
Gannyap
  Bhola relationship with, 195–96
  characteristics of, 75–76, 194
  illustrated, 196
  journey to meet, 199–200
  mantra, 197–99
  origin story, 194–95
  statue photo, 198, *pl. 13*

Garuda
  amulet, 234
  Bhola work with, 234–35
  defined, 77, 282
  journey to meet, 236–38
  mantra, 235–36
  nagas and, 232–34
  photo of, 233
  as revealer of secrets, 234
ghunring, 64
giving voice to your shamanic practice,
  147–48
glossary, 306–18
grahas
  chart of, 284–85
  defined, 277
  Graha Sarne ceremony, 286–88
  Jupiter (Guru Brihaspati), 278–79,
    281, 285
  Ketu (south node), 284, 285
  Mars (Mangal), 280, 285
  Mercury (Budh), 280–81, 285
  moon (Chandra), 280, 284
  offering mantras to, 286
  Rahu (north node), 283–84, 285
  Saturn (Shani), 282–83, 285
  sun (Surya), 279–80, 284
  Venus (Shukra), 281–82, 285
Graha Sarne ceremony
  beginning of healing, 287–88
  journey explorations, 294
  mandala, 286, 288
  materials for, 290–91
  performing the ceremony, 291–94
  places each graha holds, 288
  preliminary diagnostic journey, 287
  preparation, 289–91
  process questions, 294
  rekhi or mandala coloring, 292
  sick person in, 288, 289

grama deuta, 244
Great Mother Goddess, 166–67, 183,
    186, 191
Green Tara, 190
guardian, 75

handle (middle), 74, 76
hangsa, 47
Hanuman
    defined, 214
    journey to meet, 216–18
    mantra, 216
    mask-wearing devotee, 215, *pl. 14*
    representation, 215–16
harmony, 124
hate, 251
healing
    disharmonious planetary effects,
        287–94
    khurpa in, 71–73
    murro for, 89–90
    nagas in, 219–20
    shamans and, 4–5
    through ceremony, 254–63
Holi celebrations, 140–42
honoring the elements
    air element, 132–33
    with drumming and dance,
        135–38
    drumming in, 129–34
    earth element, 129–30
    ether element, 133–34
    fire element, 130–32
    practice, 134–39
    water element, 130
horse's head, 75
human soul
    beliefs among other cultures,
        46–47
    four aspects of, 43–44

journey to experience, 47–49
    transition, 47
human teachers, 33–34

illness, in calling to the path, 17
ishta deuta, 244

janawar ko singh and dara, 58
jhola, 58
jhyamta, 58
journeys. *See also specific journeys*
    basics for beginners, 8–13
    as bridge function, 8
    information and guidance during,
        10
    with repetitive rhythms, 10
    for songs, 147–48
journey state, 8
journey to clear and empower your
    mala, 101–2
journey to meet a power animal, 10–13
journey to meet a shamanic ancestor to
    ask for empowerment
    journey explorations, 35–36
    making the journey, 35
    materials for, 34–35
    preparation, 34
    process question, 36
journey to meet Gannyap, 199–200
journey to meet Garuda, 236–38
journey to meet Hanuman, 217–18
journey to meet Nagakanya, 229–31
journey to meet nagas, 223–24
journey to meet Shiva, 202–4
journey to meet the spirit of a local
    landscape feature, 240–42
journey to meet Vajrakilaya
    journey explorations, 212–13
    journey explorations regarding the
        khurpa, 213

performing the journey, 212
preparation, 211–12
process questions, 213
journey to receive a vision of
    ceremonial attire, 123
Jupiter (Guru Brihaspati), 278–79,
    281, 285

Kaal Bhairung
    carving photo, 205
    depiction of, 205–6
    eight Bhairung mantra, 207–8
    Maha Bhairungs, 204–5
    use of, 206–7
kalasa, 58–59
Kalchakra Katne ceremony
    journey explorations, 276
    materials for, 269–70
    materials for each person performing
        the ritual, 270–71
    performance of, 268
    performing the ceremony,
        272–76
    preparation, 269–71
    preparatory journey for the
        ceremony, 271–72
    process questions, 276
    rounds, 273–75
    use of, 267–68
Kali
    depiction of, 183
    illustrated, 184
    journey to meet, 183–85
    story of origin, 183
Kapaala Bhairung, 204
katus, 64
kaula, 64–65
kera, 65
Ketu (south node), 284, 285
khadga, 59

Khardga Puja
    ceremony of offering to the mandala,
        256–57
    completing the mandala ritual, 258
    defined, 254–63
    diagram, 255
    mandala, 255–56
Khardga Puja ceremony
    journey explorations, 263
    levels of transference and healing,
        260–62
    materials for, 258–59
    performing the ceremony, 259–63
    preparation, 258–59
    process questions, 263
khurpa
    on altar, 114
    in augmenting intent, 81
    blade (legs), 74, 76–77
    choosing, 77–78
    defined, 59, 70
    Dorje Phurba, 73–77
    handle (middle), 74, 76
    in healing, 71–73
    illustrated, 71
    journey to clear and empower, 78–80
    materials for, 70–71, 73–74
    photo of, 72
    pommel (head), 74–76
    power of, 73
    sections, 74
    thematic representations, 74
    use of, 70
    using, 81–87
khurpa mudras
    to awaken positive earth and water
        energies, 84–85
    to call in heavenly energies, 85–86
    to charge a glass of water, 86
    of communion and unity, 84

for creating ritual intention, 87
for creating ritual intention and
    dancing with the spirits, 87
defined, 82
for invoking helping spirits, 82–83
overview, 82
for personal meditation, 86
process questions, 87
for protection, 83
khurungi, 59
Krodha Bhairung, 204
kul deuta, 244

Lakshmi, 189
Langade Jhankri, 20
Lato Jhankri, 20
light, invoking levels of, 38–39
local deities, protectors, and guardians
    journey to meet, 240–42
    Masto God, 243–44
    types of, 239–40
lotus, 141
Lower World, 9

makara, 77
malas
    in chanting mantras, 100–101
    defined, 59, 97
    journey to clear and empower, 101–2
    materials used for, 97
    number of beads, 97
    as part of shamanic garb, 98–100
    as ritual attire, 121
    rudraksha, 98–99, 100
    serpent vertebrae, 113
    shamanic uses of, 98–101
    types of, 59
mandalas
    defined, 154
    drawing, 154–55

Graha Sarne ceremony, 286–88
Khardga Puja, 255–56
Mansaune ceremony, 155–57
Mansaune ceremony
    defined, 153–54
    flour dough clay recipe and, 159
    forms of, 154
    foundation of, 154
    journey explorations, 165
    levels, 162–64
    mandala, 155–57
    materials for, 158–60
    performing the ceremony,
        160–64
    preparation, 158–60
    process questions, 165
    purpose of, 153
    release, 156
    spirit umbrella construction and, 160
    sprinkling of water, 156–57
mantras
    Bhumi Devi, 186–87
    Durga, 180–81
    eight Bhairung, 207–8
    Gannyap, 197–99
    Garuda, 235–36
    Hanuman, 216
    journey to meet, 211–13, 229–31
    malas in chanting, 100–101
    meeting kul deuta, grama deuta,
        ishta deuta, 244
    naga, 228
    Nagakanya, 229
    offering to the grahas, 286
    Vajrakilaya, 210–11
Mars (Mangal), 280, 285
masculine deities
    energies, 193–94
    Gannyap, 194–200
    Kaal Bhairung, 204–8

Shiva, 200–204
Vajrakilaya, 208–13
Masto God, 243–44
mayur ko pankha, 59
mediation, 3–4
Mercury (Budh), 280–81, 285
Middle World, 9–10
mirrors. *See* aina
monkey image, 75
moon (Chandra), 280, 284
Mother Brahmchaarini, 171–73
Mother Chandraghantaa, 173–74
Mother Earth, 6–8, 38–39, 109–12,
    129–30, 152–57, 188, *pl. 12*
Mother Kaalaraatri, 177–78
Mother Kaatyaayani, 176–77
Mother Kushmaandaa, 174–75
Mother Mahagauri, 178–79
Mother Shailputri, 169–71
Mother Siddhidaatri, 179–80
murro, 88–90
mutual support, 47

Nagakanya, 228–29
nagas
    action of, 219
    ceremonies, 225–27
    creating your own ceremony of
        honoring, 227–28
    creation and, 221–23
    defined, 77, 219
    Garuda and, 232–34
    as helping spirits, 220–21
    honoring, 225–28
    illustrated, 220
    journey to meet, 223–24
    mantra, 228
    Nagakanya, 228–31
    role in healing practices, 219–20
Nag Panchami, 225, 226, *pl. 15*

Nag Raja, 152
nakshatras, 277
nali haard, 59
Nepal
    Himalayas and Mount Everest,
        pl.10
    location and geography, 2
    spiritual traditions, 2–3
    unique practices of, 8
Nepalese shamans. *See* dhami/jhankri
nine, grahas, 279–85

offering to spirits, 27, 36, 45, 48–49,
    79–80

pala-byu, 65
pancha rangi, 59–60
phurba. *See* khurpa
pipal, 65
pommel (head), 74–76
power, 16, 19
power animal
    defined, 10
    journey to meet, 10–13
    relationship with, 13
prayer beads. *See* malas
pride of birth, 251–52
pride of family, 252
protection
    altar and sacred objects, 114–15
    blessing ritual, 39–40
    khurpa mudra for, 83
    layers of, 37–40
    light visualization, 38–39
puchnu ceremony, 265
pukis, 29–30

quartz crystals, 111, 112

Rahu (north node), 283–84, 285

random rituals, 266–76. *See also*
    Kalchakra Katne ceremony
rashis, 277
rekhi. *See* mandalas
relationship with the cosmos, 277–94
renewal
    ceremony, creating, 142–44
    ceremony, performing, 143–44
    Holi celebrations and, 140–42
rice kernels, 40, 54
Ritthe Jhankri, 20
ritual intention, creating, 87
rudraksha malas, 98–99, 100
Ruru Bhairung, 204

saal, 65
saato, 47
sacred mushroom cap, 75
sacred tools/objects. *See also specific
    tools and objects*
    binding and protecting, 114–15
    creating, 107–14
    functions of, 52–53
    guidance on how to build, 69
    overview, 52–53
    plants and seeds on altar, 64–66
    reception of, 67–69
    selection of, 66–67
    types of, 53–64
    voice, 145–48
Samhaara Bhairung, 205
sankha, 60, 152
Saraswati, 189–90
sata byu, 65
Saturn (Shani), 282–83, 285
secrecy, 252
serpent vertebrae mala, 113
shaligram, 60, 113
shaman. *See also* dhami/jhankri
    altering of consciousness, 1–2

as central community figures, 3
as channel or oracle, 5
as facilitator and priest, 5
as healer, 4–5
as mediator, 3–4
nature and, 6
role, 3
as storyteller and preserver of
    cultural wisdom, 5
terms for, 3
shamanic awakening, as continual
    process, 28
shamanic candidates, 19–20, 24, 33
shame, 252–53
shila dhunga, 60–61
Shiva
    altar, 105, *pl. 9*
    as archetype, 202
    depiction of, 201–2
    illustrated, 201
    journey to meet, 202–4
    Kaal Bhairung and, 204–8
    Masto God and, 244
    overview, 200
Skandamaata, 175–76
snow lion, 75
songs
    journeys for, 147–48
    types of, 145–46
    uses, 146
spirits
    animal, 10
    dedicating yourself to, 37
    elemental, 133
    helping, invoking, 82–83
    nature, 239
    protective, 244–47
    tutelary, 133
    welcoming participation of, 124–29
spiritual/emotional unification, 295–98

spirit umbrella, 160
stupa, 75
sun (Surya), 279–80, 284
Suna Jhankri, 19–20
supari, 65–66
suspicion, 252

tapari, 66
Taras, 190–91
thaal, 61–62
thaan, 54. *See also* altar
titepati, 66
totola ko phul, 66
trishula or trident
    on altar, 105, 112, *pl. 9*
    defined, 62, 103
    journey to clear and empower, 104–6
    obtaining, 103–4
    photo of, 104
    representation, 76, 103
tulsi, 66

umbrella, 74–75, 160
Unmatha Bhairung, 204
Upper World, 9

vajra dhunga, 63–64
Vajrakilaya
    action of, 210
    calling upon, 210
    characteristics of, 208–9
    depiction of, 209
    illustrated, 209
    khurpa as representation,
        73–77
    mantra, 210–11
vajra or dorje, 62–63, 76
Venus (Shukra), 281–82, 285
vishva-vajra, 64
voice, as shamanic tool, 145–48

water element, 130
White Tara, 190, 191

About the Authors

Evelyn C. Rysdyk is an internationally recognized shamanic practitioner and bestselling author whose titles include *The Norse Shaman* and *Spirit Walking: A Course in Shamanic Power*. Along with her writings, Evelyn is an impassioned teacher and a featured presenter for the Shift Network, Sounds True, and other international, online programs.

Whether through face-to-face contact with individual clients, workshop groups, and teleconference participants, or through the printed word, Evelyn uses her loving humor and passion to open people's hearts and inspire them to live more joyful, fulfilling, and purposeful lives.

She acknowledges that as people awaken their full selves, they are much more likely and able to make their unique contributions toward transforming our world.

Still bemused that she was shape-shifted by the spirits from being solely an artist into a writer, she lives and manifests all manner of creative mischief on the coast of Maine.

Her websites are www.evelynrysdyk.com and www.spiritpassages.com.

Bhola N. Banstola is a twenty-seventh-generation, indigenous dhami/jhankri from Nepal. He also holds a degree in cultural anthropology from the University of New Delhi.

He spent long periods with the shamans of the Himalayas (Nepal, India, Bhutan, Tibet), reworking shamanic techniques that allow him to be a bridge between his ancient culture and the modern world. He participates in international conferences and lectures and facilitates courses in Europe, North America, and Nepal. With his wife, Mariarosa (Mimi) Genitrini, Bhola founded NEPAL SHAMAN, a cultural association created to promote the preservation and expansion of traditional shamanic practices and cultural knowledge from Southern Asia with a specific focus on the Himalayas and Nepal.

Bhola is committed to preserving and spreading the ancient traditions of his people through this book, through workshops, teleconferences, and videos, and by hosting travelers to his homeland.

Bhola and Mimi live in Italy as well as Nepal and spend months traveling across Asia.

His website is www.nepal-shaman.com.